PSYCHOLOGY: MAKING SENSE

CW01574502

4-50

Under the editorship of
H. Philip Zeigler

PSYCHOLOGY: MAKING SENSE

DAVID A. STATT
Fordham University, at Lincoln Center

Harper & Row, Publishers
New York Hagerstown San Francisco London

To my mother and the memory of my father

Sponsoring Editor: George A. Middendorf
Project Editor: Lois Lombardo
Designer: Michel Craig
Production Supervision: Kewal K. Sharma
Compositor: American Book–Stratford Press, Inc.
Printer and Binder: The Maple Press Company
Art Studio: Danmark & Michaels, Inc.
Part Openers and Cover: The Quinlan Artwork, Co. Ltd.

PSYCHOLOGY: MAKING SENSE

Copyright © 1977 by David A. Statt

All rights reserved. Printed in the United States of America. No part of this book may be used or reproduced in any manner whatsoever without written permission except in the case of brief quotations embodied in critical articles and reviews. For information address Harper & Row, Publishers, Inc. 10 East 53rd Street, New York, N.Y. 10022.

Library of Congress Cataloging in Publication Data

Statt, David A 1942–
Psychology: making sense.

Bibliography: p.
Includes index.
1. Psychology. 2. Perception. 3. Social perception. I. Title. [DNLM: 1. Psychology. 2. Sensation. 3. Psychophysiology. BF121 S797p]
BF121.S827 150 76-54171
ISBN 0-06-046412-7

Contents

Preface

A common problem of people who teach introductory psychology is that their students don't read the textbook. My sympathies are with the students, for these books are quite unreadable. They are gross in size and style; they are unintegrated and unimaginative.

After wading through seven or eight hundred pages of an introductory text even the most diligent student will have little idea of what psychology is all about—unless the instructor fills in the gaps. Chapters devoted to learning and developmental and social psychology, for example, will often deal with the same things and even quote the same studies. All too often these are hermetically sealed areas to the student, who can't quite figure out why they are all called psychology.

My intention in writing this book is to free the instructor from the role of interpreter by providing the student with a text containing a lot of information that is at the same time short, clear, and integrated around a theme. The instructor will now have a sporting chance that the student will have read the material before coming to class, will understand where it fits in the general scheme of psychology, and will be ready to deal with concepts in more depth.

Instead of using class time to explain the textbook, the instructor will be able to assign readings for discussion that probe issues, outline current developments, provide background or raise controversies. Time will be available for films, slides, tapes, visits, and guest speakers.

When I reflect on the difficulty of finding peace and quiet in the vicinity of New York, I'm amazed that I ever wrote this book at all. Whatever you think of its merits, you should regard its very appearance as a triumph of the human spirit over sirens, trucks, firecrackers, and screaming kids.

The progress of this book from conception to birth has been blessed with the presence of three expert attendants: Barbara Moir did a superb job of typing (and sometimes improving) the manuscript; George Middendorf, of Harper & Row, and Phil Zeigler, the outside consultant on this project, guided me deftly around the many pitfalls of textbook authorship. I'm glad I had enough sense to take most of the sound advice they offered me.

My thanks are also due Ully Hirsch, who read and commented helpfully on the early part of the manuscript, and Margot Nadien, who read the whole manuscript closely and gave me some useful suggestions along with a lot of moral support.

D. A. S.

PSYCHOLOGY: MAKING SENSE

Copyright © 1972 United Feature Syndicate, Inc.

CHAPTER 1

Introduction to psychology

My first psychology instructor said, "We don't expect you to understand what psychology is all about until you graduate." He did not have much in common with Peppermint Patty of the Peanuts cartoon—except his view of psychology. Their idea that psychology is a mysterious subject, deep and difficult to understand, is all too commonly held and is, in my opinion, profoundly wrong.

I agree instead with the view of psychology presented by George Miller in his presidential address to the American Psychological Association: "The techniques involved are not some esoteric branch of witchcraft that must be reserved for those with Ph.D. degrees in psychology. When the ideas are made sufficiently concrete and explicit, the scientific foundations of psychology can be grasped by sixth-grade children" (Miller, 1969) (see Box 1.1).

Miller advocates that psychologists "give psychology away to as many people as possible," and this book is an attempt to move in that direction. The idea for this book grew out of my experiences with introductory psychology texts, both as a student and as a teacher; I found them tedious to learn from and practically impossible to teach with. Textbooks in psychology have usually been huge, and as the quantity of psychological research increased they did little more than list the latest studies as they came out.

We have now reached the stage where the average 700-page textbook will tell you a lot more than you want to know about psychological research and theory. What it won't tell you is what psychology is all about. Typically, a textbook will define psychology as the science of human and animal behavior and then split the subject into 15 or 20 chapters, each dealing in great detail with a different area, like learning, personality, developmental, social, and so forth.

BOX 1.1

GIVING PSYCHOLOGY AWAY

In his 1969 presidential address to the American Psychological Association, George Miller proposed to his colleagues that they "give psychology away" to the general public. Miller argues that unlike other sciences the importance of psychology does not lie in its ability to produce technological products for people to use, like cars and television, but in its unique ability to provide new ideas of human nature and human possibilities.

Contributions from other sciences have, in the past, affected public images of man and society, as for example the finding of Copernicus that the earth is not the center of the universe, and Darwin's evidence that man is descended from the apes. But these changed images did not have much direct effect on the daily life of the average person. Changed images arising from an understanding of scientific psychology would have an immediate effect on our lives, because we base our behavior and our expectations of other people's behavior on our conceptions of human nature and its limits.

Miller argues that the prevailing image of human nature in our society is not only destructive but a distortion of what the psychologist has discovered about human nature. It is generally accepted that economic competition is the driving force of our society, that people work only because they have to obtain money, and that if people concentrate on achieving material things there will inevitably be losers in this competition—and therefore conflict.

But the findings of scientific psychology suggest very strongly that life doesn't have to be that way. There is evidence, for example, that if life is meaningful to people they will be creative and responsible in doing their jobs, and that people respond more to initiatives than to coercion. What Miller is suggesting is that competition and conflict are not inevitable and that the psychological basis exists for the social alternatives of cooperation and harmony. By fostering a social climate in which this alternative view of human nature can be accepted, psychologists will be making their greatest contribution to the promotion of human welfare.

Miller points out that just as people use chemistry in cooking and engineering in driving a car, so do they use psychology in dealing with people. If we are all in fact our own psychologists, it makes sense for professional psychologists to help us understand how we actually use psychology, and how we might use it better with the application of valid scientific principles.

But in giving psychology away, psychologists must not be tempted to lecture and theorize. They must give people something they can use, something that will let them feel more effective in their daily lives, whether it be encouraging the intellectual curiosity of their children or appreciating the assets of their fellow workers. Above all it is crucial that psychologists deal with the problems that people feel they have, and not the problems that psychologists and other outside experts think they should have.

Miller hopes that people will then begin to realize they can have some say in their own lives and that their changing images of what is possible may culminate in a changed society. In reply to the obvious criticism that it's a long way from here to there, Miller points out that in a time of widespread dissatisfaction and questioning, people may be less resistant to changing their images of man and society than is generally thought.

Source: George A. Miller, "Psychology as a Means of Promoting Human Welfare," *American Psychologist* 24 (12): 1063–1075, 1969.

The links between these chapters have to be made by the reader, who might as well be studying 15 or 20 different subjects. Only rarely, and in limited areas of psychology, is any attempt made to organize the work that psychologists have done and to give people who are new to the subject a sense of the unity and continuity that runs throughout psychology.

The emphasis in other words is usually on imparting information, rather than understanding, to people beginning the study of psychology. This book is on the side of understanding; information you can always get. I hope to heighten your psychological awareness so that you may come to regard human behavior with greater understanding.

THEME

A tendency that researchers have uncovered time and again in many areas of human and animal behavior is an apparent need to make sense of the environment, whether the environment is physical or social, whether the subject is alone or with others. We tend to welcome anything that helps us make sense of the situation we find ourselves in and to reject whatever does not. In particular, we tend to be threatened by the existence of *ambiguity, disorder,* and *unpredictability* in our environment. And well we might, for unless our day-to-day environments and our dealings with other people are basically unambiguous, orderly, and predictable, life as we know it would be quite impossible. Some examples might help bring this point home.

Ambiguity

A group of people were given a drug which produced symptoms of excitement like heart pounding and hand trembling (Schachter and Singer, 1962). Half of the group were told the drug would have this effect and the other half were not. All of them thought they had received a vitamin supplement. The first group then attributed their feelings of excitement to the drug they had been given, but the second group had no way of knowing why they felt excited. They were in an *ambiguous* situation. At this point in the experiment two "stooges" were introduced into this second group, both of whom were supposed to have been given the same drug. One of the stooges had been told to act happy and the other to act angry. The people in the presence of the happy stooge interpreted their feelings as happiness and acted accordingly; the people in the presence of the angry stooge behaved as though what they felt was anger. Both groups made sense out of their ambiguous situations by observing how other people behaved in that situation. But by manipulating this need to make sense of the environment, the experimenter got people with the same physiological symptoms to report very different feelings, and what is more important, to behave in accordance with those feelings.

Disorder

Our need to live in an ordered world is so taken for granted that we only notice it when it is brought to our attention. Why, for example, do we only see the following figure as three groups of two lines each, rather than as six single lines?

Probably for the same reason that we think of someone wearing a blue uniform with a badge on it as a policeman, rather than as someone who happens to be wearing a blue uniform with a badge on it. The raw information we pick up (series of lines, man in blue uniform) has to be processed before we can do anything with it, before we can make sense of it.

Unpredictability

Suppose you want to see a movie. You walk briskly up to the cash desk, deposit your money, shout "one, please" through the window, and the cashier hands you a banana. Presumably this behavior is not quite what you had anticipated. The person in question is not behaving like a cashier. Such behavior, in other words, is *unpredictable,* and if it were more than a rare occurrence would make it impossible for us to maintain ongoing relationships with other people.

Situations that contain all of these threatening elements of ambiguity, disorder, and unpredictability are sometimes so overwhelming that people have to deny what they actually see. If you believe that black people are lazy and stupid it saves you from dealing with every black person you meet as an individual, and going to the trouble of finding out what he or she is like. The same holds true if you believe that white people are evil and racist, policemen are pigs, and hippies are immoral. If you can instantly type people by their appearance, you know what they're like, how to behave toward them, and how they will behave toward you.

A serious problem arises of course when the typing breaks down. During the 1968 Democratic convention in Chicago, many people who saw on television in living color what was officially described as a "police riot" against demonstrators and onlookers later denied what they had seen and claimed that it was hippies who beat up policemen. The idea that policemen could behave in this fashion was just too much for them to handle. A group of bigoted white people were shown a drawing of a subway scene where a well-dressed black man was being threatened by a rough-looking white man wielding an open razor. The subjects were then asked to describe the scene from memory. Some of them found it so disturbing that they recalled a rough-looking black threatening a well-dressed white (Allport and Postman, 1947).

These may seem like rather dramatic and unusual examples, but in the following pages we will see that all of us are capable of what appears to be dramatic and unusual behavior if our need to make sense of the environment is strong enough.

THE RELEVANCE OF PSYCHOLOGY

The most common focal point of psychology is the behavior of a single individual. Psychologists also study the behavior of small groups, but when the size of a group being studied is larger than just a few people (say, seven or eight) we are rapidly leaving the field where psychology is the most relevant science to consult for an understanding of the behavior involved. When we come to groups as large as tribes or nations, psychology by itself is able to tell us very little about how such groups operate. The social factors impinging on each individual are simply too numerous. But what little psychology has to say is extremely important because no matter what the size of the group involved (even if it is two societies making war on each other), the behavior is actually done by individuals, each of whom is subject to the same psychological processes.

At the other end of the scale there are a whole series of factors from within each individual that impinge upon his actions, and some of these are studied by psychologists. The genetic inheritance that someone was born with, for example—physique, temperament, and the tendency to act one way rather than another in a given situation—is an important factor in determining how he will react to the world he is born into. Similarly, a person's physiology and chemistry, the way the nervous system works and how the glands function, can have an important effect on behavior.

However, if we concentrate too much on these biological processes we may come to regard human beings as just another member of the animal kingdom with a few unique features. This point of view may be useful enough from a biologist's standpoint but loses the psychologist's perspective that every individual's behavior is a unique amalgam of internal and external forces. Where those forces meet and are expressed in individual behavior is the area that forms the basis for the study of psychology.

We can represent this with a diagram as in Figure 1.1.

At either end of this hourglass figure the temptation to misuse the psychological perspective and apply it out of context is very great, and both psychologists and nonpsychologists are guilty of doing so. In dealing with international relations, for instance, I have heard people make remarks like "Germany tried to conquer the world in 1939 because Hitler was a sexual pervert." Similarly, in regarding mankind as a species of animal, some people have argued that riots in big cities can be explained by overcrowding, because when rats are confined in a small space they will turn on each other and fight to the death.

In understanding the flaws underlying these arguments—that Hitler was not Germany and people are not rats—we have to be clear that while the behavior of Hitler was important to an understanding of Germany in 1939, a great deal more of the picture is provided by studying German history and culture and the German economic and social systems. In the latter case it is vital to realize that human and animal behavior that looks the same may not be so, or may be so for very different reasons. In certain situations of overcrowding, rats will automatically, instinctively, lash out to defend their territory. People do *not* have this built-in instinct to lash out and defend their territory. Some

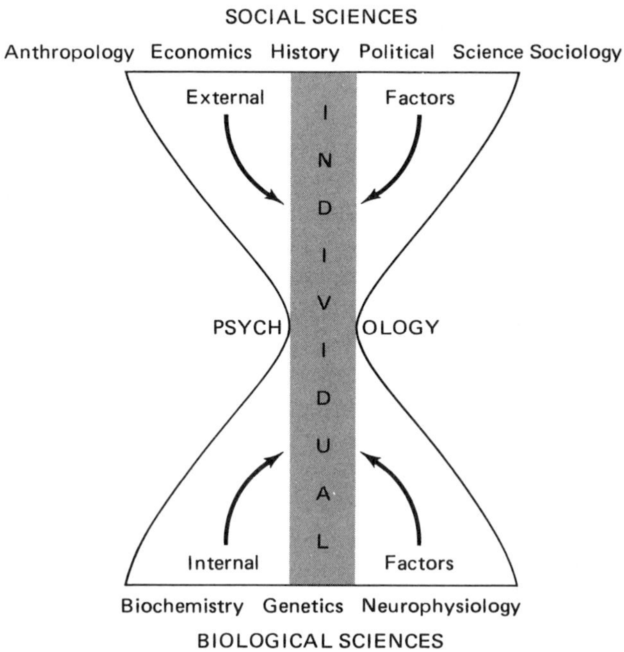

Figure 1.1 The focus of psychology.

people will riot in overcrowded conditions; most people will not. Those who do so do not riot simply because they are overcrowded. Their behavior is the tip of an iceberg composed of any number of internal and external factors that are hidden from immediate view. To equate the behavior of rats with that of people, or people with that of nations, is to *psychologize*—to misuse psychology. Doing so makes it simpler to deal with human behavior, but at the cost of achieving any real understanding.

Simplifying the world we live in is the most common way in which we try to make sense of it, and in this we are encouraged throughout our lives by the authorities we come in contact with—parents, teachers, supervisors, officers, ministers, and politicians.

The more ambiguous, disorderly, and unpredictable a situation is, the more complex it is, the greater the number of factors we have to take into account, and the stronger the push to simplify. Generally speaking, however, psychologists believe that the more *complexity* people can handle and the more they can resist the temptation to oversimplify, the greater their maturity. This is an idea we will return to at various points throughout the book (see Box 1.2).

BOX 1.2

COMMON SENSE IS CLEAR BUT CONTRADICTORY

Every society has its collection of wise sayings designed to simplify complex situations with a single piece of advice. These sayings may indeed contain a lot of good advice, but what do you do if there is more than one saying for the situation you're in and they offer you different advice?

For example:

Look before you leap	*but*	He who hesitates is lost
You're never too old to learn	*but*	You can't teach an old dog new tricks
Absence makes the heart grow fonder	*but*	Out of sight, out of mind
Birds of a feather flock together	*but*	Opposites attract
Clothes make the man	*but*	You can't make a silk purse out of a sow's ear
Two heads are better than one	*but*	Too many cooks spoil the broth
Great minds think alike	*but*	Fools seldom differ
Better the devil you know than the devil you don't know	*but*	Familiarity breeds contempt (and furthermore) Variety is the spice of life

Even the most insightful men of literature can't make up their minds. "No man is an island," said John Donne, but to Thomas Wolfe "Every man is an island."

PLAN OF THE BOOK

From now on we will deal only with the *external* factors that affect the individual, as represented by the upper half of Figure 1.1 (facing page).

There are two reasons for this:

1. A relatively high level of knowledge in the biological sciences is required to focus on the internal factors that affect individual behavior.

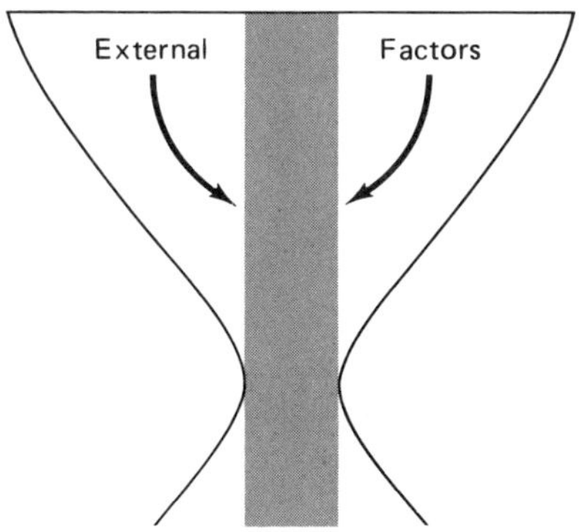

2. Most psychological research focuses on external factors and individual behavior because psychologists are mainly interested in human behavior in a social setting, in examining how people behave toward other people.

An elaboration of the previous figure may also be helpful in clarifying the way I have tried to organize the material in this book:

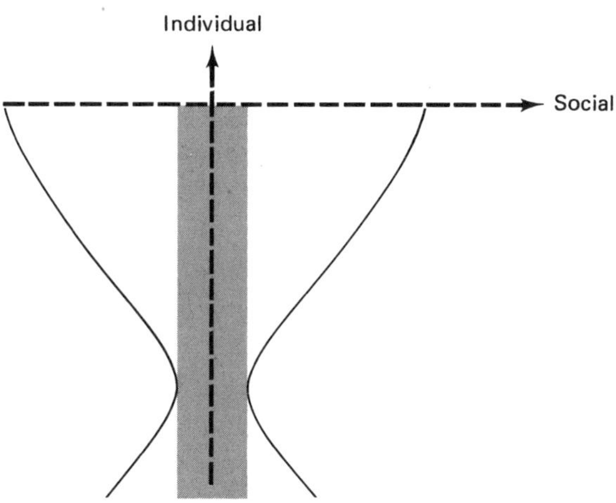

Individual

This approach focuses on the individual life cycle and the kind of psychological processes that every individual encounters as he or she goes through life. The processes of learning, perceiving, using language, and thinking would fall into this area, for example.

Social

This approach focuses on the external factors that affect the development and use of these individual processes. It deals with the effects of being born and growing up in different societies—for instance, of learning to behave in different ways and learning to expect different kinds of behavior from people. It deals with how people form attitudes about others and how people influence each other.

The Person

As a bridge between the individual and social approaches, we will examine the process whereby an individual becomes a "person," and how that person learns to understand himself, to make sense of his thoughts, feelings, and behavior.

In the final chapter we will look at the psychologist's own need to make sense of the environment, as a human being and as a psychologist, and examine the way this need can affect what we know about human behavior.

We can accept the usual definition of psychology as "the science of human and animal behavior," and while the bulk of this book deals with human behavior, we will take a brief glance in the next chapter at animal behavior and see that the need to make sense of the environment is not limited to the species *homo sapiens.*

PART ONE

ANIMAL BEHAVIOR

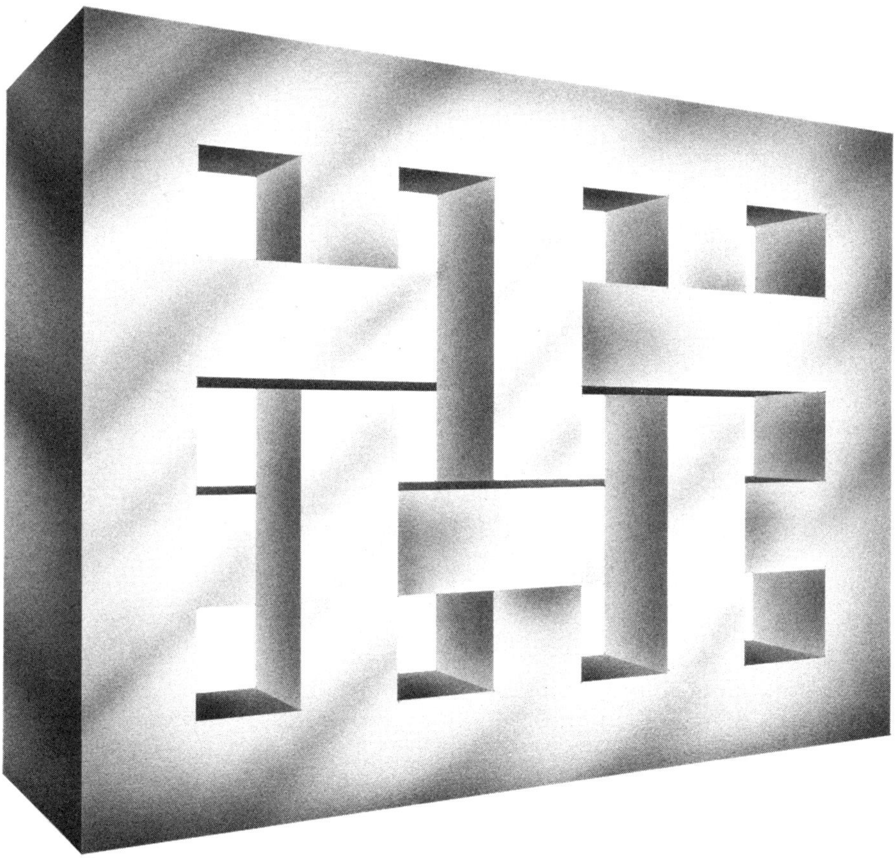

Only one chapter of this book is specifically devoted to animal behavior, but research on animals is an integral part of psychology, and contributions from this work will be referred to throughout. It has been said, in fact, that the two most commonly used subjects in psychological studies are the white rat and the college sophomore.

There are several reasons for the psychologist's interest in animals. It is often much more convenient to study animals than humans, and scientists can do things to animals that they can't do to people for both ethical and practical reasons. It is therefore possible to isolate and study basic psychological processes like learning and perception which could not be studied in humans so readily because of their vastly more complex behavior.

Psychologists are also interested in studying animal behavior for its own sake, to understand how animals do what they do and in particular to find out how some relatively simple animals can engage in some very complex behavior.

CHAPTER 2

Animals and their need to make sense

The theme of this book is relevant to animal behavior in two ways. First of all, as animals are part of our environment we have a need to make sense of their behavior. Second, it is quite clear that animals have a need to make sense of their own behavior and to understand their environment in their own terms.

A great deal of research has been done by psychologists on the ways in which animals make sense of their world, and we can only deal with a few of the more important mechanisms here. The ways in which psychologists make sense of animal behavior, however, have gone largely unexamined. As we will see in the course of this chapter (in the story of Clever Hans), this attitude can have serious consequences for our understanding of animal behavior.

In studying animal behavior we will come across some striking similarities to human behavior in similar circumstances. There are also many clear differences. And there are many areas of psychology where the similarities and differences between animals and people are unclear and controversial.

SIMILARITIES: RATS AND PEOPLE

Some human behavior looks like animal behavior under similar circumstances, although on closer inspection the similarity turns out to be more apparent than real. This is the case with the "similarity" that is often invoked between overcrowding behavior in rats and what seems like the same behavior in people. Over a certain density of population, rats will often become violent and lash out at their neighbors. They may also exhibit other kinds of antisocial behavior. From this it has been argued that people who live in overcrowded cities will also tend toward antisocial behavior such as violent crime.

This argument nicely illustrates a complete misunderstanding of psychology. Jonathan Freedman in his book *Crowding and Behavior* (1975) details this type of argument and shows up its defects. The chief aim of the rat, Freedman points out, is to reproduce. Therefore, it is concerned above all else with finding a safe place to make its nest and produce its young undisturbed. The more crowded the conditions under which it has to do this, the more upset the rat becomes and the more antisocial will be its behavior.

Freedman produces evidence to show that population density in cities is *not* directly related to the kinds of things that have been associated with it, like mental illness, shortened life expectancy, and high crime rates. Nor does overcrowding lead to increased aggression. As is so often the case in psychology, the relationship between crowding and aggression is more complex than had previously been imagined. It now appears that the effects of crowding are to *intensify* whatever situation is being experienced, so that pleasant situations seem more pleasant and unpleasant situations more unpleasant.

To understand all the reasons for urban social problems we would have to leave psychology and go to sociology, economics, and political science. To attempt a psychological explanation alone for these very complex social issues is to *psychologize,* to misuse psychology.

In this case, an attempt was made to explain human behavior in terms of animal behavior, but attempts have also been made (also mistakenly) to explain animal behavior in human terms, as the following example shows:

Clever Hans, the Talking Horse

Despite the often demonstrated differences between human and animal learning abilities, there have been frequent attempts (some of them quite honest) to prove that some particular animal is an exception to the rule. Such a case is that of the famous "talking horse," Clever Hans.

At the beginning of this century a German landowner named Von Osten selected a horse from his stables who seemed to him unusually intelligent and tried to educate him. The horse was Clever Hans and the program of instruction was the local elementary school curriculum. The training was apparently done in the usual fashion with the horse being rewarded with food when it gave the correct response.

At the end of two years' intensive training, Clever Hans was able to add, subtract, multiply, divide, change fractions into decimals and vice versa, give the date, tell the time, and even give the correct musical composition of a minor chord. Not too bad for second grade. Von Osten would typically chalk the question on a blackboard in front of the horse (e.g., $12 + 5 = \ldots$) and Hans would paw the ground with his foreleg the correct number of times. The horse practically never made a mistake—even when skeptical strangers were doing the questioning.

Clever Hans became such a celebrity that a panel of eminent psychologists and zoologists was appointed to study him scientifically. The panel concluded, after an intensive examination, that there was no trickery involved and that Clever Hans's abilities were genuine. However, a psychologist named Otto Pfungst was not convinced (Pfungst, 1911). He set up a situation where the questions were written on pieces of cardboard chosen at random and shown only to the horse. None of the observers knew what the question was, and in this situation Clever Hans was unable to answer a single question. He just pawed the ground aimlessly for a while, then stopped.

Pfungst's suspicions were confirmed. Horses are able to pick up tiny movements that would escape a human observer. When Clever Hans's previous questioners had asked him to solve a problem they of course had the answer in mind, and when the horse had pawed the ground the correct number of times they would unconsciously signify this by relaxing their position slightly and giving the tiniest jerk of the head—just enough for the horse to see. When the horse picked up this cue he stopped pawing the ground.

Clever Hans was indeed clever—for a horse. But human he wasn't, and he did not have human learning abilities. He was making sense of his behavior in his own way. His human admirers were making sense of his behavior in *their* own way, and between them they have provided us with a classic example of animal behavior that seems human but isn't.

The tendency to see human properties in nonhuman places is very strong, and stories like Clever Hans's crop up from time to time. I'm reminded of the old joke about the two rats who had just run through an experimenter's maze. One rat turns to the other and says, "You know, I think I've got this guy conditioned now. Every time I run through this maze he gives me a lump of cheese." On the other hand, there are situations in which animal behavior does parallel human behavior as in the examples in Box 2.1.

Dominance Hierarchy and the Pecking Order

When animals live together in groups there is a pattern in the way they behave toward each other. Rules and customs can be detected that govern the group's social behavior, with punishments meted out to animals that break them. One of the most powerful social influences in the animal's life is the position it occupies in the group, how much authority it has in relation to the other animals—i.e., its place in the *dominance hierarchy.*

Wolves, for example, have a very clear dominance hierarchy where

BOX 2.1

LEARNING HOW TO BE HELPLESS

Some of the parallels between complex human and animal behavior are strongly suggestive, and many psychologists believe that a direct application of ideas gained from studying animals can be made to some puzzling areas of human behavior. One such area has come to be known as *learned helplessness.*

It has often been reported, for example, that there are people in mental institutions who seem to have given up on life, withdrawing into themselves and making no attempt to do anything about their situation. People suffering from depression, a very common symptom of psychological disturbance, also show a decreased level of responsiveness to the world. They behave as though there is nothing they can do to affect their environment and help themselves. In addition, there are many reported cases of people in good physical condition dying suddenly and unexpectedly right after observing the appearance of some symptoms of illness or after some minor injury. Finally, a great deal of apathy and resignation is frequently noted among the poor, the weak, and the oppressed all over the world.

What do these areas of human behavior have in common and what can we learn about them from studying animals? Using both wild rats and domesticated rats, C. P. Richter has shown that an animal which sees no hope of surviving a dangerous situation will simply give up and die. Richter immersed the rats in water, under various conditions, to see how long they would swim to keep themselves from drowning. Laboratory rats can do this for 60 to 80 hours before they become too exhausted to continue.

When Richter clipped the whiskers of the tame laboratory rats, most of them still managed to survive for 40 to 60 hours. When he did the same thing to the wild rats, all of them died within a few minutes of entering the water, and some of them even before they were put into the water. Wild rats use their whiskers to maintain contact and to find their way around their environment. When deprived of this aid they ceased to help themselves, although they were quite capable of doing so.

Martin Seligman has suggested that animals *learn* to be helpless; they learn that their own behavior will make no difference to their situation so they stop trying, even when escape is quite possible. The question Seligman tried to answer was "How does this learning occur?"

Seligman and his associates strapped dogs into harnesses from which they could not escape and gave them electric shocks. In this situation the animals were truly helpless. They then placed each of these dogs and other dogs which had not been shocked in a box. In this new situation each dog was subjected to an electric shock that was turned on ten seconds after a buzzer sounded. But this time the dog could easily escape by jumping over a small barrier.

The dogs which had not previously been shocked quickly learned how to escape, but the dogs who had been shocked just lay down and whined, resigning themselves to their fate. They had learned how to be helpless, and Seligman argues that many people may learn the same lesson from being systematically beaten down and branded as failures early in life.

Source: C. P. Richter, "On the Phenomenon of Sudden Death in Animals and Man," *Psychosomatic Medicine* 19: 191–198, 1957, and Martin E. P. Seligman, "Fall Into Helplessness," *Psychology Today,* June, 1973, pp. 43–48.

a member of the pack who has low status must defer to a member with higher status. The life of a wolf pack is based around the hunt for food, and so the best hunter and best guardian of the pack's food and territory becomes recognized as the leader. When a conflict arises between the leader and any other animal (over food, for instance, or the selection of a mate), the other animal will always give way to the leader.

Similar dominance hierarchies occur, with varying degrees of rigidity, among social animals as different as bees and monkeys. But perhaps the most striking is the behavior of farmyard hens who establish their hierarchy by pecking each other—the most pecked having the lowest status, of course. The status relation thus formed among the hens is called a *pecking order,* and it is interesting to note how this term has passed into everyday speech (together with the graphic description, "hen-pecked").

Harlow and Surrogate Mothers

It has been clearly demonstrated that depriving an animal of its mother can have very serious consequences. This is especially true of primates (monkeys, chimps, and gorillas) which are high up on the scale of evolution.

Harry Harlow has done a great deal of work in this field with infant monkeys (Harlow, 1963). By rearing them in the laboratory he has been able to examine the functions that the animal's mother performs for it, and the effects of not having a mother on the animal's future behavior.

Harlow offered the infant monkey two artificial "mothers" to choose from. One was a model made of foam rubber covered with terrycloth and the other was made of wire. For some of the monkeys the wire "mother" had a feeding bottle attached to it and the terrycloth "mother" did not.

Even though the monkeys had to go to the wire "mother" for food, they chose to cling to the soft terrycloth "mother" the rest of the time for comfort and support. Harlow had thus demonstrated that the need for touching and holding was of enormous importance in the young animal's life.

As the monkeys grew up they seemed fairly normal, but when they were introduced to other monkeys of the same age who had been reared by their natural mothers, serious differences in behavior were observed. The lab monkeys appeared to be very fearful of contact with others, cowering in a corner and showing signs of distress. They did not learn as well as the other monkeys, and when they were old enough to mate they did not do so. They seemed interested in sexual activity but didn't know what to do about it.

The normal experience for baby monkeys is that for the first few weeks of life their mother feeds and protects them and they cling to her in time of distress. After a time the mother encourages the infant to be more self-reliant and to join the social group. She still keeps an eye on him, however, and teaches him what is appropriate behavior by the simple expedient of thumping him around the ear when he does something different.

The monkey thereby learns not to wander away from the group and to be cautious when approaching strange objects. At the same time, he learns that play and interaction with other monkeys, particularly of the same age, is good and is encouraged. He learns, in general, when it is appropriate to be afraid, to be playful, to be deferential, and so on. He also learns when and how to mate. Harlow's lab-reared monkeys did not learn these things.

When the monkeys were taken away from their natural mothers but reared with their age mates, their behavior was in between the two extremes of nature and laboratory. They interacted fairly normally with other members of their group and even mated successfully, but when they became parents they didn't seem to know how to look after their offspring. They were quite neglectful and uninterested in the whole business, as though never having experienced parental behavior themselves, they were unable in their turn to be parents.

Animal Neurosis

The term *neurosis* is applied to behavior that is disturbed, abnormal, and leads to social difficulties. It is mainly used in connection with human behavior, of course, but it can be applied (cautiously) to some animal behavior as well.

Harlow's motherless monkeys, you will recall, exhibited some strange behavior. When they were by themselves they sometimes rocked back and forth holding their heads in their hands. When they were introduced to other monkeys they were very slow to interact with them, cowering off in a corner and looking very fearful. And their sex life, of course, was most abnormal.

One of the most important contributions of Ivan Pavlov and his followers was to show that neurotic behavior can be produced experimentally under laboratory conditions, thus helping us understand something about the processes that are involved when normal behavior becomes disturbed (Pavlov, 1928). Pavlov was interested in the simplest form of learning, where a certain response is conditioned to follow a certain stimulus. We will deal with his work when we discuss the process of learning in Chapter 6.

Pavlov observed the phenomenon of neurotic behavior in conditioning his dogs to salivate on seeing a particular stimulus. He had trained a dog to salivate (by rewarding it with food) when presented with a card that had a circle marked on it. Then he presented the dog with an oval and did not reward it with food. The dog discriminated between the two stimuli without any trouble. In other words, it could tell the difference between the circle that meant food and the oval that did not.

Gradually, Pavlov made the oval more like the circle, so that the dog had greater difficulty in discriminating between the two stimuli. Eventually the two figures were so similar that the dog could not discriminate between them at all. At this point, the normally docile and obedient dog changed its behavior dramatically. It began to squeal, wriggle about, bite through the apparatus it was strapped into, and bark ferociously.

No longer able to make any sense out of the task that was being demanded of it, the animal exploded in a frenzy of disturbed behavior. A normal dog had thus been driven neurotic by being made to do a task it found impossible. It found itself in a situation where its previous training and experience was quite inadequate in helping it to adjust. It saw no way out, no solution to its problems and, unable to do anything else, it just lashed out in frustration (see Box 2.2).

HOW SIMILAR? HOW DIFFERENT?

Some of the most important issues in psychology represent gray areas of uncertainty in the comparison of human and animal behavior. A study of these issues is beyond the scope of this book, although we shall touch on them at various places in the chapters that follow. Per-

BOX 2.2

LEARNING HOW NOT TO BE HELPLESS

Psychologists working in the animal research laboratories of the Walter Reed Army Hospital in Washington, D.C. noticed a sudden increase in the number of monkeys dying from duodenal ulcers. This was a startling finding, for death from ulcers is very unusual in monkeys. It was observed that while the animals were being used for very diverse studies, the one thing the monkeys who died from ulcers had in common was that they had been required to learn a certain response which would prevent them from receiving electric shocks.

An experiment was set up involving two monkeys seated side by side, waiting to receive electric shocks. The animals were locked into the apparatus and linked to each other in such a way that the same electric shock was given to both of them simultaneously. The shock could be avoided by pressing a lever within 20 seconds after a light came on. When one of the monkeys pressed his lever, nothing happened, and he soon stopped pressing it. It was therefore up to his partner, whose lever worked, to save them both from the electric shocks. He was labeled the "executive" monkey.

After a month of this, the executive monkey died—from a perforated ulcer. When the experiments were repeated, the results were the same: the executive monkeys died of ulcers while the other monkeys remained healthy. In this case, unlike the studies of learned helplessness, it was the animal that *could* do something about its situation which suffered.

The executive monkey was subject to constant psychological stress from the environment. The other monkey quickly learned that it could do nothing to affect its situation, but since the executive monkey was quite effective in preventing shocks to both of them, it didn't suffer either from the shocks or from the stress of having to be constantly on duty.

The parallels to human situations in the executive monkey experiments are just as tempting as those in the learned helplessness studies. One factor common to both humans and animals in these situations is the overriding need to make sense of a new and threatening situation by whatever means possible. The ways in which organisms learn to deal with their environment (and especially their early learning) is therefore of the greatest importance, and we will examine these ways throughout this book.

Source: Reported in Floyd L. Ruch and Philip G. Zimbardo, *Psychology and Life,* 8th ed. (Glenview, Ill.: Scott, Foresman, 1971), pp. 48–49.

haps the most important controversy in this area is the question of whether or not animals are capable of speech and language, and this point will be discussed in Chapter 9.

DIFFERENCES

Some of the many striking differences in the ways that humans and animals make sense of their world are outlined below:

Tinbergen and IRMs

Biologists studying the way that innate factors affect animal behavior have added a new branch to the science of animal psychology, called *ethology.* Ethology deals with fixed inborn ways of behaving which the animal inherited at birth, which did not have to be learned, and which appear irrespective of the animal's environment or previous experiences.

Nikolaas Tinbergen (Tinbergen, 1951) helped to launch this field of research. Tinbergen carefully observed stickleback fish in their natural environment over a period of time, and found what appeared to be innate patterns of behavior. In the spring, he noted, the male stickleback stakes out a claim to some territory at the bottom of a stream and builds a nest. Other males who approach his territory are chased away, but females (who are pregnant in the spring) are courted. The male leads the female into his nest and then fertilizes the eggs that she spawns. The male then looks after the eggs until they hatch and watches over the young sticklebacks until they can go off on their own. At no time does the young stickleback have any contact with a mature female, yet when they reach maturity all sticklebacks follow the whole cycle of sexual behavior quite automatically and fertilize the females' eggs in exactly the same way.

Tinbergen, we noted, was struck by the fact that his sticklebacks reacted automatically to males by chasing them away and to females by courting them. If they'd never seen a female before, how could they tell which was which, and how did they know whether to fight or to woo? Tinbergen made some models that he presented to the male stickleback (see Figure 2.1).

He noticed that the fish acted aggressively only toward a model that was colored red underneath—the color of the male's belly—even if its shape was nothing like the real thing. If there was no red coloring, then no matter how real the model looked to the scientist, the aggressive behavior was not stimulated. Thus the red coloring was the mechanism for releasing the innate attacking behavior. Only on the appearance of this *innate releasing mechanism* (IRM) will the animal react in an aggressive fashion.

Ethologists have discovered similar innate behavior in birds and insects and even in higher animals like gorillas and chimpanzees. Sci-

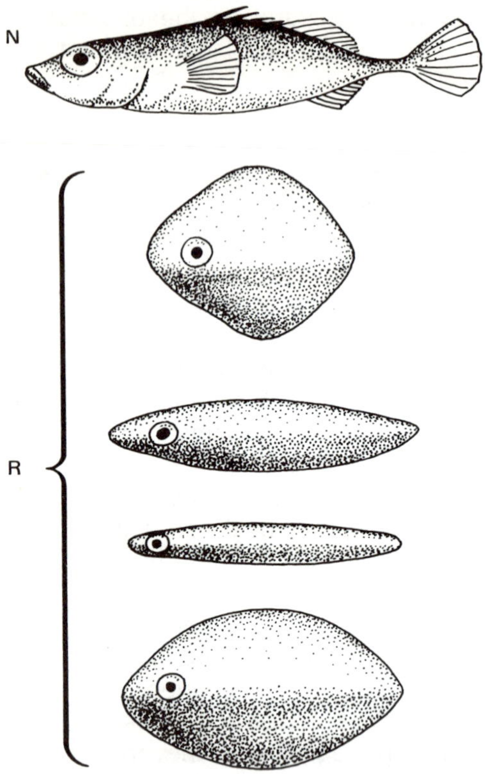

Figure 2.1 Models of male sticklebacks. (*Source: Reproduced from N. Tinbergen,* The Study of Instinct *(The Clarendon Press, Oxford, 1951). Used with permission.*)

entists, after carefully studying the innate behavior that chimps and gorillas use in their social lives, have even been able to imitate that behavior well enough to be accepted by these animals and treated as just another chimp or gorilla.

Lorenz and Imprinting

Another famous ethologist, Konrad Lorenz, has shown that by manipulating the innate behavior of animals scientists can not only manage to be accepted as one of them (like the observers of chimps and gorillas we noted above), but even as the most important member of their group—the mother (Lorenz, 1965).

In studying a group of Mallard ducks, Lorenz came up with the idea that soon after the ducklings hatched from the eggs, they were innately primed and ready to follow the first large moving object they saw. Normally, of course, this would be the mother duck that had hatched them, and she was thereby provided with a foolproof means of ensuring that her ducklings stayed with her without getting lost as she moved about.

However, Lorenz had the notion that the innate following behavior of the ducklings, which he called *imprinting,* could be released by a stimulus other than the mother duck. So one day, when a group of ducklings was due to hatch, he put the eggs into an incubator. When the ducklings emerged from the eggs they found Lorenz waiting for them—quacking like a mother duck. He quacked the mother's call note for several hours and gradually the ducklings came to regard him with confidence and trust.

As he slowly moved away from them, the ducklings quickly followed after him wherever he went. Instead of being imprinted on their mother, they had become imprinted on him. In fact, the imprinting process had been so well transferred that when Lorenz gave his ducklings the choice of following him or the mother duck, they chose him. Other investigators have since shown that ducks and geese can also be imprinted on inanimate objects like balloons, footballs, and cardboard boxes.

LEARNING PSYCHOLOGY FROM ANIMALS

Apart from the benefits of a comparison between human and animal behavior, psychologists have been able to learn about basic psychological processes from experimentation with animals. It used to be thought, for example, that we eat because we are hungry. It sounds reasonable, but it's not entirely true. The sensation of hunger that we experience when our empty stomach contracts comes to us not from the stomach, but from the brain.

Scientists working with rats have shown that destruction of a certain part of the brain called the hypothalamus will cause the animal to eat and eat, and continue eating until it becomes extremely fat. In fact, rats would eat themselves to death unless they were prevented from doing so. The eating behavior in this case has nothing to do with hunger. The same is apparently true of other basic physiological drives; they seem to be controlled by a series of very complex brain mechanisms that affect our behavioral responses.

These studies have forced us to take another, more objective look at the way we make sense of our most basic behavior. Contrary to common folklore, man's best friend may turn out to be the laboratory rat.

SUGGESTED READINGS

Birney, R. C., and Teevan, R. C. eds. *Instinct.* New York: Van Nostrand Reinhold, 1961. A collection of papers that explores various aspects of the effects of innate factors on behavior.

Lilly, J. C. *The Mind of the Dolphin.* New York: Avon Books, 1969. Both anecdotes and scientific discussions of animal intelligence.

Lorenz, K. *King Solomon's Ring.* London: Methuen, 1952. A famous naturalist and ethologist with a sense of humor discusses the behavior of domestic animals.

Southwick, C. *Primate Social Behavior.* New York: Van Nostrand Reinhold, 1963. Social bonds among groups of apes and monkeys.

PART TWO

THE INDIVIDUAL

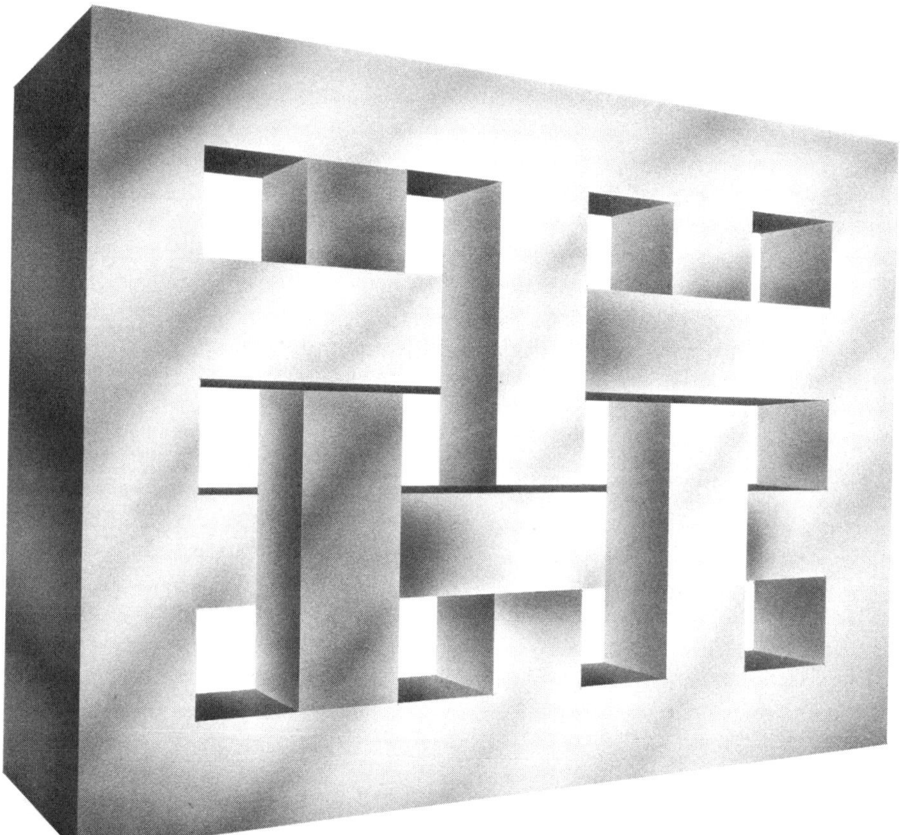

In Part Two we will examine the equipment that human beings bring into the world, and the ways in which they use that equipment to make sense of life.

We will look at the genetic inheritance that makes each human being a unique individual, and the brain structure that makes all human beings members of a unique species. The importance of the learning process will be stressed, and we will acknowledge the considerable debt we owe to studies of animal learning.

One of the most important skills an individual ever learns is how to make sense out of the tremendous amounts of stimuli that the eyes and ears and other sense organs have to cope with all the time, and we will examine how this is done. The last chapter in Part Two will take our theme into the area of individual emotions to see how we come to identify our feelings and to make sense out of them.

CHAPTER 3

What are we born with?

THE HUMAN ANIMAL

When a human infant comes into the world to start life, he or she does not seem too well equipped for the journey. Unlike many animal infants, a human baby is completely helpless for a relatively long period of time, and for several years is physically dependent on adults for sheer survival. Contrast this with several species of birds which start to walk about and forage for themselves shortly after they are born. What is important for our present discussion, however, is that the baby bird will grow up to do not much more than walk about and forage for itself, while our human baby may grow up to be Billie Holliday or Sigmund Freud.

As we saw in the last chapter, a great deal of animal behavior is preprogrammed. Human behavior, on the other hand, has many alternate routes of development: physical, emotional, and mental. The human infant's passage through life is therefore inevitably slow and fumbling compared to animal infants, and he or she is prone to make error after error in learning how to make sense out of the environment. But these errors are absolutely normal and necessary, for without them no learning could take place, and the lack of a capacity to learn—to be flexible and able to change accustomed behavior—means that an organism would be at the mercy of every new situation that came along.

Biologically, human beings form a *species* called *homo sapiens* or "wise man." Each species is different from every other species. All the members of a species have certain features in common, while at the same time each individual member is a unique organism. The fact that human infants take such a long time to develop, compared to animals, means that they have a greater possibility than any animal species for developing their individual uniqueness. The differences between human beings are therefore far greater than the differences between one stickleback and another, or even between one monkey and another. All organisms are unique but human beings are more unique than others.

GENETIC INHERITANCE

In accounting for both the similarities and the differences to be found among human beings, we have to trace their origin back before birth to examine the process of development from the very beginning—the moment of conception. Conception occurs when an egg cell of the mother is fertilized by a sperm cell of the father. The egg and sperm unite into a single cell and, by a process of splitting, this cell has become about 200 billion cells by the time a new human being is born nine months later.

In a sense, the differences between people begin at conception, for the fertilized cell contains the *genes* that transmit the hereditary characteristics of the parents. These are carried on *chromosomes,* and the chromosomes of the egg and the sperm cells merge in the new cell to form the genetic hereditary link between the two parents and their offspring. Every human being therefore has a unique genetic heredity, with the single exception of people who originated from the same fertilized cell, such as twins or triplets. These people have the same genes, which is why they are always of the same sex and look identical. Twins who did not originate from the same fertilized cell are simply brothers and sisters who happened to be born at the same time and who may not even look like each other.

Our genes are responsible for guiding our process of development from conception to death and setting the broad outlines of our abilities. We have seen that genes are concerned with our physical appearance, with color of eyes and hair and shape of face. They are also concerned with potential size and, perhaps most important, they are concerned with our learning capacity and the form it takes.

The Effects of Chromosomal Disorders

Exactly how the genes affect our intellectual capacities and the ability to learn is still very unclear, and the relationship is by no means a simple one. Parents of low intelligence can produce a genius, for example, while two geniuses may produce a child of average ability.

We do know slightly more about the effects of having abnormal chromosomes to carry the genes on, however. Normally each cell of the human body has 46 chromosomes, but in the case of mongoloid children there is found an extra small chromosome that is linked to their having mental and physical abnormalities.

These 46 chromosomes are arranged in 23 pairs with one chromosome in each pair coming from the egg cell of the mother and one from the sperm cell of the father. One of these pairs contains the sex chromosomes which determine whether the child will be male or female. These chromosomes are known as X and Y chromosomes because of their shape, and an XY pairing will always produce a male child while an XX pairing always produces a female child.

Occasionally the sex chromosomes do not simply pair up as XX or XY, and when that happens the resulting abnormality results in physical and sometimes mental defects. Females who have one X chromosome missing (Xo), for instance, do not fully develop their physical sex characteristics and are sterile. On the other hand, men who have an extra X chromosome (XXY) have similar male defects.

Perhaps the best known and least understood type of chromosome aberration is that of the man who has an extra Y chromosome (XYY). Perhaps one in a thousand male children have this abnormality, although no one really knows just what the figure is. Early researchers claimed, however, that XYY sex chromosomes were much more prevalent among prisoners and men who were mentally retarded than among the male population in general. This immediately sparked worldwide speculation in the press and elsewhere that criminals and mental retardates could be identified early in life because of their genetic make-up, and separated from the rest of the population.

More recent studies have tended to show that there is no more prevalence of XYY types among prisoners and the mentally retarded than among the general male population. In addition, it is now known that there are many XYY men who are not mentally retarded and have no criminal tendencies. About all that can now be said of XYY men is that they are taller and more active and have unusual internal physiological characteristics.

Nevertheless, the old stereotype (like every stereotype of human behavior) dies hard. It would make the study of psychology so much easier if we could just point to a particular genetic characteristic as the sole reason for a person behaving as he does. It would make it that much easier for us to make sense of someone's behavior and come up with neat solutions to messy social problems. Unfortunately (or perhaps fortunately), human behavior is not that simple or easy to understand.

NATURE-NURTURE CONTROVERSY

In discussing the effects of genetic inheritance on human behavior, we very quickly encounter the age-old question of how much behavior is accounted for by heredity and how much by the social environment the child is born into. How much, in other words, is due to what *nature* provides, and how much to the kind of *nurture* he or she receives?

One of the roots of modern psychology lies in seventeenth-century European philosophy, and two English philosophers are sometimes quoted as presenting the opposing arguments in the nature-nurture controversy. Thomas Hobbes regarded human behavior with deep suspicion. People, in his view, were ruled by inherited base instincts right from birth, over which there could be little control save that imposed by law and government. John Locke, on the other hand, argued that the mind of a newborn baby was a *tabula rasa,* a blank slate, on which anything could be written. The possibilities for producing good in each new human being were therefore unlimited. Simply find the right method of instruction and people could be taught to make love, not war. (By the same argument, of course, the possibilities of producing evil are also unlimited.)

The issue is usually phrased as nature versus nurture; heredity versus environment. When stated in an either/or fashion like this, the controversy is just plain silly. No human being could exist without having both a genetic heredity and a social environment, and both play an indispensable part in an individual's behavior. Furthermore, any piece of human behavior is the result of an interaction between a person's inherited predisposition to act in a certain way and the social environment he finds himself in.

If a man beats his wife, for instance, should we explain his behavior by saying that because he comes from a long line of wife beaters, he inherited the tendency with his genes? Or should we argue that the environment he grew up in led him to believe that wife beating was an acceptable pastime for a husband to engage in? And even if we do choose one of these "explanations," what have we learned?

Despite the apparent futility of trying to choose between these two kinds of alternatives, many otherwise intelligent people have been doing so for a long time—partly for political purposes. Down through the centuries, naturists and nurturists who held strong opinions on the subject usually had a particular view of mankind that was related to a set of strongly held political beliefs. Thus, people who agreed with Hobbes that a social order with kings and aristocrats should be maintained were usually naturists, believing that heredity should determine one's place in life and that once born into that place a person should live and die in it.

The writers who supported the American, French, and Russian revolutions, for instance, thought otherwise; and written into the official documents that emerged from these upheavals were sentiments that rejected the status quo of power and order implicit in heredity and strongly supported the influence of environment on human behavior. Affirming the equality of peoples' rights and opportunities implied that, given the right kind of social environment, the right kind of human behavior would emerge, removing the need for Hobbes's coercive laws and government.

Neither Nature nor Nurture

Splitting animal and human behavior into two categories, learned (from the environment) and unlearned (from genetic inheritance), is much too simplistic a way of dealing with some very complex processes. Because certain actions are unlearned it does not necessarily mean that they are genetically inherited. As D. O. Hebb has pointed out (1972, p. 116), some behavior is not in itself learned but couldn't appear unless some previous learning had taken place.

We came across this phenomenon in the last chapter when we discussed the experimental neurosis produced in Pavlov's dog. The dog's neurotic behavior was not learned, but it could never have happened if it had not learned in the first place to tell the difference between a circle and an oval.

Similarly, there is a well-known fear of strangers that appears in human infants about the age of six months. But why does the child fear the *first* strangers he meets? She could not have learned to fear someone she'd never met before. The baby must first learn to recognize nonstrangers, the people she is familiar with, before she can discriminate between the two.

GENOTYPES INTO PHENOTYPES

With the growth of scientific psychology over the past century, the old nature-nurture controversy has become a little less simplistic. An individual's genetic endowment is seen in terms of potentialities, called *genotypes.* There is no way of seeing a person's genotype, for genetic potentialities can only appear *in actual behavior.* All the behavior that we can observe from birth (or even before) right throughout life is thus the result of the interaction between the genotype of inherited genetic tendencies and the social environment. This result is known as the *phenotype.*

The way in which heredity and environment interact has been studied experimentally with animals. A certain species of mountain rabbit has a white coat with black patches on its extremities when reared in its natural environment. This skin coloring is, of course, genetically inherited. When the rabbit is raised in a warm cage in the laboratory, the black pigmentation does not appear. Moreover, when a part of the white area is artificially cooled, a black pigmentation develops (Sinnott, Dunn, and Dobzhansky, 1958). The particular phenotype that emerged from the genotype of skin color was partly dependent on the environment.

We can also observe the interaction of heredity and environment in our everyday lives. We know that physical size is a genotype. So how is it that children grow up to be taller and heavier than their parents? If environment played no part then, other things being equal, parents and children would be exactly the same size (see Box 3.1).

BOX 3.1

IDENTICAL TWINS AND THE NATURE-NURTURE ISSUE

One crucial problem in trying to disentangle the nature-nurture issue is that normally we can only guess at the relative importance of genetic endowment and environment in someone's behavior. A British psychologist named James Shields suggested a way out of this dilemma involving identical (monozygotic) twins and fraternal (dizygotic) twins. The identical twins would, of course, share exactly the same genes, while the fraternal twins would simply be brothers and sisters born at the same time and having nothing more in common genetically than any other two siblings.

Shields reasoned that if he could find sets of identical twins who had been reared apart from each other, he would be able to throw a lot of light on the differing effects of heredity and environment. After appealing for volunteers on British television, he was able to locate 44 pairs of identical twins who had been reared apart for most of their childhood. The twins were usually separated from the age of six months and the separation lasted at least five years.

Shields also found 44 pairs of identical twins who had been reared in the same home, as well as 32 pairs of fraternal twins. Both groups of identical twins were given a wide variety of tests including physical examinations, interviews, questionnaires, and intelligence tests. When the study was done, the subjects were mainly in their 30s and 40s, although their ages ranged from 8 to 59.

The findings of this study are strong evidence for the influence of hereditary factors on a number of personality characteristics. Smoking habits, for instance, were remarkably similar among the identical twins: 78 percent of those reared apart were either both smokers or both nonsmokers; the figure for identical twins reared together was 71 percent. But only 50 percent of the fraternal twins were alike in smoking behavior.

A similar effect was found when differences in weight were compared. Separated identical twins had an average difference in weight of 10.5 pounds, and in those raised together the amount was 10.4 pounds. Fraternal twins, however, had an average weight difference of 17.3 pounds.

But perhaps the most important finding for our purposes concerned differences in intelligence quotient (IQ) scores. Shields discovered that identical twins reared together were most like each other in IQ, followed by the identical twins reared apart, and lastly, the fraternal twins. In addition, the similarity of IQ between the sets of identical twins reared apart is more like that of the identical twins reared together than that of the fraternal twins.

The important effect of heredity on IQ scores is beyond question, but at the same time we must never lose sight of the fact that environment *can* play a crucial role as well. Even identical twins reared in the same household sometimes showed substantial differences in many ways—including their IQ scores.

Source: James Shields, *Monozygotic Twins* (New York: Oxford University Press, 1962).

Although the nature-nurture controversy is now rarely stated in either/or terms, some psychologists are interested in the *relative* importance of heredity or environment in shaping a particular piece of behavior, and some have chosen one or the other of these two areas on which to focus their attention.

Supporters of the environmental emphasis argue that we should concentrate on studying the effects of the environment, because something can be done about changing an environment while genetic heredity is fixed from the moment a child is conceived. In addition, even identical twins with the same genes have slightly different environments and can turn out to be very different people. People who emphasize heredity argue that even if a change in the environment were possible it would not affect everyone in the same way because individuals with different genetic heredities will react to changes in different ways.

Jensen and the Vexed Question of Intelligence

One of the most important phenotypes that psychologists have studied is the behavior resulting from the set of mental processes we call "intelligence." By and large, this behavior is boiled down to a single score on an intelligence test known as an IQ, or intelligence quotient. Why and how an IQ score became so important in representing "intelligence" will be more fully examined in Chapter 14, when we discuss social order and the politics of education.

It has been known for some time that blacks tend to score about ten points lower on IQ tests than whites. What this finding means is the subject of frequent and heated debate, both among psychologists and the general public. It does *not* mean that blacks are less intelligent than whites; it means they score lower on IQ tests. Naturists put the difference down to heredity, with blacks being genetically less able to score well on IQ tests. Nurturists attribute the gap to cultural differences and the material poverty that most black children have had to grow up in. It is important to note that the scores referred to here are average group scores that say nothing about the IQ of a specific individual. Thus some blacks have scored higher IQs than most whites.

Psychologists who worry about these things generally estimate that heredity is more important than environment in determining IQ. Arthur Jensen (1969) has carried this estimate one step further. He has calculated that individual IQ is 80 percent determined by heredity and 20 percent by environment, and that average *racial* differences in IQ are also largely determined by heredity. Thus, social programs of compensatory education for blacks and other minority groups cannot succeed, Jensen suggested, because these children do not have the genetic potential that would endow them with the IQ to profit from such education.

Jensen has since been subject both to hysterical charges of racism and to reasoned and comprehensive professional criticism of the soundness of his research and thinking. It is difficult to understand why he would attempt to argue about differences between large groups of people on the basis of individual test scores. Perhaps, as in the case of the extra Y chromosome we discussed above, Jensen may have been seduced by the attraction of finding neat and relatively simple genetic causes for behavior that is extremely complex, difficult to disentangle, and of wide social interest.

When all the dust has settled, we will no doubt find ourselves back in the same place. Whatever intelligence is, it is not entirely captured within an IQ score; it remains a phenotype whose genetic component is important in setting ultimate limits but which can be greatly affected by environment—thus, even identical twins with the same heredity can have a 25-point difference in IQ if reared in different homes.

The attempt to measure the relative importance of heredity and environment continues, with a definitive test remaining as elusive as ever. Lastly, there is no hard evidence that there are genetic racial differences in IQ, while there is plenty of evidence that the IQ tests currently in use are biased in favor of urban white middle-class children.

The Effects of Social Deprivation

The Jensen controversy does, however, raise broader questions about the effects of a deprived childhood on a phenotype like intelligence. At its most extreme, deprivation can rob children completely of the genetic potential they were born with. Severe malnutrition, for example, can cause irreversible brain damage whose effects can reduce the most brilliant potential to nothing.

Deprivation of such physiological severity is relatively rare, however, at least in developed countries. Much more common is the type of deprivation we encountered with Harlow's monkeys in Chapter 2. We saw there that animals who were deprived of their mothers in early infancy suffered from a retarded social and emotional development.

Similar arguments have been made about maternal deprivation in human children. It has been claimed that children raised in institutions like orphanages have lower IQs than children raised by families where a mother or mother figure is available to the child (see Box 3.2).

Psychologists are less sure of the effects of social deprivation than they used to be, and a series of unresolved questions seems to have emerged:

1. Does social deprivation retard intellectual development because the child is *emotionally* deprived by not having adults who care about him, or *mentally* deprived because he doesn't receive enough stimulation from the people in his environment?
2. Are some periods of infancy more critical than others? It is claimed that such critical periods exist for both animals and humans.
3. Are the effects of early social deprivation irreversible? Many psychologists have thought so for a long time, although the evidence was always unclear and sometimes conflicting. Recent work by Jerome Kagan and others (1972) has produced evidence to show that children who would be described as socially deprived up to the age of about eleven, and who appeared to be mentally retarded, apparently turned into normally developed and functioning children when the deprived conditions of their environment were removed.

These findings tend to support the view that individual intelligence has a relatively large genetic component which can withstand a lot of social deprivation. They may also shed some light on the fact that some children who experience the most terrible social deprivation seem to be intellectually (and even emotionally) unaffected by it. The equipment they bring into the world enables them to overcome the most severe social handicaps and make sense of their experiences in a way that fosters their development into mature human beings.

BOX 3.2

CRITICAL PERIODS IN DEVELOPMENT

It has long been accepted by psychologists that the effects of deprivation on human beings (whether it be sensory, social, or emotional) is linked to the period of life during which the deprivation occurs. Being deprived of mothering after the age of 25, for instance, is considerably less serious than being deprived from the age of six months. Some of the factors involved in the concept of "critical periods" have been examined by the animal social psychologist John Paul Scott.

According to Scott, one aspect of the critical period idea is that it is "a time when a large effect can be produced by a smaller change in conditions than in any later or earlier period in life." Being able to specify the critical periods in early human development would therefore be of great importance for education and child rearing.

Even more important than knowing *when* a critical period occurs is knowing *what happens and why*. Scott argues that critical periods in humans as well as animals occur at times when the organism is faced with the necessity of adapting very rapidly to a new set of circumstances—particularly those involving social relationships.

Human infants will start to smile at human faces when they are five or six weeks old. By the time they are six months old they will no longer smile at strangers, having learned in this period the difference between familiar and unfamiliar faces. Between six weeks and six months, therefore, infants will form their first social relationships or "primary attachments." As a result, these relationships will usually be with parents and in particular their mothers, with whom there is more contact.

Scott produces evidence to show that even a temporary break of contact with the situation in which a primary attachment was formed can be very disturbing for the infant. There is a built-in survival value to this distress; it is absolutely essential for such a highly dependent creature. Unless the infant reacted immediately and began signaling its distress (and its whereabouts) by crying, it would die helplessly in a very short time.

Permanent separation in human infants usually results in adoption by new parents, and Scott points out that if this occurs after the age of six months the baby will often have a great deal of trouble adjusting to people later on in childhood. Scott claims we can learn more about this experience from a study of dogs, who are normally adopted, of course, by people.

The adopted puppy becomes very sensitive to separation from his human "parents" and becomes more dependent on them. As Scott remarks, this may be fine for a pet but less desirable for a child. Such excessive dependency, he suggests, may be alleviated by adopting the child gradually over a period of time and thereby giving him or her more time to become familiar with a new situation without abruptly leaving the old.

Source: John Paul Scott, *Early Experience and the Organization of Behavior* (Belmont, Calif.: Wadsworth, 1968).

SUGGESTED READINGS

Birney, R. C., and Teevan, R. C., eds. *Instinct.* New York: Van Nostrand Reinhold, 1961. A collection of papers that explores various aspects of the effects of innate factors on behavior.

Bowlby, J. *Child Care and the Growth of Love.* Baltimore: Penguin Books, 1965. The effects of maternal deprivation on a child's mental health and development.

CHAPTER 4

The senses

HOW MANY SENSES ARE THERE?

Information about the environment is conveyed to the brain from the eyes, ears, and other *sense organs.* Traditionally, people have referred to the five senses of *vision, hearing, touch, taste,* and *smell.* We now know that this is an oversimplified description of the human senses. The sense of touch, for instance, is really four different senses—pressure, pain, cold, and warmth. There are four senses of taste—salt, sweet, sour, and bitter. Even the sense of vision has to be divided into two senses—color vision and black-and-white vision. In addition to these familiar senses, psychologists would now add two less familiar ones: *bodily movement* and *balance.*

Our senses are wide-ranging, complex, delicate, and sensitive, and in everyday life we normally use only a fraction of their power. Thus, on a clear, dark night we are capable of seeing a candle flame over 30 miles away, and in a quiet room the tick of a watch can be heard at a distance of 20 feet. But each of our senses, however acute, can nonetheless be bettered by some member of the animal kingdom. A hawk, for example, has sharper vision than we do and a dog can hear sounds inaudible to us. It is thus the *range* of the human senses together with their sensitivity that provides us with a unique quantity and quality of information about the environment.

The senses we know most about are vision and hearing. These senses have long been of great interest to scientists from several disciplines, and the relevant sense organs (the eyes and ears) are readily accessible to observation, experimentation, and measurement. Less is known about the other senses, but some recent work has added to our understanding of them also (see Box 4.1).

BOX 4.1

INTERACTION OF THE SENSES

Although we discuss the senses individually, like so many aspects of our psychology the human senses form a unified whole, interacting to provide us with a way of orienting ourselves to the environment.

This interaction is perhaps clearest in the behavior of blind people who can "see" their environment through other senses, particularly their sense of touch and their sense of hearing. One way of using touch, for instance, is in reading. This can be done by recognizing raised lettering by running the fingertips over it; another method using arrangements of raised dots was invented by Louis Braille. In reading Braille you would be using a set of symbols that form a kind of shorthand, enabling you to scan more material than with the laborious method of going over each letter. Blind sculptors have even used their sense of touch to produce some very striking likenesses of their models.

People who are completely blind can still find their way around busy streets with unerring accuracy. How do they do this? The study of bats provides some suggestions. Bats have no vision and live in darkness. They find their way around by emitting sounds as they fly. These sounds are reflected back off the surrounding walls into the bat's ears, and these echoes enable it to steer a safe course.

This information is known as *sonar,* and it has been suggested that human beings can also operate by sonar. Some research to test this suggestion was conducted by W. N. Kellogg. Kellogg compared the performance of blind people and sighted people who were blindfolded on a number of tasks. He found, for example, that when his subjects were asked to make sounds that would produce echoes from their surroundings, the blind people could tell whether the object they were facing was covered with velvet or denim—a skill that was completely beyond the others.

A different kind of sensory interaction has enabled dentists to reduce the pain experienced by their patients. Gardner, Licklider, and Weisz have reported that providing people with music and other sounds can inhibit the sensation of pain. At the beginning of a visit to the dentist's chair, the patient is provided with headphones through which some soothing music can be heard. As the dentist approaches with the instruments of torture, the patient can turn a dial and hear some "white noise" that sounds like a waterfall over the continuing music.

At the slightest sensation of pain, the patient can turn up the volume of noise, and this has the effect of masking the pain. There are probably several reasons for the effectiveness of this procedure. The sound of the dreaded drill is drowned out—by the patient's own actions, moreover, a factor that may give an increased sense of control over the situation and therefore reduce anxiety. Concentrating on the music through all the background noise may also help to divert the patient's attention from the sensation of pain.

Sources: W. N. Kellogg, "Sonar System of the Blind," *Science* 137: 399–404, 1962, and W. J. Gardner, J. C. R. Licklider, and A. Z. Weisz, "Suppression of Pain by Sound," *Science* 132: 32–33, 1960.

Common Properties

Before we say a few words about each of the senses, we need to look at some important phenomena common to all of them. Before we can become aware of any stimulation from the environment, a stimulus has to be strong enough for our sense receptors to pick it up. Below a certain level of intensity, we simply won't experience the stimulus. A point of light in a dark room, for example, has to be bright enough to cross our *threshold* of vision before we can see it.

This threshold is known as the *absolute* threshold because it marks the difference between sensing and not sensing. Different people have different absolute thresholds, however, and a person's ability to sense a certain stimulus may vary depending on his psychological and physiological condition at the time.

There is another sensory threshold that operates when we try to discriminate between two stimuli. Suppose there are two slices of cake left and you're trying to decide which is bigger. In order for you to decide, there has to be a difference between them sufficiently large for you to notice. The minimum amount of difference that you can detect is called the *just noticeable difference,* or j.n.d. Once you have detected a j.n.d. between one stimulus and another, you have crossed the *difference threshold* between them.

Difference thresholds are also quite variable, depending on the two stimuli in question. We can see this in our everyday experience. A one dollar increase in the price of a new car is probably not a j.n.d.; the same increase in the price of a hamburger certainly would be. As you read this book you are probably not aware of any pressure on your skin. Yet if you wear a watch, or clothes with elastic in them, you will find your skin marked by their pressure when you take these things off.

If you have ever visited a fish market, you may have wondered how the people who worked there could stand the smell. Had you asked them, they might have replied "What smell?" and assured you that people got used to it in time.

In both these cases the sense organs involved did the same thing—they adapted. Just as people in fish markets get used to the smell, you can get used to the feel of what you wear, until you stop feeling pressure on your skin. The *sensory adaptation* involved helps us live through everyday situations without the mind-boggling necessity of stopping to examine the meaning of every stimulus from the environment that our sense organs pick up. In fact, if the stimulus is constant and familiar, the sense organs become insensitive to it and stop sending information about it to the brain. If the stimulus changes, the sense organs are back in business. You are probably most familiar with the visual form of adaptation between conditions of light and dark—and so are psychologists. We will discuss this process further in the next section on vision.

There is a limit to sensory adaptation, of course—if your watch strap is so tight it causes you pain, you won't adapt to it; you'll change your environment by loosening the strap. But below the level of pain, our senses can adapt very efficiently to a wide range of environments.

VISION

The working of the human eye is often compared to that of a camera. Light falling on the eye is focused on the *retina,* the sensitive lining at the back of the eye, in a similar manner to a photographic film. The retina contains an enormous number of nerve endings that are sensitive to light. These nerve endings form an image on the retina of whatever the eye is looking at, and eventually this image is transmitted via the *optic nerve* to the brain.

The retina contains two kinds of nerve endings, known by their shape as *rods* and *cones.* The cones function in daylight, while the rods are active in the dark. The cones react to the stimulus of daylight falling on them by being sensitive to both *chromatic* colors (blue, green, red, etc.) and *achromatic* colors (black, white, and grey). The rods, functioning in a dim light, are sensitive only to achromatic colors.

If we move abruptly from light to darkness, as when entering a movie theater from the sunshine outside, the rods in our retina have to take over from the cones which become only slightly sensitive to the fainter light. After seven or eight minutes, the cones have reached the limit of their sensitivity, but the rods increase their sensitivity for a further thirty minutes, by which time the process of *dark adaptation* is largely complete and we can see as well as is possible in the dark.

This process is reversed when we come out into the sunshine again and adapt to the light, but *light adaptation* is much more rapid, taking only about fifteen minutes.

HEARING

Hearing and seeing provide us with the information about our environment that we rely on most. Our experience and our ability to make sense of the world is largely shaped by these senses. In both seeing and hearing, our sense organs react to waves of energy from the environment: our eyes to light waves and our ears to sound waves.

Just as light waves are made to activate the optic nerve at the back of the eye, sound waves are focused by the outer ear on the eardrum where they stimulate nerve endings that send messages to the *auditory nerve,* and from there to the brain.

Unlike our visual (and other) senses, the sense of hearing can be markedly affected by living in an increasingly technological civilization. With advances in technology have come increased levels of loudness and intensity in the sound stimuli that reach our ears. In fact, people living and working in a modern city are in real danger of having their sense of hearing impaired. There is no question that people who live in quiet environments have better hearing than people who live in noisy environments. Prolonged exposure to intense noise levels leads to partial or total deafness, and even lower levels of noise can cause permanent damage.

Nor is there much evidence that we get accustomed to noise and stop hearing it the way we can stop smelling unpleasant odors by the process of sensory adaptation. It is more likely that people who claim they no longer notice screaming sirens or roaring motorbikes have simply lost part of their sense of hearing.

The table that follows illustrates the loudness of our environment. Notice how much of our daily lives are lived around the 85-decibel level which represents the danger point for our sense of hearing (see Figure 4.1).

THE SKIN SENSES

What used to be called the sense of touch is now known to be four senses: pressure, pain, cold, and warmth. It is not hard to see why these senses were long considered to be one and the same, for in everyday life they are often intermingled into the same sensation. Pain, heat, and cold, for instance, are often accompanied by a sensation of pressure. Sensations of tickling and itching are caused by variations in the stimulation of these senses.

Sense receptors are found all over the surface of the skin, although they are not distributed uniformly either in amount or in type. Some areas of the skin are generally more sensitive than others, and some

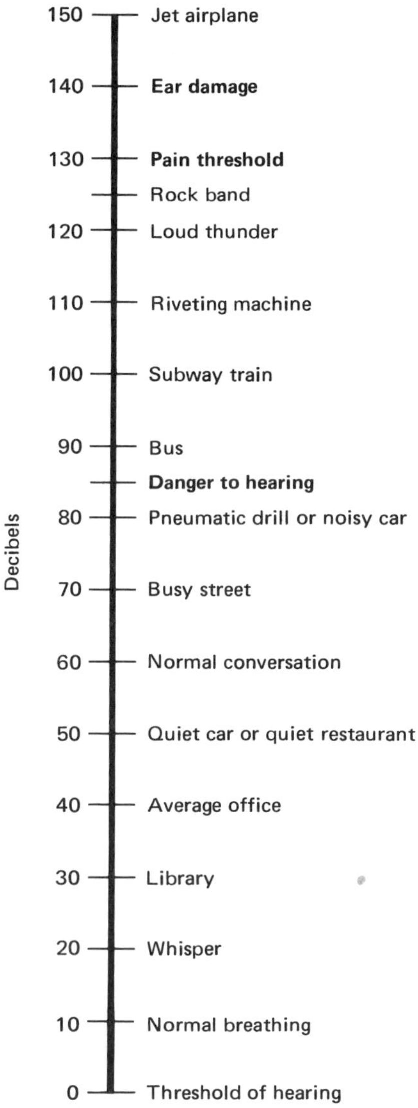

Figure 4.1 Loudness of familiar sounds, in decibels.

areas contain more of one kind of receptor than another.

Our senses are where we make contact with the environment, and a striking illustration of their importance to our functioning is the sense of pain. The stimulation of pain receptors is usually an unpleasant experience, but if they didn't work the result might be much more unpleasant, and even fatal. There are rare cases of people who don't seem to have any sense of pain, and the lack of this warning device has often resulted in their doing physical damage to themselves before they realized what was happening.

SMELL AND TASTE

The senses of smell and taste, which we normally think of as being quite different, are even more closely tied to each other than are the four skin senses. In fact, if we didn't have a sense of smell the food we eat would have very little taste. You've probably experienced this yourself when you had a head cold and your nose was blocked. If not, try holding your nose while you taste a piece of raw potato and a piece of raw apple. You won't be able to tell the difference.

The receptors for the sense of smell are high up in the nasal cavity —too high, in fact, to be in the direct line of the airflow through the nose and down into the lungs. Unless the odor is very strong, therefore, we have to sniff in order to force the air up the nose to the smell receptors which are then activated and pass their message along to the brain.

The receptors for the taste sensations are found mainly in the taste buds on the tongue. The tip of the tongue is most sensitive to *sweet* and *salt,* the sides of the tongue are most sensitive to *sour,* and the back of the tongue to *bitter.* Combinations of these four senses, together with the sense of smell, provide us with the potential for a great variety of taste sensations.

BODILY MOVEMENT

A sense that most of us don't realize we have is the sense of *bodily movement* that keeps track of the changing position of our limbs. There are sense organs embedded in the *muscles,* the *tendons* connecting muscle to bone, and the linings of the *joints* between the bones. These sense receptors respond to the environment by moving various parts of the body in an appropriate manner. Our sense of bodily movement makes it possible to walk steadily without looking carefully at each step to see where our feet are. When we go to lift a package, the same sense tells us how much muscle power we need to exert and whether we are using too little or too much. The sense of bodily movement is most useful in situations that call for rapid and closely coordinated behavior, and without it most sports we engage in would be quite impossible.

BALANCE

The sense of balance is linked to the sense of bodily movement. It too is a sense that we are normally not aware of. It is concerned with movements of the whole body rather than the limbs. The organs of balance are composed of three *semicircular canals* located in the inner ear. These canals are filled with fluid that moves when the head is moved, and they keep us oriented to the force of gravity, thereby maintaining our balance when we move.

As the sense organs are our point of contact with the environment, the information they provide us with forms the basis of everything we do. In discussing the various sense organs we noted that they pass their information along to the brain. In the brain, the information is sorted into the patterns that seem to make the most sense. Before we examine this process more closely in the next few chapters, let us take a brief look at the various *states of consciousness* we can be in as our sense organs respond to stimuli from the environment.

We are most aware of our senses and the environment they present to us when we are wide awake, alert, and interested in what is happening around us. We are at our *most conscious* then. When we are in the deepest part of a night's sleep, we are at our *least conscious* and are therefore least aware of sensory stimulation. It is perhaps preferable to think of consciousness in this fashion as a continuous scale from most to least, rather than as a definite split between conscious and unconscious.

In recent years psychologists have become increasingly interested in all aspects of consciousness, and in particular those aspects other than what we consider our normal waking state of awareness. Thus, more and more research is being done on *unusual states of consciousness* like ecstasy, delirium, and the effects of various drugs. Another fringe area of research that has become increasingly popular deals with the occurrence of paranormal or psychic phenomena (see Box 4.2).

The use of drugs to affect one's state of consciousness and heighten sensory awareness is nearly as old as humanity. Whether it be the opium of China, the hashish of the Middle East, or the peyote of the American Indian, the practice is widespread and takes many forms. Often there is a religious or ritual aspect to such practices, with the use of drugs carefully prescribed and controlled. The psychological effects of such drug use, according to the users, ranges from pleasant to nightmarish to ecstatic.

To do much more than note the existence of these different states of consciousness would lead us far afield. In the ensuing chapters, unless otherwise noted we will be dealing with a normal waking condition.

BOX 4.2

PARAPSYCHOLOGY

People in all times and places have shown a particular interest in happenings that cannot be explained scientifically. Every culture has its legacy of demons, witches, and ghosts with all kinds of magic powers at their command. Many of the occurrences that were previously regarded as being *paranormal* in this way can now be satisfactorily explained with advances in scientific understanding. We know that bubonic plague is a disease caused by lack of public sanitation and other quite explainable factors; therefore we don't need to blame its occurrence on witches.

There are still many recorded occurrences which we can't explain, and there are still many people willing to believe that these paranormal phenomena are caused by supernatural beings —no longer witches or demons, perhaps (although such beliefs are by no means dead), but how about superintelligent beings from another galaxy with spare time on their hands?

In 1934 J. B. Rhine introduced the term *parapsychology* to cover the study of what he considered to be natural functions of the mind which are not as yet understood. Rhine founded the *Journal of Parapsychology* and the Parapsychology Laboratory at Duke University, where he tried systematically to bring order into the chaotic field of psychic phenomena. Rhine divided parapsychology into two subdivisions, *psychokinesis* (PK), which dealt with the influence of the human mind on physical objects (e.g., influencing the way dice will fall), and *extrasensory perception* (ESP), which included telepathy (perceiving someone else's thoughts) clairvoyance (perception of faraway happenings), and precognition (perception of events before they occur).

A great deal of data has come out of Rhine's laboratory which he and his supporters consider to be evidence for the existence of parapsychological phenomena. But the way in which these phenomena are caused is still unknown. Gardner Murphy, a highly respected academic psychologist, has suggested that it might help if scientists knew where to look for these occurrences and if they stopped regarding parapsychology as a disreputable and taboo area for serious study.

Source: J. B. Rhine and J. G. Pratt, *Parapsychology: Frontier Science of the Mind* (Springfield, Ill.: Thomas, 1957), and Gardner Murphy, "Parapsychology," in N. L. Farberow, ed., *Taboo Topics* (New York: Atherton, 1966), pp. 56–63.

SUGGESTED READINGS

Gregory, R. L. *Eye and Brain: The Psychology of Seeing.* New York: McGraw-Hill, 1966. Deals in a readable way with the sense of vision. Discusses a great many topics like the nature of light, the structure of the eye and the brain, brightness, color, and visual illusions.

Griffin, D. R. *Echoes of Bats and Men.* New York: Doubleday, 1959. Describes the way blind people and certain animals like bats and porpoises find their way around with the aid of sound waves.

Hansel, C. E. M. *ESP: A Scientific Evaluation.* New York: Scribner, 1966. A survey and critique of past and present research in extrasensory perception and other forms of parapsychology.

Naranjo, C., and Ornstein, R. *On the Psychology of Meditation.* New York: Viking Press, 1971. Discusses various techniques of meditation and their attempts to control certain aspects of brain and behavior.

CHAPTER 5

The brain and behavior

THE CENTRAL NERVOUS SYSTEM

All but the very simplest of animals have a system of nerve cells which serves as a channel of communication, conveying messages between various parts of the organism and the environment and among the different parts of the organism itself. In vertebrates, higher animals that have a backbone, or spinal column, the nervous system becomes centralized and integrates the messages it receives from within and without. This *central nervous system* consists of the spinal column and the brain that is situated at the top of it. In humans, the central nervous system (and especially the brain) is more complex than in any other creature.

THE BRAIN AS ORGANIZER

To a psychologist, the brain is the most important part of the human body. It is at the center of our attempts to make sense of the world and to behave accordingly. Especially in recent years, scientists have discovered a great deal about the role of the brain in human behavior, and this has advanced our understanding of the enormously complex processes involved in the simplest action.

The brain is often likened to a computer that receives a constant stream of information about the environment, forms this information into a picture that makes sense, then sends messages to the required muscles that lead to the appropriate behavior being taken. Thus, as the light turns green at a busy crossing and you step out into the road, your eyes immediately spot the idiot trying to beat the light, your brain deals with the danger of a car coming at you, transmits an urgent message to the appropriate parts of your body, and you jump back out of the way. Given that you were successful, the whole incident took a fraction of a second.

The Brain: Links with Behavior

The adult human brain weighs about three pounds and fills the bony skull that protects it. It is the most complex and least understood part of the human body. We do know that the brain plays a central role in all of our activities, and that it integrates our behavior and changes it through the process of learning.

It has been suggested that learning produces physical and chemical changes within the brain. What may happen is that the electrical impulses which travel through the nervous system find it easier to follow a pathway that has already been laid down. Once a behavior is tried, a neural pathway is established in the brain and it becomes increasingly easier to do, until it is fully learned and becomes part of our behavioral repertoire.

The brain is symmetrically arranged into two connected parts or *hemispheres,* left and right. Oddly enough, the left hemisphere controls the right side of the body, and the right hemisphere the left side of the body. This is why people who suffer brain injury or a stroke on one side of the head have the opposite side paralyzed. It may also explain why most of us are right-handed. In most animals, the two hemispheres of the brain are equally important, but in humans the *left* hemisphere tends to be dominant.

STRUCTURE AND FUNCTION

The brain is often thought of as having three main sections: the hindbrain at the base of the skull, the forebrain at the front of the skull, and the midbrain in between (see Figure 5.1).

HINDBRAIN

Concerned with regular bodily activities like breathing and heart rate. It is also very important in muscle coordination, balance, and posture, and the communications between the sense organs and the limbs that carry out behavior in response to sensory information.

MIDBRAIN

Mainly concerned with visual stimuli and their relevance to the positioning of the body, but it also has the function of arousing the quiescent organism in response to a stimulus of excitement or danger from the environment.

FOREBRAIN

Deals with our habits and drives, our needs for food and water, our emotions and sexual behavior. The forebrain is also responsible for

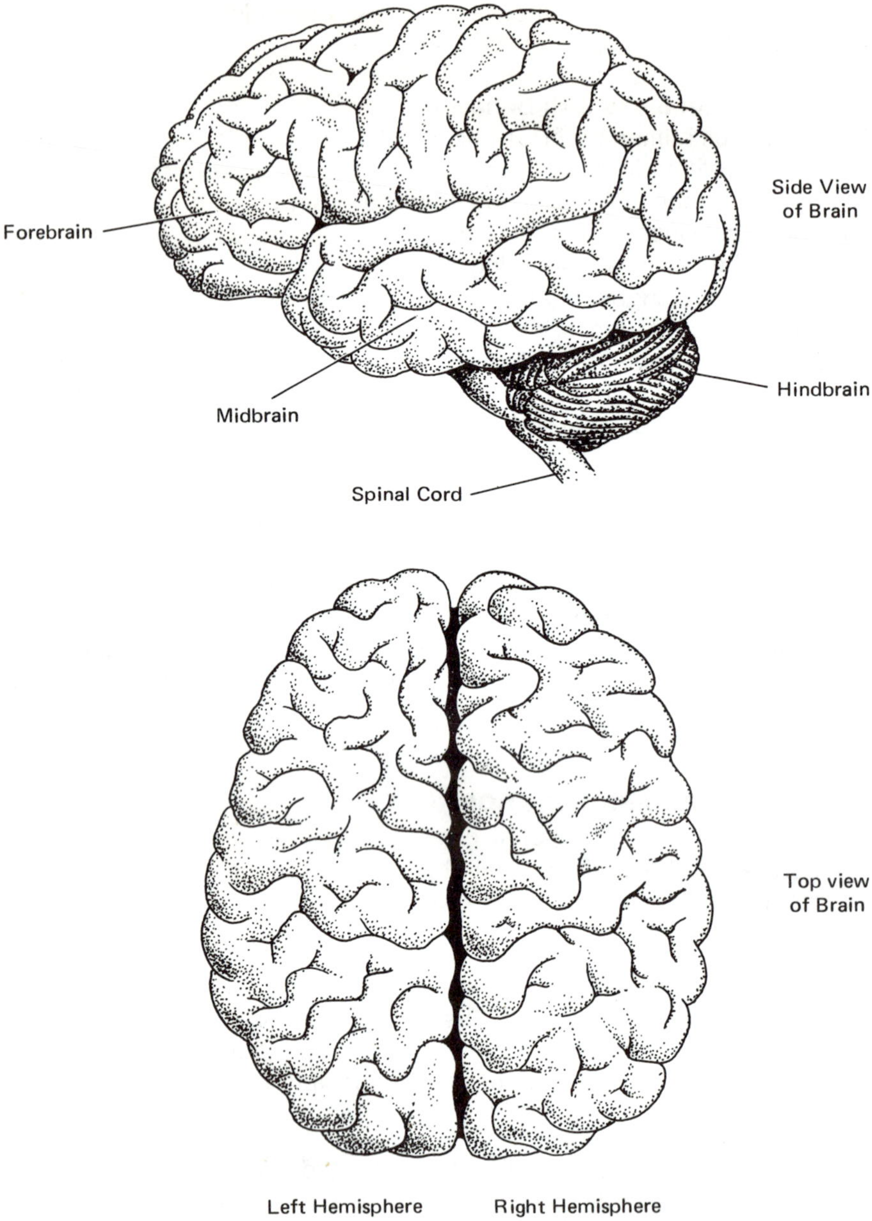

Figure 5.1 Two simplified schematic sketches of the brain.

the higher mental functions of thought, perception, speech, and learning (see Box 5.1).

It should be emphasized that while we can point to specific areas of the brain and link them to particular kinds of behavior, large tracts of the brain are still not understood, and that the brain acts as one complete highly integrated and interdependent unit. Scientists divide the brain into separate areas to help them better understand the functioning of each area, but they know that one simple piece of behavior can be the result of a great deal of activity in various different parts of the brain.

SPERRY: SPLIT BRAINS AND DOUBLE MINDS

The two hemispheres of the brain, in both animals and people, are connected by a group of nerves. Normally, information about tasks learned by the right hand or paw are stored not only in the left hemisphere that controls it but also in the right hemisphere; and similarly for tasks learned with the left. The nerves that connect the hemispheres, in other words, provide communication between them. Thus, people who learned to write or point with their right hand can perform the same skills to some extent with the left hand, without starting the learning process again from the very beginning.

In a series of experiments on cats and monkeys, R. W. Sperry discovered that if the connections between the two hemispheres were surgically cut, no information was passed between them and tasks that were learned with the right paw, for example, would have to be completely relearned with the left paw. However, apart from their inability to integrate and respond accordingly to the sensory information reaching the two hemispheres, the animals appeared otherwise to be quite normal (Sperry, 1968).

The same experiments could not, of course, be performed on human subjects, but there are quite a few people whose hemisphere connections have been cut for medical reasons (for example, to prevent the spreading of an epileptic seizure from one hemisphere to another) and their psychological functioning has been thoroughly studied. These operations usually seem to be quite successful—sensory feelings and muscle control are quite normal—and outside observers have difficulty detecting anything unusual about the patient's behavior. When tested by psychologists, however, some startling findings appear.

Just like the split-brain animals who had to learn tasks separately with left and right limbs, the human subjects lose their ability to integrate sensations from both halves of the body and to coordinate the movements of their limbs on both sides. When such a person is touched on one side of the body, he or she is unable to point to that area with the hand on the opposite side (controlled by the opposite hemisphere

BOX 5.1

STUDYING THE BRAIN

There are several ways in which scientists can study the brain directly.

1. Brain damage

It was known to many people in the ancient world that injuries to the brain were associated with changes in behavior, but their medical sciences were not sufficiently advanced to do much more than observe this connection.

In more recent times scientists have been able to identify the specific effects of damage to certain areas of the brain on particular behaviors or psychological functions. Thus scientists have shown for instance that damage to one area can lead to loss of language ability, while damage to another area can result in a loss of the capacity for abstract thought.

Brain damage may be caused by an injury or by disease. The psychological results are the same.

2. Ablation

Experiments on the brain that could not be done with humans are regularly done with animals by the process of ablation, where a section of the brain is carefully cut or removed. By this means scientists can systematically, section by section, explore the function of the brain on emotion and behavior.

3. Stimulation

By applying a mild electric current to different parts of the brain, scientists have provided themselves with a more delicate and less drastic method of relating brain function to behavior and emotion. It has been found by this method, for example, that a certain area of the brain (the hypothalamus) is concerned with regulating the state of thirst. When an animal is electrically stimulated in this area it begins to drink—and keeps on drinking until the current is switched off.

Electrical stimulation can also be used to *inhibit* behavior, as José Delgado has dramatically demonstrated. Delgado implanted electrodes in the brain of a bull, then stepped inside a bull ring and faced the animal armed only with a radio transmitter. When the bull charged him, Delgado transmitted a current to the electrodes and stopped it in its tracks. Exactly how this happens is not clear, but the net result is that the messages from the bull's brain to its muscles are intercepted and the behavior stops immediately.

Wilder Penfield, the Canadian neurosurgeon, has done a lot of research involving electrical stimulation in human beings. Many of Penfield's subjects were epileptic patients who required brain surgery. He usually gave them a local anaesthetic, injected into the scalp, so that the patient would remain conscious during the procedure. As the brain surface is quite insensitive and the patient feels no pain, Penfield could move an electrode over it to explore its effects. In this way he stimulated limbs to move, even when the patient was trying to lie still, and even more important he discovered that stimulating certain areas resulted in the patient vividly reliving long-forgotten memories.

4. Recording

Even when not stimulated, the brain has a continuous electrical activity of its own. In fact, the legal and medical definition of death includes the absence of any such activity. Brain activity is monitored by an EEG (electroencephalograph). Electrodes are attached to the scalp and the electrical information they send to the EEG machine is recorded by a pointer on a moving strip of paper. The different shapes of the resulting brain waves are related to different states of excitement or relaxation in the individual.

Source: José M. R. Delgado, *Physical Control of the Mind: Toward a Psychocivilized Society* (New York: Harper & Row, 1969), and W. Penfield and L. Roberts, *Speech and Brain Mechanisms* (Princeton, N.J.: Princeton University Press, 1959).

of the brain), but only with the hand on the same side. It is as though the same body were inhabited by two separate and completely independent brains—a split brain resulting in a double mind. Each of these brains is capable of doing all the things it could do before the split; it just doesn't tell the other one what it's doing.

Even stranger than this, each of the two split hemispheres can have the usual emotions, but sometimes these emotions are different in the two hemispheres. There is a case on record of a split-brain patient who became very angry with his wife, seized her with his left hand, and began to shake her violently—while his right hand intervened and tried to stop it (see Box 5.2).

Finally, we should note that this phenomenon is entirely due to an unusual physiological condition in the brain. It has *absolutely nothing* to do with the psychological conditions of split personality or schizophrenia, both of which will be dealt with in Chapter 14.

BOX 5.2

PSYCHOSURGERY

The various kinds of brain surgery that we looked at in Box 5.1 are not usually referred to as psychosurgery. This term is normally reserved for an operation performed on the human brain for the purpose of relieving severe emotional disorders.

The most common operation is done on the prefrontal lobes of the brain (and is therefore also known as a lobotomy) in order to make unusually violent people less violent. When this type of psychosurgery was introduced into the United States in the 1930s, it aroused an immediate controversy that still flares up from time to time.

One argument against psychosurgery is not so much that it doesn't work, but that it often produces drastic side effects. Patients may indeed be freed from the intense feelings of anxiety, inferiority, and rage that lead them to lash out violently, but at the same time their emotions and thought processes may be dulled to the point where they have difficulty maintaining a sense of who they are, and an image of their past and their future.

Critics have also pointed out that if psychosurgery is accepted as a legitimate means of dealing with abnormal behavior, it will have far-reaching social and political implications. These critics are to be found among both mental health professionals and the general public. Peter Breggin, a Washington psychologist, has argued that psychosurgery would be used on those groups in our society which are already oppressed, such as the poor minority groups, and the populations of our coercive institutions. Other scientists and practitioners have organized themselves into pressure groups to oppose the use of psychosurgery for social control.

Because of these controversial issues, and the fact that psychosurgery is irreversible, such operations are rarely performed today and then only as a last resort. Nevertheless, as an article on this subject in *Science* magazine puts it, psychosurgery, while "it is really at the extreme end of a massive spectrum of increasingly sophisticated ways people are learning to manipulate each other . . . may spur people to find ways of assessing how new behavioral technologies encroach on individual freedom and to decide on the extent to which they are desirable."

Source: C. Holden, "Psychosurgery: Legitimate Therapy or Laundered Lobotomy?" *Science* 179: 1109–1112, 1973, and M. F. Robinson and W. J. Freeman, *Psychosurgery and the Self* (New York: Grune & Stratton, 1955).

BRAIN DAMAGE: INJURY, NUTRITION, DRUGS

Having seen something of the paramount role the brain plays in human behavior, we can readily appreciate the serious effects of brain damage. *Injury* to the brain can lead to impairment of behavior at any time, but it is particularly serious from birth through the first year of life. The brain is particularly vulnerable at birth, when even the slightest head injury may have severe consequences for behavior and for psychological functioning.

Until the age of 12 months, for instance, a blow on the head can result in mental retardation later in life. After this age, the brain becomes much less vulnerable and the same injury would not be nearly as serious. A different kind of injury to the brain can also occur at birth, leading to mental retardation later on. If the delivery of the baby is difficult so that breathing is restricted and the supply of oxygen to the brain is insufficient, certain crucial areas of the brain may be permanently damaged.

In Chapter 3 we noted that severe malnutrition in young children has an adverse effect on their potential intelligence by impairing their brain functioning. The most serious aspect of such malnutrition is the absence of protein which is especially vital to the growth and maintenance of a healthy brain. However, inadequate *nutrition* takes its toll even before a child is born. The fetus in the pregnant mother's womb is totally dependent on her for its nutrition, and if the mother's diet lacks sufficient protein, premature birth and defects of the brain and the nervous system may result.

Apart from diet, whatever affects the pregnant mother may possibly affect the child in some way as well, both for good or ill. (It is much easier to point out examples of the "ill" than the "good," of course. In psychology, the irregular occurrence is a lot easier to spot than the regular.) Illness is a case in point. If the mother has rubella (German measles), for instance, her pregnancy may be terminated lest the child be infected and suffer brain damage from the infection.

The abuse of *drugs* is another way in which a child's future development can be adversely affected during pregnancy. The abuse may be completely inadvertent, as in the case of women who for medical reasons are given certain drugs which turn out to have unforeseen, and sometimes tragic, side effects for the fetus. There are also cases of pregnant drug addicts whose children are born with, and sometimes die of, the same addiction.

LANGUAGE IMPAIRMENT

The human capacity for language and speech is one of the few things that distinguishes us psychologically from animals. In fact, the human brain has an area dealing with language and speech that is not found in the brain of even the most intelligent animal. This area is located in the usually dominant left hemisphere. About seven percent of all people are left-handed, and their right hemisphere is normally dominant. But even among left-handed people the speech center is usually still found in the *left* hemisphere of the brain.

Damage to this speech center can lead to impairment of the ability to speak coherently or to understand spoken language. This is known as *aphasia.* Surgeons and physiologists have done a great deal of work with aphasiac patients (often people who have suffered strokes where the blood supply to the speech center of the brain was cut off). Due to the clear links between the speech area of the brain and the act of speaking, the work done on these patients has helped psychologists interested in language to understand a great deal about the functioning of the brain that underlies normal speech and the use of language in everyday life.

One interesting aspect of the speech center's location in the left hemisphere takes us back to our discussion about split brains and double minds. If a split-brain patient is shown the word *heart* in such a way that the letters *he* are in the left field of vision, and the letters *art* are in the right field of vision, he or she will not be able to integrate the two separate parts into the whole word *heart* because the connections between the right and left hemispheres have been cut.

The patient will report that he sees *art* but will say nothing about *he.* As *art* is what he sees with his right eye, the message gets passed to his left hemisphere and, this being the hemisphere with the speech center, he can report what he sees. His left eye transmits *he* to his right hemisphere, but without a speech center there he cannot report what he sees; and of course with the connections between the hemispheres cut he has no access to the speech center in the left hemisphere. However, as the visual information the patient receives through his left eye is still stored as normal in the right hemisphere, he is able to *recognize* what he sees even though he cannot say it. Thus, when he is shown *he* among a group of other letters, he can point quite correctly to what his eye has seen.

SOCIAL IMPLICATIONS

Whatever the differences are between human and animal behavior, they can be traced back to differences in the brain. Or to put it another way, our brain is what makes us human, and the more we use it the more human we become.

At the beginning of human history, one of our apelike ancestors (Harvey, I think it was) learned how to make weapons for hunting and self-defense, and tools for digging and shaping the world around him. Here was an animal whose brain had evolved genetically to the point where he could begin to evolve *culturally* and manipulate his environment by the power of thought. Instead of adapting to the environment and dying out when the environment changed (as the dinosaurs did), humans could now begin to adapt the environment to *their* needs. Where animals grew fur to protect themselves from the cold, people learned to slay animals and make themselves fur coats.

By now it looks as though we may have adapted our environment up the spout. The complex societies that we have created with our brain power seem to have acquired dynamics of their own that could conceivably result in the destruction of us along with our environment. If we do avoid catastrophe, it will be by emulating old Harvey and using our brains to find a better way.

SUGGESTED READINGS

Asimov, I. *The Human Brain: Its Capacities and Functions.* New York: New American Library, 1965. The famous science fiction writer is himself a scientist who can write clearly on many scientific topics. Here he describes how the brain organizes and guides an individual's behavior.

Crichton, M. *The Terminal Man.* New York: Knopf, 1972. A novel based upon scientific research about connecting a human brain to a computer.

Delgado, J. *Physical Control of the Mind: Toward a Psychocivilized Society.* New York: Harper & Row, 1969. The uses of electrical stimulation of the brain in both humans and animals.

Jones, K., Shainberg, L., and Byer, C. *Drugs and Alcohol.* New York: Harper & Row, 1969. The effects of drugs and alcohol on behavior and the social problems they present.

Williams, M. *Brain Damage and the Mind.* Baltimore: Penguin Books, 1970. A survey of the different kinds of brain damage and their psychological effects.

Wooldridge, D. *The Machinery of the Brain.* New York: McGraw-Hill, 1963. A nontechnical account of physiological psychology.

CHAPTER 6

Learning how to make sense

MODIFYING BEHAVIOR THROUGH LEARNING

Learning, according to E. R. Hilgard (1975), a leading authority on the subject, is "a relatively permanent change in behavior that occurs as the result of prior experience." Most psychologists would probably define learning in a similar fashion, so let us accept Hilgard's definition and examine it a little more closely.

By *relatively permanent* we mean behavior that is not due to the effects of temporary situations like taking alcohol or drugs or being very tired, any of which can dramatically affect the way we behave for a limited period of time. When we say that learning is the result of prior experience, we exclude the changes in behavior that accompany the process of growing up and maturing in both animals and people. And we also exclude, of course, the behavioral changes that may follow brain damage or any other disability.

These exclusions seem to add up to a lot of behavior, and we may begin to wonder how much of our behavior is actually changed by learning. But in fact a truly enormous amount of behavior change is due to learning. Some psychologists would argue that learning is the most important process in human behavior, ramifying through every area of our lives. Even those popular old pastimes, sex and aggression, are largely learned behaviors. We have to *learn* how to fight and, like Harlow's monkeys, we have to *learn* how to mate.

The effects of learning on behavior are easiest to see in young children, for whom the world is new and waiting to be discovered. As they become increasingly aware of their environment, their society *socializes* them, instructs them in how they should behave. In the process of being socialized, children must learn the approved ways of walking, talking, eating, excreting, and thinking, to name just a few of the more obvious kinds of behavior. They must also learn how to make sense of life in the fashion approved by society; whom to like and whom to dislike; who is friendly and who is dangerous.

In place of the term *prior experience* in the definition of learning, the word *practice* has been used.

We tend to associate practice with repeated attempts at the same behavior, like piano exercises. But in the more precise way the term is used by psychologists, it could also refer to staying out of the rain, putting your left sock on before your right, or leaving half your paycheck at the race track every week. All of these behaviors are learned, and learned from experience by *repetition.* Like all psychological processes, practice is quite neutral in its social implications, and bad habits seem to be distressingly well learned.

At the same time, as we saw in our nature-nurture discussion in Chapter 3, learning can take place without the individual practicing anything. I quoted the example of the baby learning to fear strangers before it had ever encountered a stranger to practice its fears on. As in the case of repeated practice, the child had learned by experience. But in this case, the experience was that he *should not* be afraid of familiar faces—and therefore that he *should* be afraid of strangers.

We noted in Chapter 5 that the human brain is largely what distinguishes us from animals. This difference shows up in behavior where our superior brain gives us a much greater capacity for learning. Even newborn human infants are capable of some learning, and this ability to learn increases greatly as the sense organs, the nervous system, and the brain rapidly mature.

Because so much of the pioneer research on learning has been done with animals, we will discuss the basic principles of this work first, then examine their operation in humans. We will also look at some other forms of learning that are specific to humans.

Pavlov, Skinner, and Conditioning

The term *conditioning* is closely associated with one of the most famous names in psychology, Ivan Pavlov. Yet Pavlov never considered himself a psychologist. He was trained as a physiologist and spent a good deal of his long career studying the digestive system of dogs. In fact, he was awarded the Nobel Prize for his work. But in the course of his research on digestion, he clearly demonstrated the working of a learning process that was psychological.

Pavlov had known for a long time that when dogs are fed, their digestive glands start to function and they salivate. What he began to observe in the course of his research was that the dogs in his lab began to salivate *before* they were fed, as soon as they recognized the man who was coming to feed them. This aroused Pavlov's curiosity, and he designed an ingenious series of experiments to find out what was going on (Pavlov, 1927).

A dog salivating when he is given food displays a perfectly automatic inborn response. It does not depend on any other conditions being present, so that both the *stimulus* of presenting the food to the dog and the dog's *response* of salivating are *unconditional*—unconditional stimulus (US); unconditional response (UR).

A dog salivating when he is merely shown food or sees someone bringing him food is not producing an inborn response because there is a condition attached to it. The condition is that the dog be able to associate what he now sees with what he has previously tasted; that he be able to recognize it as food. When the dog recognizes food, his brain flashes a message to his digestive system and he starts to salivate. Thus, the *stimulus* of seeing the food and the *response* of salivating are both *conditional*—conditional stimulus (CS); conditional response (CR).

What Pavlov now wanted to find out was what kinds of conditional stimuli could produce the conditional response of salivating. After starting out by simply showing the animal food and getting it to salivate, he substituted a whole host of conditional stimuli like bells, buzzers, metronomes, and lights, and found that with any of them he could produce the conditional response and get the dog to salivate.

The experimental procedure he used is known as *conditioning:*

1. Food (US) leads to salivation (UR).
2. The sound of a bell (CS) by itself leads to nothing.
3. The sound of a bell (CS) followed by the presentation of food (US) leads to salivation (UR).
4. When this process has been repeated often enough that the dog begins to associate the bell (CS) with the food (US), he will salivate (UR) at the sound of the bell alone.
5. At this point, the animal's salivation has become conditional on hearing the bell rather than unconditional on being given food. Thus, the bell (CS) now results in salivation (CR) just as effectively as the food (US) had resulted in salivation (UR). The animal, in other words, has been *conditioned* to salivate at the sound of a bell.

Having conditioned an animal to salivate in response to some arbitrary stimulus, Pavlov wanted to find out if it would stay conditioned. He discovered that after a time, if the ringing bell was not accompanied by food, the dog's conditional response was extinguished and it stopped salivating. This *extinction* could be counteracted if he occasionally followed the sound of the bell with some food. Such *reinforcement* of the conditional response was enough to keep the animal salivating indefinitely whenever the bell was sounded.

As Pavlov systematically varied the different factors in his conditioning experiment, he discovered that the dog would not only salivate at the sound of the regular bell or buzzer that was used, but at other bells or buzzers that had a similar sound. The animal was generalizing from the particular stimulus it had been conditioned with to a wider range of stimuli that were similar to it—*stimulus generalization.*

At the same time, Pavlov demonstrated that a dog can also be trained not to generalize to any other stimulus. He showed that the animal could be trained to discriminate its original conditioned stimulus from any other conditioned stimulus. He simply reinforced the animal with food if it salivated to one particular sound and did not reinforce it for responding to any other sound. The dog thereby learned *stimulus discrimination.*

We have seen that classical (or Pavlovian) conditioning is a very basic form of learning that depends on a stimulus (S) being given to an animal which results in a particular response (R). The animal's behavior in this pattern of stimulus-response is said to be *elicited* from it. The animal does not initiate the conditioning process by its own behavior. However, much of animal behavior is not elicited by outside stimuli but is *emitted* by the animal's own spontaneous actions. Without waiting for a push from outside, an animal will often begin to explore its surroundings, to "operate" on its environment. An animal engaging in such activity is said to exhibit *operant behavior,* and this brings us to the work of another famous psychologist—B. F. Skinner.

Skinner carried Pavlov's work on conditioning a step further and showed that it was possible to *shape* an animal's behavior in some very ingenious ways by using conditioning techniques (Skinner, 1938). This process is known as *operant conditioning.* He designed a cage for an experimental rat that completely controlled the animal's environment. With this cage (now known as a "Skinner box") he could control the amount of light, heat, and sound that the animal was exposed to. But the crucial feature of the Skinner box was a small bar set low down on one wall. When this bar was pressed, a food pellet automatically dropped down into a tray below it.

As the rat explored the Skinner box, it accidentally pressed the bar, winning itself some food. It ate the food, but didn't make the connection. In the course of moving about it pressed the bar again, and this time the idea clicked. The rat now made the connection and associated the bar pressing with the appearance of food. It then proceeded to press the bar as often as it could. As with classical conditioning, as long as the rat's operant behavior of bar pressing was reinforced by the appearance of food, it continued with the behavior. When Skinner withdrew the food and the rat was no longer rewarded for this particular operant behavior, it stopped doing it.

Skinner also neatly demonstrated that the avoidance of pain is at least as important in reinforcing operant behavior as the gaining of a reward. Through the floor of the box, he produced a mild electric shock which could be turned off by pressing the same bar that had produced food in the previous experiment. The rat went through the same random movements before pressing the bar accidentally and turning off the current. As before, it quickly learned to press the bar as soon as the current came on, thereby avoiding further shocks. Skinner called this *aversive conditioning.*

When discussing Pavlov's work, we saw that animals could learn to generalize from one conditioned stimulus to others and conversely to discriminate between one particular stimulus and any other stimuli. Skinner has shown that these principles also apply to operant conditioning. In fact, by building up the animal's learning step-by-step he has shown that animals can learn some very complex tasks. Animal trainers in zoos and circuses are actually applying operant conditioning by reinforcing the animal with food when it exhibits the desired behavior. By this means they can get horses to dance and dolphins to perform acrobatics. Skinner himself has actually taught pigeons to play ping pong, and has demonstrated it to his students.

Kohler's Insightful Apes

In our discussion of conditioning, we were looking at a very simple and basic form of learning behavior. Even in an operant conditioning situation, where the animal took some initiative, the learning involved was accomplished by trying out the behavior many times until it was satisfactory to the trainer. Circus tricks performed by animals require a great deal of patient step-by-step training, a lot of tries and lot of errors corrected, before the animal has learned the trick. *Trial and error* learning is thus a slow and laborious process. People, as well as animals, learn by this means, but a lot of human learning is due to *insight,* where the understanding of a situation or the solution to a problem seems to occur quite suddenly and without any careful step-by-step process of learning.

This phenomenon, where everything seems to click all at once (an "aha" reaction), also occurs among the most intelligent animals. Wolfgang Kohler, for instance, has described some striking examples of insight in the behavior of the apes he studied (Kohler, 1925). In a typical experiment, a banana is placed outside a chimpanzee's cage but well out of his reach, even with the aid of the short stick that Kohler has provided him. Just outside the cage is another sick, long enough to reach the banana from the cage. The animal reaches for the fruit, first with his hand, then with the short stick lying inside the cage. He is unable to reach the banana, of course, and gibbers about in frustration. After a time he calms down, backs off, and surveys the whole situation once more, taking in all the elements of the problem. Suddenly the answer comes to him. He uses the short stick to pull in the longer stick, then successfully hauls in the banana with the new tool at his disposal.

By such a process of *insightful learning,* Kohler's apes have solved much more complex problems than this. They have made tools and used them, and they have combined various elements in their environment (like ropes and sticks) to reach distant objects. But there is a limit, of course, to animal insight, and even the brightest chimps cannot learn beyond the level of a three- or four-year-old child.

The greatest advantage of an insightful solution is that, unlike trial and error learning, it can be applied to new situations. No specific skill or set of movements is learned, but an understanding of the relationship between a means and an end is gained.

A THEORY OF LEARNING

Because the learning process is so important to human behavior, learning theory based on animal research has given rise to a long series of controversies within psychology. Generally speaking, there are two main schools of thought. One of these schools emphasizes the *associations* that link a stimulus to a response to form a new connection, a new way of behaving. The classical conditioning of Pavlov is the prime example of this type of new behavior. Learning, to the psychologists of this school, is thus the formation of new *habits,* like the habit of associating the word *ball* with a round object, or the habit of laughing and crying in particular ways. The organism must go through a process of trial and error before learning is accomplished in this way.

The other school of thought emphasizes the importance of understanding and insight; some higher mental processes like the "aha" reaction of Kohler's apes as opposed to the conditional responses of Pavlov's dogs. Psychologists of the insight or cognitive school feel that the sheer formation of habits, no matter how complex, cannot entirely account for the ability of people and animals to cope successfully with problems they have never experienced before. Some other process, they argue, takes place inside the learner's head that allows him to use the habits already learned and then go a step further into unknown territory.

Harry Harlow (1949) has done some research that suggests a way in which these two schools of thought might be reconciled. He presented his monkeys with a series of problems where they had to choose between two objects, under one of which some food was hidden. The two objects were either different colors or different shapes, and their position was alternated randomly from trial to trial, with the food always under the same object.

Over 300 such problems were presented to the animals, and in the course of the experiment Harlow noticed an interesting phenomenon. On the first trial of each problem the monkeys had to guess the answer, and so they chose the correct object about 50 percent of the time. For the first few problems, the monkeys didn't do much better than chance. On the tenth problem, they could manage about 75 percent correct choices by the sixth trial. But by the three hundredth problem they had the correct solution 98 percent of the time by the second trial.

At the beginning of the study the monkeys had approached the problem in a trial and error fashion, making no systematic use of what they discovered on the first trial. By the end of the study they understood that if the food wasn't under the first object they chose it had to be under the other one, and they correctly chose this object on all subsequent trials regardless of its position.

The animals had acquired what Harlow called a *learning set* for the series of problems they were given which enabled them to transcend the original trial and error approach and use their insight to make sense of, and master, the situation. The animals were, in fact, "learning to learn."

Studying the Learning Process

It may be as well to mention at this point that we have a fundamental difficulty in trying to study the learning process—we can't see it. What we can see is the *performance* of some behavior, and it is this performance we study in trying to understand the learning process. We have to infer from someone's performance whether any learning has taken place inside his head.

Making such inferences from performance to previous learning would be very difficult unless the process were simplified for study. How do we know whether the subject learned the task he was given entirely during the course of the experiment, or was aided by some earlier learning he'd done elsewhere?

Psychologists therefore try to devise tasks that will be completely new to the subject, so that old learning will not interfere with the new. Thus, instead of giving people lists of words and measuring how well they can learn them in a certain order, psychologists devise lists of nonsense syllables like MYV, ZOJ, and PEM for the same purpose. Their reasoning is that people are not able to associate these nonsense syllables with anything they have previously seen, and thus everybody has to learn them from scratch, making it possible to measure individual learning abilities and to compare them with others (see Box 6.1).

BOX 6.1

A BRILLIANT USE OF NONSENSE

A study reported in 1885, whose findings are still accepted today and whose methods are still being used, unquestionably deserves the overworked adjective *classic.* Such is the work of the German psychologist Hermann Ebbinghaus.

Before Ebbinghaus, psychologists had generally believed that there was no way to study the workings of complex mental processes like those involved in learning, memory, and thinking. Ebbinghaus showed that there was such a way and that all you needed to find it was brilliant insight, scientific rigor, and a lot of hard work.

Furthermore, Ebbinghaus showed that a classic contribution could be made to psychology without the aid of university facilities, costly apparatus, research assistants—or even subjects. Ebbinghaus worked entirely on his own, in his own home, and studied his own process of memory. Systematically, and over a period of years, he observed the way in which he learned poems and other written material.

Ebbinghaus noted how past experiences and emotions were associated with the words he memorized, playing an important part in what material he remembered and what he forgot. He reasoned that any attempt to measure remembering or forgetting would have to start with a base line of material that had no previous associations in his experience—and what he came up with was the *nonsense syllable.*

Ebbinghaus formed his nonsense syllables by using the formula *consonant-vowel-consonant,* as in NOV, ZOJ, and PEM. Because the syllables had no meaning associated with them, Ebbinghaus reasoned that they would therefore be of uniform difficulty when he came to learn them. So, having made up some 2300 of these nonsense syllables, he randomly selected about a dozen and proceeded to memorize them.

Ebbinghaus made up hundreds of these lists and memorized each list in the same fashion. He sat down at exactly the same time each day to learn a list of nonsense syllables and repeated each syllable once, to the beat of a metronome, thus ensuring that each syllable received exactly the same amount of attention.

The number of repetitions necessary to memorize each list was noted. After a certain time interval (an hour, a day, a week, or a month), Ebbinghaus noted that in order to memorize a list completely, he needed fewer repetitions of it than he had when memorizing it the first time. The difference between the two attempts to recall the material, by learning then re-learning the same lists, gave him a measure of forgetting, and his results have been verified many times since then. Most of what he learned was forgotten within a few hours, after which the rate of forgetting slowed considerably over the following weeks.

Source: Hermann Ebbinghaus, *Memory: A Contribution to Experimental Psychology* (New York: Dover, 1964).

READINESS TO LEARN: MOTIVATION AND AROUSAL

There is currently a hot debate in some psychology circles as to whether or not people can learn while they sleep. The prevailing opinion seems to be that if we are capable of learning in our sleep, what we learn certainly can't be much. There is a great deal of evidence, in fact, that the wider awake, the more *aroused* we are, the better we are likely to learn.

While a state of arousal is probably necessary for a person or an animal to learn, it is not by itself a sufficient condition for learning to take place. Something more is required—the will, drive, urge, need, or desire to learn. The organism, in other words, must have the right *motivation* for learning.

Motives represent a kind of energy within us that push us in a certain direction, toward the fulfillment of a certain goal. Some of these motives, such as hunger and thirst, are very evident. If we are hungry, we are in a high state of arousal and are very motivated to look for food. When we have eaten our fill, the arousal level drops and the food-seeking motivation disappears. This is a biological motive that animals as well as people are born with.

However, you will remember from our discussion of genotypes and phenotypes in Chapter 3 that whatever we are born with (genotype) has to be expressed in behavior (phenotype) that can be observed. So it is with biological drives or motives. A person's need for food, drink, and sex can be satisfied in many different ways, resulting in many and varied behaviors; and each of these behaviors is learned. Oriental and Arabian food and ways of eating may seem strange to us, as ours no doubt seem strange to them, but all these customs represent different ways that people have learned to deal with the same unlearned motivation of hunger.

There is some evidence that people and many animals have a biological motivation toward exploring their environment—curiosity, perhaps. In exploring the environment, a certain amount of learning may happen incidentally without there being a deliberate attempt to learn something specific. For human infants, such *incidental learning* might be that mother is soft and warm and the source of food.

Adults are also capable of incidental learning. You learn the location of certain landmarks on your way home not because you deliberately set out to do so, but simply because you see those landmarks every day when you walk past them and your brain registers that information for you. You needn't learn how to do it, as it were.

However, any other kind of learning must be learned. It is a far cry from curiosity about the environment to studying accounting in college, for instance, and people have to learn that this kind of learning is rewarding. An accounting student has already learned the rewards society gives for going to school, for studying, for passing exams. These rewards are *extrinsic;* they are awarded because a task has been performed, but the task itself may not be rewarding enough to motivate anyone.

On the other hand, our accounting student may have learned that he likes working with figures and learning how to use them. This would be an *intrinsic* reward, where the person would be motivated to perform the task for its own sake. In everyday life, of course, the learning we do is extremely complex and we are usually motivated by a combination of intrinsic and extrinsic rewards.

We noted earlier that a high degree of arousal is necessary to motivate learning successfully. We should now note in passing that there is such a thing as too much arousal, and this is often detrimental to learning. If a person in a learning situation is so aroused about it as to be anxious, the anxiety can interfere with learning. Thus, there is some evidence that people with high anxiety get poorer grades in school than people with low anxiety (see Box 6.2).

CONDITIONING IN HUMANS

Earlier in this chapter we discussed some basic forms of learning that were discovered from research on animals. We will take a look here at some of the implications this research has for humans, and then discuss some forms of learning that have been discovered by research on humans.

Both classical (Pavlovian) conditioning and operant (Skinnerian) conditioning exist in human as well as animal learning. Psychologists have long realized the frequency with which conditioned responses appear in everyday human behavior. In the early years of this century, J. B. Watson provided a convincing demonstration of how children can learn to fear something they have previously liked (Watson and Rayner, 1920).

Watson took an eleven-month-old child named Albert and showed

BOX 6.2

FREEZING UNDER PRESSURE

Most of us are all too well aware of the situation where it's important to do well, say something intelligent, or make a certain impression. What can make these occasions especially memorable is the awful realization that your brain has decided to go home early that day, leaving you blank, tongue-tied, and helpless.

Although psychologists are also liable to "freeze" under pressure, they have attempted to figure out what goes on under these circumstances. There appear to be three factors involved—motivation, emotion, and performance. Any performance of any kind of behavior is affected by motivation and by emotional arousal, but not always in the same way.

When motivation and arousal regarding a given task are low, it will be poorly performed. Increasing motivation and arousal results in increasingly good performance—up to a point. Beyond this optimum point, any increase in motivation and arousal will lead to a poorer performance. This finding is known as the Yerkes-Dodson Law, after the two psychologists who first proposed it.

It has also been found that different kinds of tasks have different

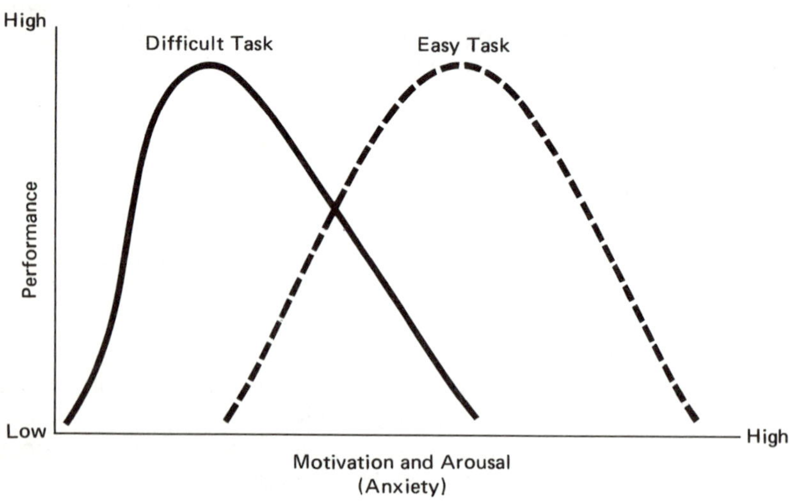

Figure 6.1 Relationships between anxiety and performance. (*Source: R. M. Yerkes and J. D. Dodson, "The Relationship of Strength of Stimulus to Rapidity of Habit Formations,"* Journal of Comparative Neurology and Psychology *18:459–482, 1908*).

optimum levels of motivation and arousal. Simple tasks have a higher optimum level than complex tasks, meaning that you can feel more anxiety about simple tasks before you begin "freezing" under pressure. So if you are mowing the lawn you can be very anxious about your performance and still perform well. But if you are taking the Graduate Record Exam and feel the same level of anxiety, your performance will suffer accordingly (see Figure 6.1).

him a rat. Albert was quite unafraid of the rat and wanted to play with it. Then Watson showed Albert the rat again, and this time he accompanied the appearance of the rat (CS) with a loud noise (US). Very young children are automatically frightened of unexpected loud noises (UR), and Albert was no exception. After the appearance of the rat had been paired with the noise a few times, Albert showed signs of fear when the rat appeared (CR), even if the noise was not sounded. He had now learned to fear rats.

The child even behaved in accordance with the stimulus generalization principle we noted earlier. He now showed fear when presented with other furry objects, like a rabbit or a man with a beard. History does not record whether Albert was left with his new fear but we can presume he wasn't, for it should have been a simple enough matter to recondition him by associating the appearance of the rat with something pleasant.

More recently, it has been experimentally shown that adults can also be conditioned to learn a new response by the use of unconditioned automatic reflexes like the knee jerk or eyelid blink. If a light is flashed just before a puff of air, people will eventually blink when the light is presented by itself.

Outside the laboratory, many psychologists would argue that classical conditioning is of fundamental importance in everyday human learning. Generally speaking, it would appear that our emotional responses are basically set in early childhood by a process of classical conditioning, with all the tremendous implications this has for adult behavior.

There is a case on record of a woman who had an irrational fear, a *phobia,* of running water and the splashing sound it made (Bagby, 1923). She had no idea how she came to have this phobia. Eventually, under treatment for her phobia, the woman remembered an important incident from her childhood. Despite her parents' instructions to the contrary, she had gone wading in a stream with a fast current and found herself trapped beneath a waterfall with the water splashing over her. She was found by an aunt, and being very much more anxious about having disobeyed her parents than about her physical safety, she begged her aunt not to say anything. The aunt agreed and the child quickly forgot the whole incident. Shortly thereafter, her phobia appeared. She had been conditioned to fear waterfalls and had generalized the stimulus to include any kind of running, splashing water.

Operant conditioning, where the subject must deliberately emit some kind of behavior in learning a new response, can likewise be seen in many common (if less dramatic) human behaviors. In the laboratory the effects of operant conditioning can be demonstrated quite simply. In conversation with a subject, an experimenter can get him to increase the number of opinions he gives by reinforcing all such statements. Thus, whenever the subject begins a sentence with "I think," or "In my opinion," the experimenter responds with "Right," "I agree," or "M'hmmm." Conversely, statements of opinion can be decreased by disagreeing with such statements or just being silent when they are made (see Box 6.3).

The skills we learn in doing things are a result of operant conditioning, and these skills include writing, driving, typing, riding a bicycle, and even answering the telephone. But perhaps the most important skill we learn via operant conditioning is the ability to speak our native language.

Babies are born with the capacity to speak any language on earth, and when they discover that they can produce sounds, they start to babble. This babbling contains all the sounds the human voice is capable of making, and the language that this babbling will grow into depends entirely on which language his parents happen to speak. Out of their child's babble, parents will pick up what seems to them recognizable sounds—like "Dada."

The emission of these sounds will quickly be reinforced by cries of parental delight, and the child will thus be encouraged to continue. When he learns "Dada," he will probably generalize from this stimulus and affix the label to any male he sees. By appropriate reinforcement and extinction, he will gradually learn to discriminate and apply the word "Dada" to his father alone. In this way, by trying to make sense of their child's babbling, parents teach their children what language to speak.

TRANSFER OF TRAINING

If we had to learn a new response to every new situation we found ourselves in, we would have to lead very restricted lives indeed. But fortunately for us, much of the learning done in one situation can often be transferred to other situations. If you learn to drive a car in one particular model, you can probably drive most other models too. If you've already learned Spanish, it will help you in learning Italian. The

BOX 6.3

CONTROLLING THE UNCONTROLLABLE

Until the mid-1960s, psychologists believed that classical and operant conditioning were two different forms of learning, relating to two different kinds of nervous systems. It was generally thought that involuntary responses like salivation and eye blinking were quite automatic when stimulated, and thus the province of the *autonomic nervous system.* Voluntary muscle responses like bar pressing and typing were considered to be under the control of the *central nervous system.*

Neal Miller considered this difference between classical and operant conditioning to be more apparent than real. In Miller's opinion, they were two examples of the same learning processes under different conditions. In order to support his idea, Miller had to show that automatic responses were susceptible not only to classical conditioning but also to operant conditioning.

Miller carefully conducted an elaborate series of studies with rats, where the animals' muscles were temporarily paralyzed with curare to ensure that they could not voluntarily produce the desired involuntary effects. The reward to the animals took the form of a pleasurable electrical stimulation. Thus, Miller tried to affect the rats' heartbeat by waiting for a spontaneous increase or decrease in the rate of heartbeat, then rewarding them with the pleasurable stimulation.

The results of Miller's experiments were startling. He and his associates had apparently trained the animals to control their heart rates, blood pressure, intestinal contractions, and urine formation. They had even trained them to send blood to one ear and not the other.

The implications of Miller's work for the medical treatment of humans are, of course, quite dramatic, and they were immediately seized upon by other scientists who began to figure out practical applications for patients suffering from a variety of diseases.

There are still many problems to be overcome, however, before routine operant conditioning of blood pressure or heart rate becomes a therapeutic reality for human medical problems. Although some successes have been reported, it seems that the conditioning is often quickly extinguished when the patient leaves the hospital.

Finally, the relation between classical and operant conditioning has not been entirely cleared up. Although there is no reason to doubt the scientific rigor of Miller's original experiments, neither he nor anyone else has been able to repeat his findings. As usual in psychological research, the problem seems to be more complex than scientists had thought.

Source: Leo Di Cara, "Learning in the Autonomic Nervous System," *Scientific American* 222 (1): 30–39, 1970, B. T. Engel, "Operant Conditioning of Cardiac Function: A Status Report," *Psychophysiology* 9: 161–177, 1972, and N. E. Miller and B. R. Dworkin, "Visceral Learning: Recent Difficulties with Curarized Rats and Significant Problems for Human Research," in P. A. Obrist et al., eds., *Contemporary Trends in Cardiovascular Psychophysiology* (Chicago: Aldine-Atherton, 1973).

transfer of training involved in these examples is *positive:* your present performance or learning is helped by learning you did in the past.

But if you learn how to drive a car, then how to steer a boat with a tiller, your learning will be made *more* difficult. In a car, you turn the wheel the way you want to go; in a boat, you push the tiller in the direction opposite to the way you want to go. Your experience in driving a car is thus a *negative* transfer of training because it hinders your new learning.

Similarity of stimuli (similar cars) and similarity of responses (similar ways of driving them) result in a positive transfer of training. Dissimilarity of responses (steering systems of cars and boats) result in a negative transfer of training.

The previous learning that we transfer to a new situation is not just a matter of particular skills or specific information that may be relevant. We also transfer ways of learning. Like Harlow's problem solving monkeys, we learn how to learn. However, research on both animals and children has shown that learning to learn is only possible when the original learning is thoroughly mastered. If simple things are not properly learned, there can be little positive transfer to more complex learning. It is quite useless to introduce a sixth-grade child to Shakespeare if he has not yet mastered a first-grade reader. If a child has not learned how to learn, putting him into increasingly complex learning situations, simply because of his age, can only pile frustration upon frustration.

VERBAL LEARNING

Perhaps the most important kind of learning, and one that may be unique to human beings, is *verbal learning.* Learning the use of words is the basis for practically all of the formal learning we do in school, and for a great deal of the informal learning we do outside school.

Verbal learning is necessary for the acquisition of language, and language is closely bound up with thought. We put problems and concepts into words, communicate them, think about them, and reason our way toward future behavior. We will pick up this topic again in Chapter 9, when we explore the implications of verbal learning for becoming a person.

REMEMBERING AND THE NEED TO FORGET

Whatever we learned would be of no use to us unless we had some way of storing it, ready to be retrieved when needed. Whenever we learn something, the brain engages in various activities that probably result in some kind of physical traces. We then store this information and experience in our *memory.* Exactly how this happens or what these physical traces are like, psychologists can only speculate about. It is quite conceivable, however, that some trace of past learning will always remain. The problem is to retrieve it. Whatever can be retrieved is *remembered;* whatever cannot be retrieved is *forgotten.*

There are several ways in which you can try to retrieve previous learning from your memory. If you have been given a poem to learn and you are then asked to recite the poem, you are being urged to *recall* what you learned. Similarly, if you have essay questions on an exam, you have to recall previous learning in order to answer the questions.

If the exam was composed of multiple choice questions instead of essays, then only *recognition* of previous learning would be called for. You would normally be able to recognize more of the material learned than you could recall.

The most reliable and sensitive measure of remembering the material you had learned would be obtained if you were asked to *relearn* it. In fact, if you ever have to relearn something, you will probably find that things you thought were long forgotten can be remembered quite clearly. Your second learning should therefore be easier than your first, as you would benefit from a positive transfer of training.

The most famous study of relearning concerns a fifteen-month-old boy who was read passages of ancient Greek every day until he was three years old (Burtt, 1941). The poor child had absolutely no understanding of this material, of course. When he was eight years old (and still knew no Greek), he was asked to memorize these same passages, together with similar passages that had not been read to him in his earlier experience. The difference was striking. He required 30 percent less effort to memorize the old passages than the new.

These three processes of recall, recognition, and relearning are three different kinds of response to the same stimulus; to the same jogging of the memory. In discussing how much learning has been retrieved or remembered by these means and how much forgotten, it must be understood, as we mentioned earlier in this chapter, that we have no direct access to learning processes. When we look at test results and say that Joe learned more than Moe but less than Flo, we are talking about *performance.* And, as we noted in our section on motivation, various factors other than what is learned and what is remembered can affect performance.

The actual process of committing something to memory seems to involve three distinct stages. When the sense organs react to environmental stimuli by sending information to the brain, a fleeting trace of the stimulus remains after the message is sent. For example, if you just glance at a telephone number you will have a very brief memory of it as it registers in your brain. This *sensory memory* lasts for less than a second, and if you want to use the information from your senses it has to be transferred onto the next stage of memory.

This second stage lasts for a slightly longer period of time (up to 30 seconds), long enough to decide whether or not the incoming information is worth keeping. As most of the information is not worth keeping, it gets tossed out or, in other words, forgotten. If you call half a dozen local stores to see if they have a certain make of camera, you will not remember their telephone numbers for very long. Nor would you want to remember this kind of information; it would be a waste of time and effort, and confusing to boot. But some of the information that we have to consider in this *short-term memory* stage is important enough to be kept in a permanent record, and it must then be transferred to the third and final stage in the process.

This third stage is called *long-term memory,* and in order to get there the information has to be processed while being held in short-term memory. New information is constantly passing from sensory memory into short-term memory, and as it does so it pushes out the information already there. Information that is earmarked for long-term retention is therefore repeated or rehearsed (e.g., by saying it aloud or writing it down) so that it sticks. It is then coded in such a way that what we consider essential about it is retained and the rest is discarded. The information is then ready to be placed alongside similar information in long-term memory storage, where it will probably remain forever.

Contrary to widely held belief, memories that are filed away in long-term storage do not fade with time, although they may change somewhat. Our memories of school, for instance, may become distorted as we add things that didn't occur or subtract things that did, in an attempt to make better sense out of what actually happened and the way we experienced it at the time.

If our memories are permanently stored and do not fade away, why then do we forget things that have happened and information we have learned? The answer depends on *why* we cannot remember. It may be that the stimulus we are given is not sufficient for us to *retrieve* the memory, or it may be that we don't want to retrieve the memory.

As we saw in our discussion of recall, recognition, and relearning, the form in which the stimulus is presented can determine how much is remembered and how much is forgotten at any given time. Another sign that the stimulus given may not be sufficient to retrieve the desired information from memory lies in the feeling, familiar to everyone at some time, that the answer is on the "tip of the tongue" but can't quite be produced.

It seems that verbal information which is stored away in long-term memory is filed under at least three different systems—the way it sounds, the way it looks, and what it means. Thus, if the word you want is the navigational instrument *sextant* but you can't get it past the tip of your tongue, you may actually produce the word *sextet* which looks and sounds similar, or the word *compass* which has a similar meaning.

A failure to retrieve information because we don't want to is a different matter altogether. Our earlier example of the woman who was conditioned to avoid running water is a good example of this kind of forgetting. The woman's childhood fear had been so great that the only way she could cope with it was to blot out the entire incident from her memory as if it had never happened. She had a *need to forget it.*

Of course, the memory was not really blotted out, it just went underground where she was not conscious of it. When she acquired her phobia, the psychological effects of the memory surfaced in her behavior. It was only when she went for help with her phobia that she was able to remember her childhood fear and deal with it. Such a need to forget is by no means rare or bizarre. Repressed memories, though usually less dramatic in their effects, are a central concern of the methods for treating emotional disturbance employed by many clinical psychologists. This is a topic we will return to in Chapter 10.

The most striking instance of the need to forget is the case of *amnesia.* Amnesia can occur as the result of brain injury or disease of the brain or in severe alcoholism. But the type of amnesia that has captured the popular imagination is where someone is found wandering around, unable to remember who he is or where he lives. This kind of amnesia does indeed happen, but probably occurs more often in fiction than in real life.

Such amnesia is the result of extreme repression of painful personal memories dealing with severe emotional conflict. It can last for days or years and is often accompanied by a physical move to get away from the agonizing conflict, which is why amnesiacs frequently turn up in strange surroundings far from home. As with other instances of the need to forget, amnesiacs can remember everything unconnected with their conflict—in this case, everything that would not remind them of their identity—and if they can deal with their problems in therapy, their memories are usually restored.

It was Sigmund Freud who established the importance of early experiences on later life, and he therefore considered memories of early childhood to be of great importance. He soon noted, however, that these memories were very sparse compared to memories of later years, and he was rather struck by what seemed a kind of "childhood amnesia." Psychologists would now advance two ideas to explain this phenomenon: The world perceived by the child is not the same as that perceived by the adult, and most of our memories depend on the use of language, which the child of course is still in the process of developing.

MAKING LEARNING MEANINGFUL

The desire to make human learning as efficient as possible has promoted an enormous amount of research for many years. A lot of this research has been devoted to the study of competing methods of learning:

1. MASSED VERSUS DISTRIBUTED PRACTICE

There is a lot of evidence that learning something a little at a time is usually more efficient than trying to learn it all at once. For instance, if you have a week in which to learn a list of French vocabulary and you can only spare three hours to study it, you would be much better advised to divide that time into half an hour a day for six days than to spend three straight hours on it.

Apparently our brain needs some time after each learning period to *consolidate* the changes that have occurred and thus allow the information to be permanently recorded in our long-term memory bank. For this reason, it is useful to have a learning period shortly before going to sleep.

2. WHOLE VERSUS PART METHOD OF LEARNING

Another basic problem in learning is whether it is more efficient to study something as a whole, or broken up into a number of parts. Is it easier, for example, to learn a ten-line poem as a poem consisting of ten lines or as ten separate lines of poetry? In this case, as in most human learning (especially verbal learning), the whole method is definitely superior to the part method. Occasionally, if the task falls naturally into separate parts, the part method may be quite effective. This is true of some sporting skills like those required in golf or tennis—but not in swimming or cycling, where the skill is best learned as a whole.

3. READING VERSUS READING AND RECITATION

It is well established that some people learn better by reading and others by hearing the same material. It has also been found that, even for people who learn best by reading, simply reading over some material is a much less efficient way of learning it than reading combined with recitation. The recitation of the material, whether out loud or to oneself, has the effect of fixing it in the memory.

4. RULE VERSUS ROTE LEARNING

Learning by rote requires simply the repetition of material until it is learned. Learning by rule involves finding some pattern, meaning, or logic in the material and learning that rather than the material itself. We learned arithmetic in school using both methods. We learned by rote that three times five is fifteen, but we also learned by rule that if you divide fifteen by five you get three. We learned multiplication *tables,* but we learned *how to* divide.

Most school learning is a combination of rote and rule. If it is possible to learn something by rule, then it is certainly preferable to do so as it makes both learning and remembering much easier. But some learning simply requires the grind of sheer repetition. To make this grind easier, we have to take our time and go over the material frequently and attentively, attempting to learn only one set of materials at a time.

5. FEEDBACK

No matter what you are learning or how you are trying to learn it, it is extremely helpful to know how you are doing—one reason students may welcome mid-term exams. Any feedback you receive on your learning performance enables you to pick out problems that have come up and generally makes the learning more interesting. This principle is the basis for teaching machines and programmed learning units where the learner receives feedback at every step of the way.

6. MNEMONICS

In ancient Greece, public speaking was practically a spectator sport, and orators were highly skilled at making long and elaborate speeches without notes. They were able to do this in the same way that modern entertainers perform amazing feats of memory for a living; they developed their own system of coding the information they wanted to remember into "chunks" that could easily be retrieved from their long-term memory bank.

Thus, the Greek orators would break up their speech into paragraphs and associate each paragraph with a statue in their favorite temple. As they were making their speech, they would take an imaginary walk through the temple, and each succeeding statue they came to would be the stimulus to trigger the retrieval of the paragraph associated with it. Such devices are called *mnemonics,* from the Greek word for remembering.

We sometimes use mnemonics ourselves. Most of us learned the number of days in each month by reciting the jingle, "Thirty days hath September. . . ." Spelling was made a little easier by putting "*i* before *e* except after *c.*" Even in the absence of mnemonics, we like to group and cluster things together, as if we were making keys that would unlock doors where more information is stored away. As long as we remember where we put the keys, we're in business.

For instance, if I'm sitting in my university office in Manhattan and I want to call someone in Westchester County whose number I don't have, I will have to dial eleven digits to get the information I need: 99145551212. Now, if that's how the number was presented to me, I would have a hard time remembering it. The normal memory span is able to cope with about seven digits. However, all the memorizing I have to do is in three or four chunks, thus: 9-(914) 555-1212. I know you have to dial 9 to get off campus, and I know the area code for Westchester County is 914. So all I really have to learn is the directory assistance number, 555-1212.

Meaningfulness

The thread running through these methods of learning is the search for meaning, for understanding, for ways of making sense. In making sense of our learning processes, we are learning how to make sense of our whole world. We search for patterns, codes, keys, and rules that will make our learning easier, and we *must* do this because there is so much to learn. We learn new things by linking them with things we already know. We interpret the unfamiliar new information in terms of what is familiar to us. We strive constantly for logic and order and have difficulty learning if we don't find it. So important is the search for meaning that the rest of this book is really concerned with examining its implications for human behavior.

SUGGESTED READINGS

Burgess, A. *A Clockwork Orange.* New York: Ballantine Books, 1971. A novel that portrays how the personality of an antisocial young man is altered by the use of operant conditioning techniques.

Halacy, D. *Man and Memory.* New York: Harper & Row, 1970. A nontechnical review of studies on memory and some factors like drugs, sleep, and dreaming that relate to it.

Kohler, W. *The Mentality of Apes.* New York: Random House (Vintage Books),

1927. A series of studies on the intelligence of chimpanzees, focusing on their ability to engage in insightful behavior.

Luria, A. *The Mind of a Mnemonist.* New York: Avon Books, 1969. The story of a man who cannot forget, by a leading Soviet neuropsychologist who details the unique problems of an almost perfect memory.

Skinner, B. F. *Walden Two.* New York: MacMillan, 1948. A novel of a planned Utopian society where behavior is based on Skinner's theories of operant conditioning.

Talland, G. *Disorders of Memory and Learning.* Baltimore: Penguin Books, 1968.

CHAPTER 7

Making sense of what we see

PERCEPTION AND THE SENSORY APPARATUS

As we saw in Chapter 4, the sense organs through which we make contact with the world provide our brain with a steady flow of information about our environment. The brain's task is then to take this raw material and use it to help us make sense of that environment through the process of *perception.* And the brain does its job so smoothly and well that we're not even aware of what it does.

Occasionally we come across incidents in our daily lives where the "sense" we have made of our environment is seen to be illusory. Walking home late at night, we turn a corner and jump as we see a mugger lurking in the shadows. A split second later we realize the "mugger" is a tree. Why did we make the mistake and what did we actually see? Well, what we *saw* was a tree, but what we *perceived* was a mugger.

Presumably, if we lived in an environment where there were no muggers, and only sabre-toothed tigers lurked in shadows, we might well have seen a sabre-toothed tiger as we turned the corner. The raw material provided by our sensory apparatus is thus a very important component of perception, but it is not the only one. What we see, hear, and feel is quite unlearned, but if we had to rely on only these sensations to make our way about the world, we would be as helpless as an infant. We have to learn how to interpret and order these sensations in such a way that the environment becomes secure and predictable.

Not only does our past experience of dealing with the world enter into our perceptions, but so does our current emotional state and our needs, wishes, and desires. Some people are more likely than others to mistake trees for muggers (or sabre-toothed tigers). There are times and places in which we would all make the same mistake.

In perceiving, we are led to make sense of our environment, but at the same time there is some evidence that our environment can also have a striking effect on what we see, the raw material for our visual perceptions. The brain may even be physically affected by our environment.

SENSORY DEPRIVATION

To isolate the effects of physical environment on perception, two British physiologists took a couple of newborn kittens and raised them separately (Blakemore and Cooper, 1970). The environment of one kitten was adorned with nothing but vertical white lines, while the other kitten saw nothing but horizontal white lines. After six months of these conditions, the animals were removed from their environments and placed in a cage containing two obstacle courses, one with vertical white bars and one with horizontal white bars.

The experimenters wanted to know if depriving the kittens of the chance to see either vertical or horizonal lines for the first six months of their lives meant that they would be unable to see such lines even if they were present in a later environment. That is exactly what they found. The kitten reared with the vertical lines walked quickly through the verticle obstacle course but was completely baffled by the horizontal obstacles, and instead of jumping over the bars, barged into them as if they weren't there. The other kitten did just the opposite.

From the animals' behavior, it appeared that they received no visual sensations from the vertical lines in the one case and the horizontal lines in the other; they simply didn't see them. To check this idea, the animals were given an anaesthetic while the experimenters examined the visual area of their brains. What they found was that the brain cells dealing with vertical lines in the one cat and horizontal lines in the other had not developed as they would normally have done. Thus, the sensation of seeing horizontal or vertical lines had never been recorded in the brain. There was no message for the brain to interpret, and so nothing for the cat to perceive.

In our discussion of nature and nurture in Chapter 3, we decided that our genetic inheritance probably sets the upper limits of our achievements, and that environmental influences could either help us achieve this potential or lead us to fall short. The kittens in the visual deprivation experiment are an example of the latter effect. Their environment had not allowed them to develop the visual skills for which they had the genetic capacity. Whether or not these effects are permanent is an important question to which we still don't have a complete answer.

Hebb and Making Sense of Nothing

A different kind of environmental influence on perception was observed by a group of scientists under the direction of D. O. Hebb

(Heron, 1957). In Hebb's laboratory, a number of student volunteers were paid to lie quietly on a comfortable bed for as long as they could. The investigators wanted to see what the effects on healthy young adults would be of sensory deprivation, so they reduced the amount of sensations impinging upon their subjects as much as they could. The subjects wore face masks and cotton gloves with cuffs, and the only sounds were the hum of the fan and the air conditioner controlling the climate of the cubicle. The subjects were allowed out to eat and to go to the bathroom, but otherwise they just lay there for 24 hours a day.

At first the students took advantage of the situation to catch up on lost sleep and to lie there thinking, pleasantly relaxed. After a while, however, the lack of sensory stimuli from the environment became very boring. After boredom had set in, something very striking happened—the subjects began to hallucinate. Some people reported hearing and feeling things that didn't exist, as well as having vivid visual hallucinations of objects and scenes. It was almost as though, having nothing in their environment to make sense out of, they felt a need to provide their own sensations and make sense out of nothing (see Box 7.1).

FOCUSING AND ATTENTION

In our day-to-day environment, there is usually no lack of sensory stimulation. In fact, our problem is normally the opposite of sensory deprivation. Why is our perceptual process not continually swamped by the enormous amount of stimuli picked up by the sense organs? As we noted in our discussion of memory in Chapter 6, very few of the stimuli that impinge on us at any given time are of any importance. We filter out the ones which are important simply by paying attention to them, and we ignore the rest.

We focus on whatever stimuli are most important in the environment at any given time. We ignore a constant hum from an air conditioner, for instance, but immediately focus on the machine if it suddenly stops, providing us with a new and possibly important stimulus. If the steady hum returns, the sound of the air conditioner becomes unimportant once more and it recedes to the edge of our awareness. It is this process of *focusing* our perceptions, bringing them in from the edge, that we refer to as *attention,* and attention is crucial in learning something and committing it to memory.

By attending to certain sensory stimuli and not to others, we give them access to our sensory memory, the first stage of the memory process, and they can then move from there to short-term and to long-term memory. Underlying this series of psychological processes are corresponding physiological processes. Thus, when one channel of communication between a sense organ and the brain is occupied and has our full attention, the other physiological pathways to the brain are

BOX 7.1

THE PHANTOM LIMB

There have long been reports of people who had an arm or leg amputated, yet still could "feel" the missing limb. The person may report feelings of pain or itching; he may try to move the missing limb, momentarily forgetting that it is no longer there. Why do people perceive these imaginary sensations?

The phantom limb phenomenon has been intensively studied by M. L. Simmel, who has provided a psychological explanation for its existence. By researching medical journals and conducting a great many interviews with amputees of all ages (and, in the case of children, with their parents as well), Simmel has come up with some interesting findings.

From her data it can be established that the frequency with which amputees report feeling phantom limbs increases with age, so that after the age of eight everyone who has an amputation reports feeling a phantom limb. Simmel suggests that the way we learn to perceive our own body (our *body schema*) follows the same kind of processes of cognitive and perceptual development as any other ability that increases with age.

Simmel has also worked with people suffering from leprosy. With leprosy the fingers and toes will gradually disappear, sometimes over a period of many years. This process is usually painless. Simmel found that even in advanced cases of leprosy, no phantoms were reported. Yet when the remnants of fingers or toes were amputated, phantom replacements invariably occurred.

Simmel explains these findings in a fashion similar to her developmental data on amputations. The leprosy patient's body schema is able to change gradually, keeping pace with the progress of the disease. Thus phantoms will not appear. Amputation, however, is a sudden and painful process, producing changes in the physical reality of the body without any process of psychological adjustment taking place. When this happens, the patient has no choice but to do what he can with his existing body schema, the way of perceiving himself that he's always had. Hence the appearance of a phantom limb, and the continuing perception that what was always there before still exists.

Source: M. L. Simmel, "Developmental Aspects of the Body Schema," *Child Development* 37: 83–95, 1966.

apparently blocked so that we don't become confused and overwhelmed by the other sensory messages.

Selective Perception and Distortion

We have seen that in order to make sense of our sensations, our perceptions have to be selective. But how do we go about making the selection? In order to perceive something, we have to give it our attention. But we know from our own experience that our attention is continually shifting. What determines which stimuli will capture our attention?

Psychologists refer to external and internal factors in trying to understand attention-getting and selective perception.

EXTERNAL FACTORS

In our example of the air conditioner, we noted that the sound of the machine stayed at the edge of our awareness until it stopped, whereupon it captured our attention. It is the stimulus provided by a *change* in the environment that is most important. The change can take many forms. *Contrast* (between sound and silence, for example) is one of them. A man seven feet tall stands out much more on the street than he would on a basketball court. A television newscaster wearing a see-through dashiki would attract more attention than one in a gray pin-striped suit.

Movement in the environment is another important kind of change. People are very responsive to visual movement, quite automatically. Even the youngest infants will try to follow movements with their eyes, and adults will have their attention caught by moving neon signs rather than by stationary ones.

The *repetition* of a stimulus can sometimes be effective—a phenomenon well known to mothers calling their offspring in from play. *Size* can also be an important factor, hence newspapers grade the importance of their headlines by the size of the type. The *intensity* of a stimulus can also catch our attention, so bright colors and loud sounds are often effectively used to gather a crowd to a public event or to sell a product.

INTERNAL FACTORS

The external factors outlined above refer to the stimuli from the environment. However, the person perceiving these stimuli does not do so as a neutral observer; different people react to the same sensations in different ways. A woman may put on a sweater because the room is too cold, while her husband throws open the windows. She may sleep through the ringing alarm that wakes him up for work, but is instantly awake at the baby's first whimper. When they read the same magazine, she will pick out the sales of women's clothing, and he the men's.

This man and woman have different interests and motives that they bring to each situation they share. Their emotional and their physical states will change, and if they don't happen to feel the same way at the same time they may well have different reactions. But the most important internal factor in perception is what people expect to see or hear in each situation. The woman has a *mental set* to hear her baby cry. She expects it to happen. The man has a mental set to hear the alarm go off at the same time each morning—so much so that he has come to wake up a few seconds before it goes off.

Sometimes this set may be so habitual or so important to a person that he may perceive things that aren't there—like the tree we mistook for a mugger at the beginning of this chapter. Psychologists have discovered some striking examples of such perceptual distortion.

In one study, a group of white people who were known to be highly prejudiced against blacks were shown a picture and asked to describe it from memory (Allport and Postman, 1947). The picture depicted a subway carriage with several people in it. The central characters in the scene were a black man and a white man. One of these men was well-dressed and standing quietly in the middle of the carriage. The other was poorly dressed and rough-looking and he was standing in front of the first man, threatening him with an open razor. The first man was black; his attacker was white. But the prejudiced white subjects in this study did not have a set to see what the picture showed, and so they reported a rough-looking black man threatening a well-dressed white. They had distorted their perception to fit what they expected to see (see Box 7.2).

Illusions

Internal factors can thus lead us to perceive things differently from the way they really are. But so can external factors. The important difference is that while each person brings a unique group of internal factors to a perceptual situation, the external factors, for all the members of a given society, are the same. There are some perceptual situations, for example, where we will all react the same way, perceive the same thing, and be completely wrong.

In Figure 7.1 the top line is obviously longer than the bottom line.

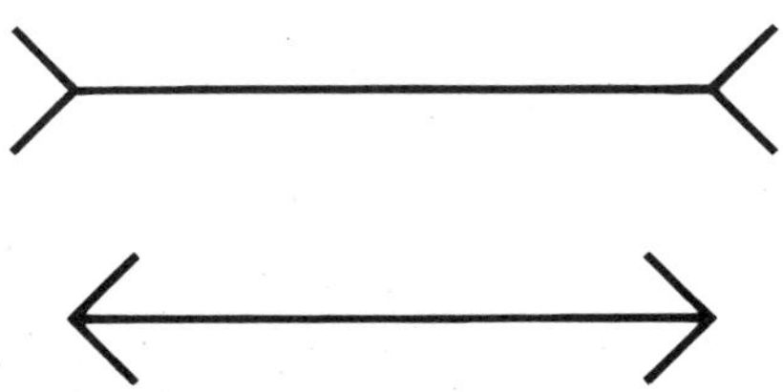

Figure 7.1 Length of line illusions.

BOX 7.2

SEEING AND BELIEVING

A striking demonstration of the way in which different people can have very different perceptions of the same sensory stimuli is provided by Albert Hastorf and Hadley Cantril. The occasion was a college football game in 1953 between Princeton and Dartmouth. This game turned out to be one of the roughest grudge matches in the history of college football.

It seems that Princeton had a star named Dick Kazmaier on their team, and Dartmouth was intent on putting him out of the game. They succeeded: Kazmaier left the game with a broken nose. Many more injuries were sustained by both teams before the "game" ended.

Fortunately for our purposes the match was filmed, and our two psychologists, Hastorf of Dartmouth and Cantril of Princeton, came up with the idea of using this objective record to examine the perceptions of students from both campuses about what really happened. They began by giving a questionnaire to a sample of students from each campus, asking for their attitudes toward the game. Then they showed each group the same film of the game and asked them to record every infraction of the rules made by both sides.

When the data were examined, it was found that practically all the Princeton students thought the game was extremely rough, and 90 percent of them believed that the rough stuff was started by the other team. This was entirely to be expected, of course, but what was less expected was the way these students viewed the film.

The Princeton students found that Dartmouth had committed twice as many infractions as their own team. The Dartmouth students also thought the game was very rough but they believed that both teams were equally to blame, and moreover, when they saw the film they found an equal number of illegalities on each side. The two groups of students saw the same game and the same film of that game, but ended up with very different perceptions of what they had seen.

Seeing apparently *is* believing—whatever you're predisposed to believe.

Source: Hastorf, Albert and Cantril, Hadley, "They Saw a Game: A Case Study," *Journal of Abnormal and Social Psychology* 49: 129–134, 1954.

But if you measure them, you'll find they are exactly the same length

Would you believe that the brim of the top hat in Figure 7.2 is the same length as the height?

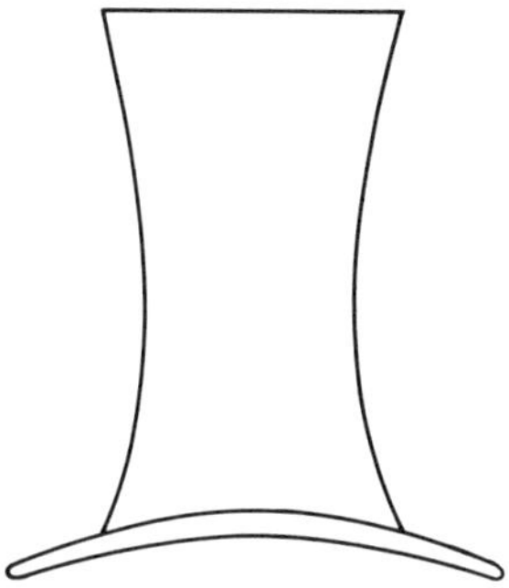

Figure 7.2 The vertical-horizontal illusion. (*Source: Reproduced from G. A. Kimble, M. Garmezy, and E. Zigler,* General Psychology, *4th edition. Copyright ©1974, The Ronald Press Company, New York. Used with permission.*)

And how about the impossible tuning fork in Figure 7.3?

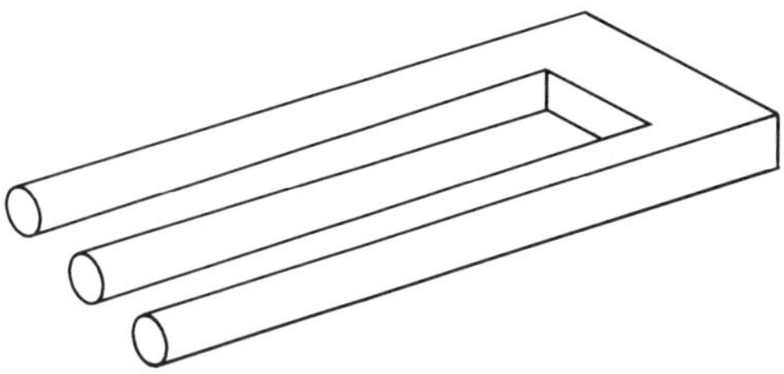

Figure 7.3 The impossible tuning fork. (*Source: Reproduced from G. A. Kimble, M. Garmezy, and E. Zigler,* General Psychology, *4th edition. Copyright © 1974, The Ronald Press Company, New York. Used with permission.*)

ORGANIZING PERCEPTUAL CUES

These perceptual illusions are very exceptional, however, and in our daily lives our perceptions are normally accurate and perfectly reliable. But the existence of such illusions has been helpful to psychologists interested in the normal process of perception. Out of a vast number of careful studies has emerged the understanding that the way in which we perceive is highly organized and well ordered. We do not live in a world of changing sound and light waves but in a world of objects, people, music, and events. With our perceptions we make sense of our sensations, according to some well-established principles that are partly learned and partly due to the structure of the brain and

Figure 7.4 Vase and profiles.

the nervous system. These principles allow us to navigate our way through the world, but they are not perfect—hence impossible tuning forks and trees as muggers.

FIGURE AND GROUND

Perhaps the most basic of these perceptual principles is the way we perceive things against a background; the way we need a background before we can pick out an object in the environment. Where we cannot separate *figure* and *ground* in this way, we are unable to see the object we may be looking at; it is hidden or camouflaged. Many animals make use of this principle to evade their predators, like the chameleon that changes color to blend in with its background.

You are also making use of this principle in reading this book. You are perceiving black print against a white background. When you close the book and put it on the desk, it doesn't disappear. You can see it clearly outlined against the background of the desk. We can separate figure and ground in this fashion because of our ability to perceive *contour.* Contours mark off one thing from another, an object from its background, and even a musical theme from its surrounding chords. Figure and ground are both necessary for our perception and, as Figure 7.4 shows, they can be interchangeable at times.

When you perceive the white figure, the vase, the black part is the ground. When you perceive the black profiles, the white part becomes the ground. Notice that you can't see both figures at the same time, and that no matter how hard you try to focus on one of these figures, your attention will shift after a time and focus on the other.

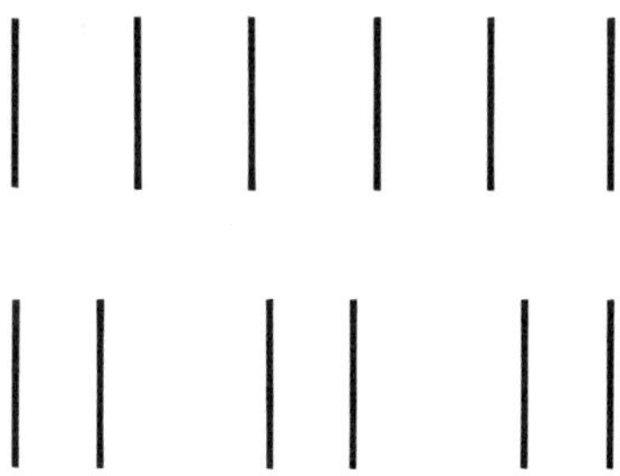

Figure 7.5 Organization of lines.

GROUPING

Another important way in which we structure our perceptions is by grouping things into patterns. In Figure 7.5 we see six single lines on top but *three pairs* of lines on the bottom.

If you remember our discussion on memory in Chapter 6, you will recognize here a process similar to the clustering, "chunking," or grouping of information that we use to store things in our long-term memory bank.

CLOSURE

Despite the fact that they are incomplete, you recognize the three drawings in Figure 7.6 as a triangle, a square, and a circle. If certain things are familiar to us, our perceptual process will close the gaps in the picture, thereby providing the necessary contour lines for us to perceive it as a distinct object. We do much the same thing with our language when we read a telegram or a newspaper headline.

GESTALT

The principles of perception we have been discussing are due mainly to the work of some German psychologists, who took the view that what we perceive is more than just the sum of the sensory stimuli

Figure 7.6 Incomplete figures.

that impinge on us from the environment. We perceive something, they argued, as a *gestalt,* a German word meaning "form" or "structure." Each gestalt has a lot more meaning to the perceiver than just its sensory properties of size, color, or weight. An apple, a book, or a painting may have meaning for us (and be able to affect our behavior) far beyond a cataloging of its physical properties, no matter how detailed.

Therefore, in perceiving, not only is the whole greater than the sum of its parts but the parts in themselves are not important or even perceived. We search constantly for patterns, for order, for wholes that make sense of the parts.

Perceptual Constancy: Color, Size, and Shape

There are several other factors we must consider in discussing the way our perceptions are organized. One of these is the fact that while the sensations we receive from the environment are ever changing, our perceptions of things remain constant. You know, for instance, that as the eye operates like a camera, images of the objects you look at will appear on your retina as they would on a photograph. So if you set your coffee cup down in front of you and take a picture of it, the picture will show what you see—an elliptical object. But you *know* your coffee cup is not an ellipse. It's round. How do you know that?

When you're surrounded by people on the street, it's quite easy to judge how tall each person is, and you would be accurate to within a few inches if you did so. When you're on a country road and you see someone coming toward you from a great distance, the image of him on your retina would make him about as tall as an insect. How do you know he's not?

Apparently what we see is not always what we perceive, not just in visual illusions but in our everyday perception. We have to learn the *meaning* of what we see. Among the things we learn are that black snow at night is really white, that an opening door does not disappear into a vertical line, and that buildings seen from the air are really bigger than matchboxes. Young children do not yet have this ability to perceive their changing sense impressions in constant ways, and a child looking down on a highway from a great height may perceive the cars as toys to play with.

Depth and Distance: The Visual Cliff

Just as perceptual constancy is so completely a part of our lives that we take it for granted until it is pointed out to us, so the fact that we see a three-dimensional world seems totally unremarkable until we realize that the retina, like the lens of a camera, is a two-dimensional surface. How do we use the two-dimensional information of right-left

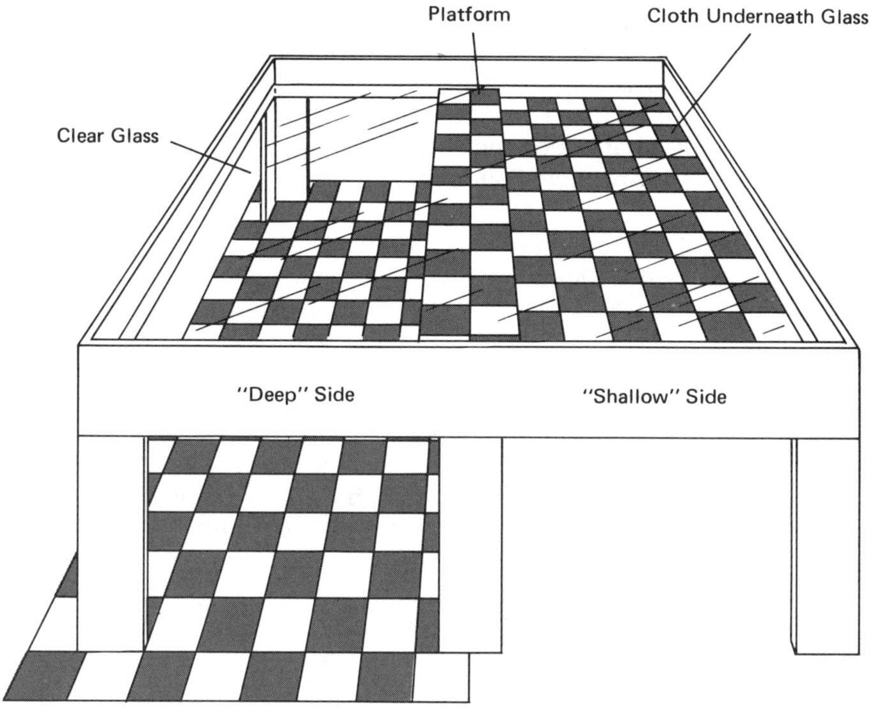

Figure 7.7 Sketch of "visual cliff" apparatus.

and up-down that our eyes see to perceive a world of objects, of depth and distance?

It appears that in judging the distance of objects, we are very sensitive to various cues from the surrounding environment, in a fashion similar to the figure-ground phenomenon we noted above. These cues include the play of light and shadow, perspective, and the positioning of other things in the environment. The fact that we have two eyes which give us slightly different images of what we're looking at also plays a part in judging distance.

The judgment of depth is one kind of distance perception, and it has been studied particularly in children and young animals. One series of studies was carried out with an apparatus known as a *visual cliff,* consisting of a heavy sheet of glass suspended a few feet above the floor of a cubicle (Gibson and Walk, 1960). A long, thin platform covered with checkered cloth is placed at the center of the sheet of glass. To one side of the platform, a piece of the same checkered cloth is fixed directly under the glass; on the other side, the cloth is laid on the floor. To an infant, the first side looks solid and the other side seems to be a sheer drop, or "cliff" (see Figure 7.7).

Infants old enough to crawl, as well as young chickens, goats, lambs, rats, and cats, seem to perceive the visual cliff as a dangerous drop and refuse to venture onto that side of the glass. But none of them is afraid to crawl onto the other, "solid" side. The ability to perceive depth is thus of great importance to people and animals, and is either innate or learned very shortly after birth.

Movement: Movies and the Phi Phenomenon

The final area of perception we should examine in trying to make sense of what we see is that of movement. Some of the movement we perceive, like a bird flying past the window, can be explained simply as visual stimuli, moving across our visual field and stimulating different parts of the eye. However, much of the movement we perceive is also quite illusory and cannot be explained in this fashion.

The most common illusion of movement is perceived in watching a film. A film consists of a series of still photographs, each one slightly different from the preceding one, flashed onto a screen at the rate of about twenty frames per second. At this speed we don't perceive a series of stills, we perceive movement on the screen.

This illusion was studied extensively by the Gestalt psychologists at the beginning of this century when movies were first introduced. They were able to isolate the simplest form of the illusion and examine the conditions under which it appeared.

They discovered that if they flashed two lights on and off in quick succession, given the right time interval between the flashes, people perceived the light as moving between two points. They called this illusion of movement the *Phi phenomenon,* and in addition to being active in our perception of films, it underlies the effectiveness of the moving neon light displays that attract our attention in big cities.

HEIDER AND MICHOTTE: SEX AND THE SINGLE TRIANGLE

In dealing with our environment, we not only perceive many different objects, we also perceive interactions between these objects. We see rain beating on the roof, birds searching for worms, a man chopping wood for the fire, buses halting at stop signs, and countless other interactions involving people, animals, and inanimate objects.

Central to the way we make sense of these interactions is our need to explain things that happen in terms of cause and effect. By placing yourself at a bus stop (cause), the driver will see you and stop the bus to let you get on (effect). Now, how about my neighbor chopping firewood? Unlike myself, he doesn't live in a house with a fireplace; he lives in a modern apartment. He's not chopping firewood at all, as it turns out; he's making splints to support the potted plants on his terrace. I

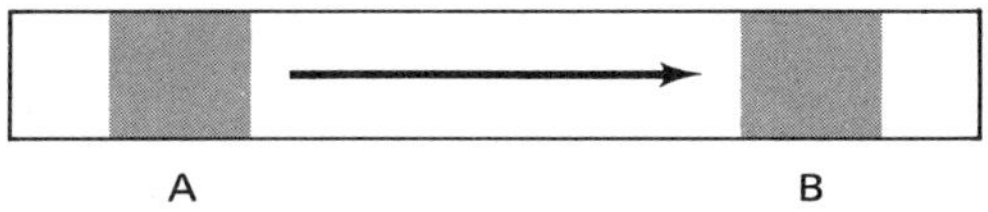

Figure 7.8 Illusion of movement.

have attributed the wrong cause and effect to his behavior. However, I could have been right, and until I knew where he lived my explanation of his behavior was at least plausible—even if it was the middle of July.

We have already seen how our need to make sense of our perceptions can lead us to see things that aren't there and to give false explanations for certain events. Fritz Heider took this problem into the laboratory, where he devised an animated cartoon consisting of a large triangle, a smaller triangle, and a small circle arranged in a series of different positions (Heider, 1944).

Because of the animation, people saw the three figures moving about. But they saw a lot more than that. When they were asked to describe the cartoon, they reported an "aggressive" triangle "bullying" a smaller one in "rivalry" over a "shy, timid female" circle. Not only did they perceive causation, but they saw causation in human social terms.

The Belgian psychologist Albert Michotte has taken this work a step further by trying to isolate the conditions under which people will attribute causality in this way (Michotte, 1954). He gave his subjects a very simple situation to deal with, consisting of a slot with two rectangles, A and B (see Figure 7.8).

Michotte moved the rectangles back and forth within the slot at different speeds and in different ways, then asked the subjects what they saw. If A was moved quickly to B, and then both were moved together to the end of the slot, A had *pushed* B. If A was moved quickly to B, then slowed down while B was moved quickly to the end of the slot, A had *hit* B. If A was moved slowly to B, then stopped, they were *getting together.*

These examples from Heider and Michotte show quite clearly the tremendous influence of the social context in which we live on the process by which we make sense out of what we see. Without that social context, we would have little idea of what it was we were seeing. In Chapter 8 we will examine the influence of that same social context on making sense of what we *feel.*

SUGGESTED READINGS

Gregory, R. *The Intelligent Eye.* New York: McGraw-Hill, 1970. Examines visual illusions and argues for the importance of inferences based on sensory information in the way we perceive.

Keller, H. *The Story of My Life.* New York: Doubleday, 1904. Helen Keller became completely blind and deaf shortly after birth. Her story tells how she learned about the world through her fingertips with the aid of an exceptional teacher.

Zubek, J. *Sensory Deprivation: Fifteen Years of Research.* Englewood Cliffs, N.J.: Prentice-Hall, 1969.

CHAPTER 8

Making sense of what we feel

PERCEIVING: EXTERNAL AND INTERNAL

In the last chapter we saw how we organize and interpret sensory information to make sense of our environment. But while it is crucial for us to perceive what is happening around us, it is also important for us to perceive what is happening within us. Making sense of what we feel is a part of daily life and is closely related to all the other ways we try to make sense of what is happening in the world. We find a pattern of meaning in the internal stimuli our brain receives, just as we do with external stimuli, and our internal patterns are likewise influenced by our perception of the environment around us.

WILLIAM JAMES AND THE MEANING OF EMOTION

If I asked you to describe your emotions right now, you would probably begin with the words "I feel . . ." When someone talks very volubly, bright-eyed and gesticulating as he does so, we refer to his behavior as being "highly emotional." A theater audience, gripped by a dramatic production, will "feel" what the actors "emote."

It seems, therefore, that in everyday life we use the terms *feeling* and *emotion* to mean the same thing. Psychologists, however, make a distinction between the two. Every emotion has an important feeling aspect to it, but it has more than this; it has a thinking or *cognitive* aspect as well. And it is this cognitive aspect which links a person's feelings with his environment.

The common sense view of emotional behavior is that we feel something inside ourselves, then act accordingly. We learn of a friend's death, feel sad, then cry. We see a mob, feel scared, then run. This view of emotional behavior seemed so obvious and so much a part of everyone's experience that it was taken for granted until fairly recently. The cause and effect involved seemed quite clear, and as we saw in our discussion of perception in Chapter 7, understanding the causes of things that occur is crucial to our making sense of the world.

At the end of the last century, William James suggested that this way of regarding emotional behavior might not be correct (James, 1890). Suppose you were walking in the forest, he argued, and suddenly found yourself face to face with a ferocious looking bear. As soon as you perceived the bear, certain bodily changes would occur: your hands would tremble, your heart would pound, and so on. Physiologically, you would be in a state of excitement.

This excitement, said James, you would *interpret* as fear, rather than joy or anger or any other strong feeling, because of your *cognition* that bears are fearsome. You *know* that bears eat people, so the bodily changes you feel on meeting a bear are translated into the emotion fear. Common sense would say you trembled because you were afraid of the bear. James proposed it would be more correct to say you were afraid of the bear *because* you trembled. Similarly, we are sad because we cry and we are angry because we lash out.

SCHACHTER AND THE LINKS BETWEEN COGNITION AND FEELING

What James's theory implied was that if we need cues from the environment to help us label our emotions, we won't know what we're feeling if these cues are missing. At first glance this proposition seems rather absurd, and for a long time nobody was able to produce much scientific evidence for it. But in the early 1960s, a study by Stanley Schachter and Jerome Singer threw some valuable light on the relation of feelings and cognitions to emotions (Schachter and Singer, 1962).

Schachter and Singer wanted to duplicate the physiological state of excitement that accompanies strong feelings but without the kind of environment in which these feelings are normally found. So instead of introducing a bear into the lab or telling their subjects they'd won a million dollars in a lottery, they gave them an injection of adrenalin. Adrenalin is a stimulant that causes a strong physiological reaction, with symptoms like trembling hands and a pounding heart.

Some of the subjects were told about the physiological effects of the injection and some were not. The subjects who were not told of the effects were divided into two groups. In the first group, when each subject came to the lab he was asked to sit in a waiting room where he was soon joined by another person who had supposedly received the same injection. This second person was not a subject in the study, however. He was Schachter's assistant and he had a carefully written role to perform.

The assistant, or stooge, began to behave in a very carefree and happy manner, telling jokes, playing with a hula hoop (that just happened to be lying around), making paper airplanes and flying them around the room, and playing basketball with the waste basket. In the course of his act, the stooge invited the subject to join in—and sure enough he did, and they both had a whale of a time.

The second group of subjects met the same stooge in the same waiting room, but this time he behaved very differently. He had been programmed to appear angry and aggressive, and he climaxed his act by ripping up a questionnaire he had been asked to fill in, and throwing it on the floor. Once again the subject shared the stooge's emotions and behavior as he too became angry and aggressive.

All these subjects, you will recall, were experiencing the effects of the adrenalin injection, effects which they had not been told about. In another part of the study, the subjects who *had* been told what effects to expect were divided into the same two conditions and met either a "happy" stooge or an "angry" stooge. But this time the stooge's behavior had no effect on the subject. They refused to join in either his happy or his angry behavior.

What caused the difference? Where the subjects knew what symptoms to expect from the injection, they attributed their feelings of physiological excitement quite simply to the adrenalin. To them, the stooge was just a guy acting strangely, whose behavior was irrelevant to their feelings. The people who did not know what symptoms to expect had no way of knowing why they were starting to feel physiologically excited. But they couldn't leave it at that, of course. They needed some way of explaining their feelings—and that's exactly what the stooge gave them.

In Chapter 7, we noted the great importance of environmental cues for our perceptions. People are often the most influential providers of such cues, particularly if we think their experience is the same as our own. Thus, the people who encountered the happy stooge interpreted their feelings as "happiness," while the people who met the angry stooge interpreted *the same feelings* as "anger." It is the experience of the physiological change, the feeling, together with the cognitive process whereby we interpret that feeling within its social context, that results in our labeling an emotion one way or another.

WHAT IS THIS THING CALLED LOVE?

The publication of Schachter and Singer's work has led to an increase of psychologists' interest in the study of emotions, including romantic love. Serious study of this emotion is just beginning, but it has been suggested that our experience of love (as opposed to liking) may be similar to our experience of the powerful emotions that Schachter and Singer were dealing with (see Box 8.1).

Being "in love" implies a feeling of excitement, of physiological arousal, and as Schachter and Singer pointed out, such feelings are essentially neutral; they take their emotional identity from an interaction between the individual and his interpretation of the social context. If a man's arousal is based on fear, pain, or sex, and his social context contains an attractive woman, it is at least plausible that he will associate her with his feeling, label those feelings "love," and feel himself to be in love with her (Walster and Berscheid, 1971).

TO SAY NOTHING OF AGGRESSION

The meager amount of research on love is in striking contrast to the enormous number of studies on aggressive behavior and the emotions that underlie it. But then, love is not a social problem.

The discussion of aggressive behavior brings us to the links between feeling an emotion and expressing it in behavior. We have seen that two people with the same feeling can have very different emotions and express those emotions in completely opposite behavior. What kinds of emotions lead to aggressive behavior—how and why?

Psychologists have a variety of definitions for *aggression,* some more inclusive than others, but the essence of an aggressive act is that it is an intentional effort to harm another person. The kind of emotions that would lead to such behavior are obviously unpleasant ones like fear, anger, pain, and especially *frustration.* It had long been observed, especially with children, that when someone was prevented from doing something pleasurable, he or she became more ready to engage in aggressive behavior.

This proposition was tested in the laboratory when a group of children were shown a roomful of attractive toys, then were made to wait a long time before they could get at them. Another group of children were also shown the toys, then were allowed to play with them right away. They did so happily. But the children who had been made to wait did not play happily with the toys. They smashed them and stomped on them and generally wreaked havoc. Apparently their frustration had led directly to an outburst of aggression (Barker, Dembo, and Lewin, 1941).

From studies like this it became commonly accepted by psychologists that frustration usually leads to aggression. However, while there are many cases where this is so, there are also situations where frustration does not lead to aggression, and aggressive acts are committed by people when they are not frustrated. Like so much of our behavior, aggression is mostly learned. We learn both how to be aggressive and how not to be aggressive.

When a teacher frustrates a child or an army officer humiliates a soldier, neither victim is likely to retaliate aggressively unless unusu-

BOX 8.1

LOVE EXPERIMENTS

A Measure of Love

A study done by Zick Rubin has examined the various psychological factors involved in romantic love. Using a large number of written questionnaire items, Rubin developed both a love scale and a liking scale which he administered to 182 dating couples who were in college. Each of the subjects also filled out these scales regarding a friend of the same sex as their partner. Thus there was a measure of liking and of loving for the dating partner and for the friend of each subject.

In his scale of *loving,* Rubin included such processes as dependency, caring, and exclusiveness; the *liking* scale included factors like maturity and intelligence. Although there was of course some overlap between people's judgments of loving and liking, it is quite clear that they are not the same thing. The women in the study were much more inclined to make this distinction than were the men. In addition, while men and women loved each other an equal amount, the women liked their boyfriends much more than their boyfriends liked them.

Both men and women, as expected, loved their partners much more than they loved their friends, but the women loved their friends more than the men did.

Source: Zick Rubin, "Measurement of Romantic Love," *Journal of Personality and Social Psychology* 16: 265–273, 1970.

The Romeo and Juliet Effect

A great deal of prose and poetry has celebrated the notion that true love cannot be denied, that love will always find a way, and that obstacles placed in love's way will only serve to intensify the emotion. At least three psychologists have taken these notions seriously. A study done by Driscoll, Davis, and Lipetz has found that there may be some psychological substance to the old clichés, but that the whole business is of course more complex than the clichés would suggest.

The investigators were specifically concerned with seeing whether interfering parents had the effect of strengthing a couple's love for each other. Twenty-nine dating couples were asked to complete a questionnaire dealing with their relationship and the attitudes of their parents toward it.

The results do indeed seem to indicate that parental opposition does lead to a strengthening of a couple's love—the Romeo and Juliet effect. But there was one interesting complication. Although the couples became more loving toward each other, they also became less trusting and more critical. Perhaps the influence of parents has an effect that nobody anticipated.

Source: R. Driscoll, K. E. Davis, and M. E. Lipetz, "Parental Influence and Romantic Love: The Romeo and Juliet Effect," *Journal of Personality and Social Psychology* 24: 1–10, 1972.

ally provoked. They will inhibit their aggression against the person frustrating them because they have learned what the consequences would be if they didn't. At the same time (as we will see in Chapter 11), it is possible to induce normal children to be more aggressive simply by letting them see people behaving aggressively.

Furthermore, the social context is once again an important factor in translating emotions of anger and frustration into actual aggression. Leonard Berkowitz has shown that objects just lying around a room can affect the amount of aggressive behavior a subject will display.

Berkowitz made two groups of subjects angry. The people in one group were sitting in a room that contained a gun; the people in the other group saw a badminton racket instead of the gun. When given the opportunity to retaliate later by handing out electric shocks, the subjects in the room with the gun were clearly more aggressive. In this instance an aggressive object, the gun, literally "triggered" aggressive behavior (Berkowitz and LePage, 1967).

MAKING SENSE OF WHAT OTHER PEOPLE FEEL

If we have such difficulty deciding what emotions we feel, it seems that another person observing us should have an even tougher time identifying those emotions. All he has to go on is our outward expressions and behavior. If the situational cues are unclear and we feel ambiguous about our emotions, this ambiguity will be conveyed to the observer—unless we deliberately try to convey a particular emotion. Even if we are sure of our emotions, we can still try to mislead someone about them, scowling when secretly pleased, smiling bravely when hurt, and so on.

Usually, however, people have a fairly good idea of each other's emotions and can gauge their behavior accordingly. We learn to use the cues from someone's voice, gestures, and expression in judging what emotion is being conveyed, just as we learn the appropriate ways of expressing whatever emotion we ourselves feel.

BOX 8.2

JUDGING OTHER PEOPLE'S FEELINGS

Psychologists interested in how we judge the feelings of others have found a very high measure of agreement among people on what basic emotions such as fear, anger, happiness, or surprise look like. At least for simple emotions like these, there does not seem to be much difficulty in linking someone's facial expression with the emotion he is experiencing.

As we have seen in this chapter, however, social cues can play a decisive part in the identification of emotion. Among the most important social cues in our culture are the color and sex of the person expressing the emotion and the person perceiving that expression.

A study by Gitter, Black, and Mostofsky systematically examined the effects these factors had on 160 college students evenly divided by color and sex. They hired 20 professional actors (also evenly divided by color and sex) and filmed each actor portraying a range of seven basic emotions—anger, distrust, fear, happiness, pain, sadness, and surprise. A group of outside judges selected the one frame that best portrayed each emotion by each actor, and these frames were made into still photographs.

Each of the student subjects then saw the photographs and made a judgment as to which of the seven emotions was being portrayed. These judgments were then compared with the emotions that the actors had *intended* to portray.

The results showed that female expressions of emotion (in both black and white women) were much more accurately judged than male expressions. This was true both of men judging women and of women judging women. White expressions of emotion were more accurately judged than black expressions of emotion—with the exception of pain—but blacks perceived emotion more accurately than did whites.

In general terms, the most accurate judgments of emotion were achieved when women rated other women, a finding that may be related to the greater degree of emotional expression that our society permits women to have. Perhaps both men and women found it easier to identify emotions in women than in men because women have a greater opportunity to express emotions.

Source: A. G. Gitter, H. Black, and D. Mostofsky, "Race and Sex in the Perception of Emotion," *Journal of Social Issues* 28: 63–78, 1972

The more cues provided by the social context, the more accurate our perception of other people's emotions become. When asked to judge emotion solely from photographs of someone's face, we can sometimes be quite mistaken, although we are still more often right than wrong. The same is apparently true of judging emotions solely from hand gestures or from the sound of a person's voice. When all these cues are put together, they give us a way of checking and correcting and refining our judgment (see Box 8.2).

The way we learn to make sense of what other people feel depends, of course, on their learning the same thing. *We* learn one way of expressing our own emotions and identifying those of others; in different cultures people learn different ways. What would we make of men crying on a public occasion, for instance, as often occurs in Latin countries? Or of people laughing when they're embarrassed, as in Japan? And what writer in our culture would have his characters clapping their hands when they are worried and scratching their ears when they are happy—as they do in Chinese novels?

SUGGESTED READINGS

Darwin, C. *The Expression of the Emotions in Man and Animals.* University of Chicago Press, 1965. A reissue of Darwin's original and readable book with an introduction by Konrad Lorenz.

Fromm, E. *The Art of Loving.* New York: Harper & Row, 1962. A discussion of love in all its aspects, stressing the reasons for its importance to a satisfying life.

Schachter, S. *Emotion, Obesity and Crime.* New York: Academic Press, 1971. A report of a number of studies exploring Schachter's theory of emotion.

PART THREE

THE PERSON

By the end of Part Two, we had begun to focus on internal human processes and the way we make sense of the stimuli from within. An awareness of ourselves—literally a "self-consciousness"—is probably one factor in making our species distinctly human.

In Part Three we will concentrate on this self-awareness, exploring its development, its implications for our behavior, and the role it plays in making an individual human being a person.

CHAPTER 9

Becoming a person

AN INDIVIDUAL AND A PERSON

We tend to use the terms *individual* and *person* interchangeably. But we also recognize, in our language, that *person* means a lot more than *individual.* We can talk about individual chairs, individual dogs, individual pieces of a jigsaw puzzle. We can even talk about individuals in a flock of sheep. What we are doing is separating one animal or object from similar animals and objects. But the differences between the individuals are often barely noticeable, and are quite trivial compared to the differences between persons.

Webster's Dictionary defines a *person* as "a human being; a particular individual," and therein lies the important psychological difference. Any thing or animal can be an *individual;* only a human being can be a *person.* In previous chapters, we have examined some of the basic psychological processes that are shared by all the individuals of our species, *homo sapiens.* In this chapter and the next we will look at the ways in which each of those individuals becomes a person—"a human being; a particular individual."

ACQUIRING LANGUAGE: SYMBOLS, CONCEPTS, AND THOUGHT

Thought and the creation and use of language are often described as the crowning achievements of mankind. As psychological processes, they are closely bound up with each other. We are born into a world of talking people. As we grow up, we learn how to make sense out of the sounds they make; we learn words and how to use them. We learn that the animal who lives in our house is called Maynard and that Maynard is a doggie. Thus we have learned a *symbol,* for when we use the word *doggie* we are referring to something other than the word itself; we are referring to the dog Maynard. When we learn that Charlie next door and Marmaduke across the street are also doggies, we have learned a *concept,* and we will no longer apply the symbol *doggie* to parrots or pussycats. They have their own concepts.

Most words are therefore both symbols and concepts, and both are used in the mental processes of thinking. How would we ever cross a busy street, for example, unless we (and all the drivers on the road) understood the symbol *stop* and the concept *red?* The symbol of the American flag and the concept of *freedom* mean very different things to Barry Goldwater and Angela Davis. But both would still have to use language to describe and communicate their thoughts to us (see Box 9.1).

When a child is old enough to use words, he will often use them in thinking about and controlling his behavior. If he goes near an electric socket, his parents will cry, "No! Don't touch." After a while, when the child finds himself drawn to the socket he may repeat his parents' command to himself, "No! Don't touch." Eventually, whenever the child gets close to the danger zone he will stop and look at the socket, then withdraw from the scene. It is as though he were silently giving himself his parents' command. The child has *internalized* speech. He no longer reacts to the same old stimulus with the same old response. The concept of danger which he has learned from his parents' words now comes between stimulus and response, and he does not touch the socket. In a similar if more complex fashion, we also use labels, symbols, and concepts to manipulate the environment in our heads and make sense of it before deciding what to do. By thinking, we can cut out a lot of wasteful behavior.

This is not to say, however, that all our thinking is done in words. When we try to recall the places we played as children, a series of impressions, pictures, and images, flashes through our minds. They may concern very specific things and events, but often we don't think of them in words. As with concepts of justice and freedom, however, the only way we can tell anyone else about them is by using words. Language therefore expresses thought, whether the thought is simple or complex, whether the language is English, Chinese, or mathematics.

Psychologists used to be quite confident that language and thought clearly distinguished man from the animals. Then they discovered that animals are capable of thought, and now they're not so sure about language, either. Kohler's apes, you will recall from Chapter 6, were able to form simple concepts and use them to solve problems. They were quite clearly capable of thought. Although no other species has both the physical structure and the brain mechanism necessary for speaking language, various fruitless attempts have been made to teach

BOX 9.1

WORDS AND PICTURES

What goes on inside a person's head when he thinks of symbols (like the American flag) or concepts (like *freedom*) has long been of considerable interest to psychologists. Are our memories of symbols and concepts stored in the form of words or pictures, for instance?

Allan Paivio has done a considerable amount of research on this issue and concluded that we seem to operate on the basis of two different systems, a *visual* system and a *verbal* system. Depending on the words we're being asked to think about, we may use one or the other. If the word has a definite picture associated with it (like *flag*) we will use the visual system; if the word is abstract (like *freedom*) and therefore difficult to visualize, we will use the verbal system.

Paivio has shown that if we can provide visual images for abstract words we are then able to make use of both the verbal and visual systems, giving us a much better chance to learn and recall the abstract word or concept. Our system of numbering is a good case in point. The way the numbers 1 through 9 were originally written, each symbol contained within it the appropriate number of angles, thus:

1 2 3 . . . 9

And as children, some of us learned these numbers with the help of a nonsense rhyme:

One is a bun
Two is a shoe
Three is a tree
Four is a door
Five is a hive
Six is a stick
Seven is heaven
Eight is a gate
Nine is a line
Ten is a hen

Pictorial images have another advantage for our thought processes—they can link together several different elements of a situation in a way that makes sense and thus can be more easily remembered than a series of words taken individually. How many words would it take to make up a "Kafkaesque" situation, for example, or to describe a "southern belle?" There does seem to be some psychological basis for the old Chinese saying: "One picture is worth a thousand words."

Source: Allan Paivio, *Imagery and Verbal Process* (New York: Holt, Rinehart and Winston, 1971).

chimpanzees to understand spoken language by bringing them up from birth with human infants.

Allen and Beatrice Gardner have now suggested a way in which chimps might be able to use language to communicate with humans (Gardner and Gardner, 1971). They have tried to teach a chimp the sign language used by deaf people. In four years and three months, the chimp had learned 132 signs and was able to combine some of them into simple sentences likes "You me go out hurry." This is a remarkable achievement for both chimp and psychologists, and it may help us understand more about the nature and function of language in people.

Whether or not this constitutes speech or language, however, is still a matter of controversy in psychology, and like so many other controversies it shifts our attention from an important issue. Even if the Gardners' chimp is capable of speech and language; even if thought and language do not clearly distinguish man from animal—*so what?* Psychologists were certainly premature in the past in predicting the limits of animal learning, but the limits of human learning can't even be visualized. For all practical purposes there are no limits, and even within the limits of our known achievements in language and thought, there are things that every school-age child can do that no animal could ever begin to emulate.

The reason for this is very simple: we have a much more powerful brain. Furthermore, in the dominant left hemisphere of our brain there is a specialized area called the *speech center* that no animal has. This speech center enables us to vocalize language, to utter sounds and sounds with meaning in the form of sentences. It also enables us to conceptualize and act on highly sophisticated linguistic images and symbols such as *nation* and *democracy.*

The way in which children learn how to speak their language in correct sentences is still not fully understood. We saw in Chapter 6 that the child learns to speak the same language as his parents by a process of operant conditioning. But this only tells us what language he will form his sentences in, not *how* he forms them.

It is inconceivable that a child learns all the language he speaks simply by listening to it, repeating it, and being reinforced for doing so. How is he able to form sentences he has never heard before? By the time a child goes to school, he can speak a language fluently and correctly. Before he has a single English lesson, he has mastered the rules of grammar. He knows how to use subjects, predicates, and objects years before he ever hears of these terms.

How this occurs is still largely unknown, but we have a few clues. Presumably, there has to be some prewiring in the human brain of the ability to use linguistic rules. As the child matures, the wiring is activated and the behavior appears. There is a critical period in the child's life when he will begin to speak grammatically, and no amount of adult urging can hurry this stage along. If the child is not ready, he will not be able to respond. So leave him alone. On the other hand, if the child reaches the critical period and he does not hear language spoken, he may lose the ability to speak grammatical language entirely.

Some psychologists, influenced by the ethology research we looked at in Chapter 2, have suggested a reason for this. They argue that hearing spoken language acts as a *releasing mechanism* for the *innate* capacity to speak (an IRM, in other words). If spoken language is absent from the child's environment, there is nothing to trigger the capacity lying there dormant—and no reason to do so. Studies of children who were virtually abandoned before they could speak and who grew up in isolation tend to show that they are practically incapable of learning to speak when they return to human society. At the same time, though, there are striking examples of children who survived the most appalling deprivations in early childhood and who did not lose the capacity for speech. There is apparently a very complex interplay here of genetic, maturational, and environmental factors that we have not yet been able to unravel.

PIAGET AND THE WAY CHILDREN MAKE SENSE OF THE WORLD

The development of children in their growth as persons is an area where researchers have made some very important discoveries. Foremost among these are the contributions of a man who was originally trained in biology in the early part of this century, the famous Swiss psychologist Jean Piaget.

Piaget worked in Paris at the start of his career, administering intelligence tests to school children. The work was routine and unstimulating to a man of his ability and imagination, until he noticed something that aroused his curiosity. When children gave wrong answers to his

Figure 9.1 Understanding conservation.

test questions, they seemed to do so in a particular manner. It wasn't just that some children gave more wrong answers than others, but that all of the children at a certain age seemed to give the same kind of wrong answers to the same questions.

By simple and systematic experimentation, Piaget was able to demonstrate that children perceive things in a different way than adults do. The nature of the child's world, the one he has to make sense of, is quite different from the world of the adult. Before Piaget's discoveries, these worlds were cut off from each other. Children could not convey their perceptions to adults in ways (i.e., by language) that adults could understand, and adults themselves, having crossed into the adult world of adult perception, could no longer perceive the world as they had when young.

Piaget's insight lay in not taking for granted that children perceive the same world as adults. Instead, with the wrong answers to intelligence tests as his clues, he asked them how they *did* perceive and was rewarded with some fascinating answers. For example, an adult knows that if two small, fat jars contain the same amount of water and the contents of one jar are then poured into a tall, thin jar, the amount of water remains the same (see Figure 9.1).

If you ask a seven-year-old child about this procedure, he will also understand it. But four-year-old children, no matter how intelligent, will tell you that the tall, thin jar contains more water because it is higher, or less water because it is thinner. But there is no way they will believe that the amount of water has not changed—even when they themselves do the pouring. Their intellectual equipment has simply not matured to the point where they can understand the principle of conservation involved.

The seven-year-old child seems to understand this principle intuitively. In fact, he may look at you in amusement, wondering why you are asking him such an obvious (such a childish) question. He may only have acquired this ability a few months ago, but now he can't imagine the world being any other way. It is clear, therefore, that between the ages of four and seven some very important developments take place in the way the child views the world around him.

STAGES OF DEVELOPMENT

The process of development from child to adult is not a gradual increase in knowledge, says Piaget, but rather a progression from one way of organizing the world to another, more complex way. The human infant does not so much grow from a small person into a larger person, as from a childlike person into an adultlike person. In doing so, he seems to pass through what Piaget claims are several well-defined and typical *stages* of development (Piaget, 1952).

Sensory Motor Stage (birth to two years)

At this stage language, and therefore symbols, play a very small part in the child's development. He is concerned with discovering his own body and his growing power to act on his environment, shaking rattles and kicking and thumping in his crib.

The major achievement at this stage is the discovery of *object constancy.* By the end of the first year of life, objects that are removed from the child's field of vision no longer cease to exist for him, as they had before. He realizes that objects have a separate existence from him, and he can hold images of them in his mind.

Preoperational Stage (two to seven years)

The acquisition of language and the use of symbols characterize this stage of development. In fact, words and especially names of things come to have a magic quality for the child. He believes that the name of an object is part of the object, that it couldn't exist without its name. He calls a stick a rifle and treats it as if it were. And he becomes very upset if someone calls him "a bad name."

At this stage, the child does not yet understand the principle of conservation as illustrated in Figure 9.1. This lack of understanding also extends to social relationships, for instance, where he doesn't understand that if he has a brother, then so does his brother, or that someone can be Catholic and American at the same time. He hasn't yet grasped that people and objects can belong to more than one category.

Concrete Operations Stage (seven to eleven years)

After the age of seven, the child can understand conservation and is able to classify things and people into more than one category. This achievement marks a great watershed in the child's cognitive development. He has begun to grasp that the physical properties of things, their quantity, number, weight, and volume, remain the same even if their appearance changes.

The child learns that there is order to the physical world and that there are rules he can learn to find out what that order is. He is thus in a position to *know* what the world is really like even when it does not agree with his *perceptions* of it. The child who has not yet achieved the stage of concrete operations is tied to the perceptual cues he receives from the environment in trying to make sense of it. However, as the name of this stage implies, the child can only apply the new rules he has learned to concrete objects in his environment. Abstract thinking is still beyond him.

Formal Operations Stage (eleven years on)

The ability to form concepts and to think abstractly are the final achievements in the child's intellectual development, and these appear some time after the age of eleven. The use of logical reasoning in solving problems is the particular accomplishment of this stage. No longer is the child dependent on the physical presence of objects that he can see and manipulate. Now he can work things out in his head and come up with the answer to a problem. By late adolescence, he is cognitively an adult.

ASSIMILATION AND ACCOMMODATION

As the child's maturation unfolds, he is at the same time trying to adapt to a more and more complex world presenting him with new information all the time. Piaget suggests that there are two parts to this process of adaptation. In one part, the child assimilates new information about the world into his cognitive system, his existing way of thinking. This is called *assimilation.*

The other part comes into play when the child's existing way of thinking is not sufficiently complex to let him make sense of some new information. The child is then forced to reorganize his cognitive system to include the new situation. This is called *accommodation.* When a particularly crucial accommodation has been achieved, the child may be ready to move into the next *stage* of development.

We should note that Piaget's stages of development seem to hold true for a wide variety of cultures and not just his native Switzerland. It appears that children mature intellectually at roughly the same age in roughly the same way in Europe, America, Hong Kong, and Africa. There are of course individual differences between the children in all of these cultures. Some children understand the principle of conservation at the age of six and others at the age of eight.

Piaget, however, despite (or perhaps because of) his early work in intelligence testing, is not very interested in individual timetables of maturation. He thinks it might be possible to speed up a child's passage through the stages of development by training him to do certain things, but he doesn't see much point in doing so. In fact, it may be harmful. Sooner or later, he reasons, everybody goes through all the stages of development, and as a biologist he feels there may be a good reason for letting this process take its course. Perhaps we need the experience of maturing at our own pace to prepare us adequately for the adaptations we will have to make for the rest of our lives (see Box 9.2).

FROM EGOCENTRIC TO RECIPROCAL

At the earlier stages of development, the child's world centers around himself. He knows how the world looks to him, but cannot visualize how it would look to other people. Piaget calls this view of the world *egocentric.* To a five-year-old child, for example, a foreigner is always somebody else. A person from another country is a foreigner even in his own country, but the child is not a foreigner no matter where he goes.

As the child develops, he acquires the ability to "decenter" from himself and put himself in someone else's place. He learns the relativity of the concept foreigner, for instance, and he also learns to play games by fixed rules, even if it means he has to lose. He acquires what Piaget calls *reciprocity,* a cognitive achievement that forms the psychological basis for adult social behavior in all organized human societies. With reciprocity, we are able to deal with concepts of equity, impartiality, justice, and fairness.

DIFFERENCES MAKE MORE SENSE THAN SIMILARITIES

Although Piaget is not very interested in the educational implications of his work, they are nonetheless of far-reaching importance. Perhaps one of the more simple yet striking derivations of his work is that children can understand *differences* between people and things much more easily than they can *similarities.* Questions about similarities and differences are a standard feature of the commonly used intelligence test, the Stanford-Binet. On this test, six-year-old children, for instance, can usually tell us that summer is hot and winter is cold. But not until they are much older can they tell us that summer and winter are both seasons.

The ability to see similarities as well as differences is often a difficult intellectual task even for adults, and there is a suggestion that it may require more cognitive complexity than is needed to identify differences alone. It is thus easier to learn and to teach differences than

BOX 9.2

SPEEDING UP CONSERVATION

Despite Piaget's reluctance to engage in research on ways to speed up the acquisition of certain concepts in children, other psychologists are not so reticent. The concept of conservation has been of particular interest to investigators, perhaps because of the striking differences the acquisition of this concept makes to a child's thinking.

Three psychologists, named Price-Williams, Gordon, and Ramirez, have studied the effects of a child's environment on his ability to understand conservation. There are several different areas of conservation, and these investigators studied the concepts of number, liquid, substance, weight, and volume. Their subjects were a group of children between six and nine years old who lived in rural Mexican villages.

The psychologists were specifically interested in the differences they might find between children whose families specialized in making pottery and children whose families specialized in other skills. They reasoned that children who grew up in a pottery-making family would have the experience of manipulating things in their environment and should thus attain at least the conservation of substance concept earlier than other children. The investigators left open the possibility of there being a transfer of training from the conservation of substance to the other concepts of conservation.

As it happens, the conservation tasks of number, liquid, weight, and volume did not reveal any significant differences between the children from pottery-making families and the others. But on the tests dealing with conservation of substance they found, as expected, great differences between the two groups. For example, in one village the pottery-making children exhibited conservation in 77 out of 80 tasks, compared to 10 out of 80 for the others.

The researchers argue that manipulation may be necessary for children to attain conservation, and that training in manipulative skills of all kinds may hasten and ensure that attainment.

Source: Douglas Price-Williams, William Gordon, and Manuel Ramirez III, "A Study of Pottery-making Children," *Developmental Psychology* 1 (6): 769, 1969.

similarities, a factor that is reflected in the educational curriculum of any school system. Differences of dress, manner, language, customs, behavior, and appearance are very evident and are frequently stressed by all the social institutions (like family, school, church, and play group) that children have to deal with. Similarities have to be sought out, and even when the child is intellectually capable of handling such concepts, there is little reward in doing so.

LANGUAGE AND CULTURE: MAKING SENSE OF A DIFFERENT WORLD

Earlier in this chapter, we noted that thought gets expressed in language. However, this is just one aspect of the intimate relationship between thought and language. If the child grows up among talking people, he develops his intellectual abilities using the symbols and concepts of the language that these people speak. If the people speak Navajo, he learns one set of symbols and concepts; if they speak English, he learns another.

A language reflects the things that are important to the people who speak it. To people who speak English, time is of great importance. Time flies for us; to people who speak Spanish, it walks. We surround ourselves with clocks and watches and divide the passage of time into hours, minutes, and even seconds. We need to know what time trains leave, classes start, and programs end. We usually know what day of the week it is, and we certainly know whether our vacation started last week or starts next month. Imagine how disoriented we would be if our language did not have separate words for past and future. Yet such is the case with the African language of Schambala, in which there is only a "today" and a "not today."

Evidently the people who speak Schambala don't have many trains to catch. Time plays a different part in their lives. It is perceived and thought about differently. If they speak only Schambala, they will never know what it's like to live in our kind of culture. The language they speak affects the way they perceive the world and how they make sense of it. Thus, the thought and culture that is reflected in a language is also shaped by the use of that language (see Box 9.3).

DOES MORALITY CHANGE WITH TIME AND PLACE?

One aspect of social living that the thought and language of all cultures are concerned with is *morality,* a generally accepted distinction between "right" behavior and "wrong" behavior. It is well known, of course, that specific behaviors like incest or killing off the aged, deemed wrong or immoral in one time or place, can be considered quite acceptable in another.

BOX 9.3

THE PERILS OF LANGUAGE

Misunderstanding the Same Language—I

George Bernard Shaw once said jokingly of the English and the Irish that they were two peoples divided by a common language. The inhabitants of Britain and the United States are also supposed to speak the same language, and even between these two closely linked peoples there are differences in the way they use English that may be reflective of important differences in their two cultures.

Some of the differences are merely amusing (although they may illustrate a problem in communication), like the phrase "I'm mad about this flat."

In New York, if you said this you'd be angry about a punctured tire, but in London you'd be delighted with the place you live in.

And what do you make of these differences?

AMERICAN	BRITISH
He ran for office	He stood for office
They took a vacation	They went on holiday
I took a shower	I had a shower
She took an exam	She sat an exam
Coffee break	Teatime
Movies	Pictures

Here is an example that periodically causes problems at international meetings. When a Briton and an American wish to *table* an item on the agenda for discussion, they do not want to do the same thing—in fact, they want to do opposite things. The American wants to take the item *off* the agenda, but the Briton wants to put it *on* the agenda.

Misunderstanding the Same Language—II

The gap in communication becomes wider, of course, when the people trying to communicate in the same language come from very different cultures. An Arab psychologist named Shouby studied Arabic language and culture and concluded that in comparison to the use of English by English speakers, it was full of overassertion and exaggeration, flowery and unrealistic.

Thus, Shouby notes, "If an Arab says exactly what he means

without the expected exaggeration, other Arabs may still think that he means the opposite. This fact leads to misunderstanding on the part of non-Arabs who do not realize that the Arab speaker is merely following a linguistic tradition." The corollary of this is also true, Shouby argues—namely that an Arab finds it hard to take a simple statement at face value.

Shouby reports a real-life encounter that gave him a chance to observe his conclusions in action. The people trying to communicate with each other were both friends of his, an English woman and an Arab man. The woman told Shouby that the man persisted in declaring his amorous intentions toward her despite an unequivocal refusal on her part. The man told him that the woman was leading him on but that he hadn't really shown much interest in her. Both were quite sincere, Shouby argues, and both were being true to their cultures. The resultant meeting between Arab exaggeration and British understatement produced something less than perfect communication.

Source: E. Shouby, "The Influence of the Arabic Language on the Psychology of the Arabs," *Middle East Journal* 5: 284–302, 1951.

Nevertheless, as in so many aspects of human behavior, the differences in moral values may be more apparent than real. The similarities may be of more lasting importance. People in all societies have many things in common. In fact, the anthropologist G. P. Murdock has listed 73 of them, all the way from age-grading and athletic sports to weaning and weather control (Linton, 1945).

Because of our human capacity for language and thought, we can equip ourselves with *cultural* ways of dealing with these common needs; we don't need to have solutions built into our genes. A system of moral rules and values is at the core of all the cultural solutions to the problems of meeting and regulating these needs. It is the *particular* solutions to these problems that vary from time to time and from place to place.

How Do We Learn to Be Moral?

One of the most important ways in which the developing individual becomes a person is by learning his society's concept of morality, and this is another area of developmental psychology in which we are indebted to Jean Piaget. Piaget's idea of the intellectual progress from egocentricity to reciprocity seems to be just as valid in the area of moral judgment.

Until about the age of seven, children regard right and wrong as absolutes. There is nothing in between; people's motives don't count, it is only the outcome that matters; two people with different views can't both be right. After the age of seven, there is a change toward moral relativism. Motivation is taken into account and there is an increasing emphasis on equality and fairness in making moral judgments of behavior. To younger children, telling lies is bad under any circumstances. But older children realize that under exceptional circumstances, exceptions to this moral rule might be justified. They begin to understand that moral rules don't exist naturally but are made by people to reflect the prevailing values of their society.

Kohlberg and Moral Development

Many psychologists have been stimulated by Piaget's work in this area, including Lawrence Kohlberg who has extended and refined Piaget's account of moral development (Kohlberg, 1964). Kohlberg has studied children from the ages of seven to seventeen. Like Piaget, he claims that children go through a series of distinct stages of development, and also like Piaget his scheme has been tested and found to be valid in several different cultures.

Kohlberg identifies three main levels of moral development. He does so on the basis of the answers to questions about moral dilemmas that he gets from his subjects, and the way these answers are arrived at. For example, he poses the problem of a man whose wife is dying of cancer. A new drug might save her, but he can't afford it. Is he morally justified in stealing it?

1. PRECONVENTIONAL LEVEL

At this level the child is concerned about obeying the rules and whether the behavior will result in reward or punishment.

2. CONVENTIONAL LEVEL

The child at this level is mainly concerned about conforming to the expectations of others.

3. POSTCONVENTIONAL LEVEL

By this level, a person is concerned about the dictates of conscience and abstract universal moral principles.

When this last level of moral development is achieved, Kohlberg believes the individual has come to hold certain values which (although they may be expressed differently) are universal to all times and all places. These are values of concern for the welfare of others, and for justice and equality in society.

SUGGESTED READINGS

Brown, R. *Words and Things.* New York: Free Press, 1968. A fairly gentle introduction to psycholinguistics. Brown uses the case history of a "wild boy" discovered in a French forest in 1797 to illustrate a number of topics.

Chukovsky, K. *From Two to Five.* Berkeley: University of California Press, 1968. Translation of a book by a Russian writer of children's stories. Chukovsky discusses language and thought in young children and gives many actual examples.

Fraiberg, S. *The Magic Years.* New York: Scribner, 1968. Describes the development of emotion in childhood.

McNeill, D. *The Acquisition of Language.* New York: Harper & Row, 1970. Deals briefly with language in young children, emphasizing the biological basis of language.

CHAPTER 10

Dealing with ourselves

SELF-CONCEPT: THE ENVIRONMENT AS MIRROR

At the end of the last chapter we traced the development of morality in a person's behavior and saw that the end point of that development lay in the formation of a conscience with a system of abstract moral principles. A person at this stage of development is capable of guiding his behavior according to his internalized conceptions of right and wrong. Such complex behavior also represents the end point in the development of a parallel concept, the concept of *self*.

We are not born with a sense of self, of who and what we are; it develops throughout our childhood and youth, and continues to change for as long as we live. As the newborn infant develops into a person, his concept of himself is the most important concept he will ever form. It is of crucial importance to how he perceives the world and everyone in it.

As with all other concepts, the self-concept is formed in the process of interacting with other people. From the moment of birth, people respond to an infant's behavior and the infant reacts in turn. From the very beginning of life he receives messages from other people about himself, how he is regarded, the effects of his behavior.

At first the infant has difficulty knowing where he ends and the environment begins. Gradually he begins to be aware of his own body and starts to distinguish "me" from "not me" at about the age of ten to twelve months. During the first few years of life, while he is in Piaget's sensory motor stage of development, the infant is closely concerned with exploring his own body, seeing what's there, and finding out what it can do. As various groups of muscles mature he takes delight in using them, gaining more and more mastery over himself, and exploring the environment.

By about the third year of life, the child begins to be aware of himself. He can think of himself as a separate object, but still has only the crudest idea of himself as a person. He has trouble, for example, in distinguishing processes internal to himself alone from the rest of the environment. When Piaget talked to young people about their dreams and asked them where the dreams were located, he received answers like "in the room" and "beside the bed."

Children also have great difficulty, as they acquire language, in using personal pronouns. A child will start to use the word "I" to refer to himself when he is two or three years old, but he won't use it consistently. He hears people talking about objects called "table," "dog," and "ball," and he very quickly learns to use these terms correctly. But he hears people refer to *him* both as "you" and as "George," and so he may also refer to himself in both these ways. At the same time, he is learning that people announce their wants and intentions with the word "I," so he tries that one out, too.

SOCIAL CONTEXT OF THE SELF-CONCEPT

All of this early exploratory activity takes place, of course, within the social context provided by the child's family and in particular by his mother, with whom much of the activity takes place. The feelings other people have about him and the way these feelings are expressed can exert the most crucial influence on his development. If the child feels secure and loved and encouraged in his earliest explorations of himself and his world, he is off to a good start in his development as a person. If not, both his intellectual and his emotional development may suffer.

With the broadening of the child's horizons that comes with increased language and mobility, there also appears a more detailed self-concept. As at every other stage of life, the self-concept is a product of the interaction between the child and the people around him; what he perceives and interprets as their judgment of him. But whereas later in life it is possible to reinterpret the judgments of these others or to seek out different judgments, the young child has no alternative but to believe that he is what his parents tell him he is. If the message from his parents is that he is ugly and unlovable, then that is the judgment he will make of himself. We should not be surprised to find that he may then start to behave in an ugly and unlovable fashion.

While the child is growing physically from birth through puberty, the most important aspect of his self-concept is the way he looks to other people. Judgments of children are frequently made (in their presence) in terms of their size, shape, and appearance: "He's a big boy for his age"; "She's a pretty little thing"; "They look like nice kids." Judgments are also made by other children: "You're fat, he's skinny." These judgments are extremely influential in forming a child's body image, and they may also have surprising long-term effects. A thirty-year-old woman of 5'3" may still consider herself an Amazon because at the age of seven she happened to be the biggest and most athletic child in her class.

In one sense, our self-concept is never completely formed. We interact with other people all our lives, and so continue to receive judgments about ourselves that we have to deal with. However, it is quite clear that by the end of adolescence when we stop growing physiologically, the outlines of our self-concept have been set and the crucial question of whether we like ourselves or not has been answered (see Box 10.1).

SEX AND COLOR

When a baby is born, the first thing people notice about it is whether it is male or female. From then on, the baby is treated as a boy or a girl. The effects on the individual of this simple and universally accepted behavior cannot be overestimated. For quite a while the baby itself is not conscious of any sex differences. The first emotional task in developing into a person is to realize that he or she is a human being and not an animal or an inanimate object like other things that may be present in the environment. Normally an infant identifies with the person who looks after it, and thus the mother usually provides the first model of being human.

The growing child learns about himself and how he should behave by modeling his behavior on the people around him. Gradually he perceives that he is a boy and that boys and girls are treated differently, long before he knows why this is so or what the physical differences are. Adult expectations of sex differences in behavior are communicated very quickly to children. As early as age two, the behavior of boys seems to be more aggressive and less fearful than girls. Children are already acting out what their parents consider to be the masculine and feminine roles in their society.

By the age of four, practically all children know what sex they are —although they may still be confused about the genital basis for sex differences. Usually they make judgments of sex from outward cues like dress, manner, and appearance. They now have some definite ideas of appropriate behavior for boys and girls. Initially this is very specific, like whether they should go to the boys' or the girls' bathroom. By the end of adolescence, however, the idea of sex role differences has become practically universal. Men and women are supposed to feel differently and behave differently about virtually everything.

BOX 10.1

THE SELF-CONCEPT CONSPIRACY

Many psychologists believe that at least some aspects of one's adult self-concept can be changed by situational factors.

In one study by Elaine Walster a group of female college students were waiting (as they thought) to take part in an experiment when they were approached by a handsome and personable young man. The man was an assistant of Ms. Walster who had been instructed to make nice with the young ladies and ask each one for a date.

When this happened, the experimenter arrived on the scene and ushered the young woman into a different room to begin the experiment. She was told that the study dealt with some personality tests that she had previously taken. In the course of this study she read an evaluation of herself based on these tests. The evaluations were rigged, of course; half of them were very positive and half were very negative.

The women in the "negative" condition would thus receive a negative judgment of themselves that should, temporarily, lower their self-esteem. The women in the "positive" condition would have their self-esteem raised. To finish off the experiment, each woman was asked to rate her liking for a wide range of people, including the nice young man she had met in the waiting room.

In the situation of lowered self-esteem the women rated the young man much more highly than those whose self-esteem had been raised. In the face of negative judgments about themselves these people were more receptive to alternate sources of judgment that were favorable to them.

A study with a similar theme but a longer-lasting effect was reported by E. R. Guthrie. This investigator wanted to see whether a shy and awkward college woman could blossom into a campus favorite by being treated as such. He enlisted a group of college men who were instructed to invite her to all the local social events and to see to it that she had all the attention they would normally give to a highly attractive woman.

By the end of the year, Guthrie reports, "she had developed an easy manner and a confident assumption that she was popular." Furthermore, the young woman retained her new self-image when the experiment was over and the young men likewise continued to regard her as attractive and popular. But for this experience, Guthrie suggests, the woman would have resigned herself to being unattractive and unpopular, and following interests and pursuits compatible with this self-image.

Source: Elaine Walster, "The Effect of Self-Esteem on Romantic Liking," *Journal of Experimental Social Psychology* 1: 184–197, 1965, and E. R. Guthrie, *The Psychology of Human Conflict* (New York: Harper & Row, 1938).

It is important to note that in learning what is considered appropriate masculine and feminine behavior, children can learn both concepts from *both* parents. Girls obviously have their mothers in mind as a model and boys their fathers, when they come to play out the roles of female person and male person. Yet in much of our society both boys and girls see a lot more of their mothers than their fathers. It seems, therefore, that while girls can model feminine behavior all day by directly observing their mothers, boys have to rely largely on their mothers' perception of what masculine behavior should be. To a lesser extent, fathers also impart to their daughters their conception of what feminine behavior should be.

All through childhood, sex role is of primary importance to the child's self-concept. The question "What are you?" to a young child brings the response, "I am a boy" or "I am a girl." Follow-up questions usually produce a variation on the same theme: "I am a good boy"; "I am a nice girl." There is, however, at least one other important aspect to the self-concept of some children in our society—skin color.

There is evidence that black children know they have a different skin color than whites by the age of three. More importantly, they are aware of certain cultural implications of that fact. Studies of black children in the 1940s found some evidence that they regarded black people as socially inferior to whites (Clark and Clark, 1947). They consistently chose white dolls as being "nicer" than black dolls. When a follow-up study was done in 1969, however, the children preferred black dolls to white (Hraba and Grant, 1970).

Because they try to identify with who and what their parents are, children are very sensitive to the content of their parents' self-image. Whatever is emphasized by the culture, as skin color and sex differences are in ours, will be transmitted via the parents to the children. So also will cultural changes (like women's liberation and black power) come to be reflected in the self-concepts of the young.

THE NEED TO BE PREJUDICED

In every human society the family is the first social grouping the infant encounters. The way he relates to it will by and large be the way he relates to society in general. What he learns about life and people in the family will be the basis for his judgments of life and people outside the family. In our society the immediate family and especially the relationship between parent and child, is of particular importance. If this relationship is characterized by mutual love, affection, and respect, if the child feels secure and trusting, then his family experience should give him a flying start on the way to becoming a fulfilled, loving, and happy person.

If a child's home environment is not of this nature, all is not lost—only harder. If parents are harsh, critical, repressive, and inconsistent in their treatment of children, if the child does not feel basically loved, secure, and trusting, then it is more likely that he will have difficulty fulfilling his potential as a person. Such a child might conceive of the world as a place where relations between people are based on power, status, and authority rather than on trust, affection, and fellow-feeling.

A child of such an authoritarian home will be totally dependent on pleasing and obeying his parents in order to obtain their approval of him. Placing such conditions on the granting and withdrawing of approval and love will leave the child in a constant state of insecurity. He is bound to feel resentful, afraid, and hostile about such treatment. But he knows only too well what will happen to him if he expresses those feelings, so he bottles them up by repressing them into his unconscious where he no longer has to be aware of them all the time. Outwardly, such a child grows up to be a rather rigid, conventional person with a great respect for his parents and all other authorities. Inwardly, he may be very angry and filled with hate that he dare not express directly (Adorno et al., 1950) (see Box 10.2).

Such a person is often a willing participant in the sentiments of group prejudice that can always be found in a large and complex society. In such cases, the anger and hatred within is often directed onto a convenient social scapegoat. From the time the child first thinks of himself as "I," he does everything he can to support his self-image and to protect it from negative experiences and interpretations. In an authoritarian environment, he inevitably comes to feel and to see himself as being weak, insecure, and powerless. Because it is painful to think of himself in that way, he uses a variety of devices to defend his self-image.

This person may try to identify himself with the strong and despise the weak; he may cling to ideals of order, continuity, and tradition and be very threatened by the thought of change; he may blame others for all the problems he has and find no fault with himself; he may have learned to fear and distrust his own impulses (particularly sexual ones) and come to attribute these feelings to other people, seeing *them* rather than himself as licentious and immoral, and finding obscenity where none exists.

BOX 10.2

THE AUTHORITARIAN PERSONALITY

The Second World War produced a tremendous social upheaval, the effects of which were felt even in the quiet groves of psychological research. A great deal of research was stimulated by the war, and one of the most ambitious studies resulted in a report of almost one thousand pages called *The Authoritarian Personality.* This massive work was done at the University of California at Berkeley under the direction of four psychologists, Adorno, Frenkel-Brunswik, Levinson, and Sanford.

The authors were particularly concerned with what had happened to the Jews in Nazi Germany, and aimed to get at the psychological roots of anti-Semitism. The investigators soon found, however, that psychologically anti-Semitism seemed to be one species of a more general tendency to be prejudiced against other groups of people.

After a great deal of trial and revision, the authors succeeded in devising a scale of items which could differentiate people who were predisposed to be highly prejudiced from those who were relatively unprejudiced. They called this the F- (for "fascism") scale, and the interesting thing about the items is that none of them seems to be concerned with prejudice. People were asked whether they agreed or disagreed with statements like:

> Obedience and respect for authority are the most important virtues children should learn.
>
> If people would talk less and work more, everybody would be better off.
>
> There are two kinds of people in the world, the weak and the strong.
>
> Nobody ever learned anything really important except through suffering.

But the authors found that people who agreed with such statements also tended to be anti-Semitic, racist, and generally prejudiced in their attitudes toward other social groups.

Subjects high on prejudice and subjects low on prejudice were then given an intensive clinical interview and several personality tests. The picture that emerged of the highly prejudiced person has come to be known as the authoritarian personality. Such a person is rigid, conventional, moralistic, impersonal, simplistic, and judgmental.

The childhood of the authoritarian personality is likely to have been less than idyllic. His parents were invariably harsh and demanding, highly punitive yet arbitrary in their rules and regulations, and quite intolerant of any expression of resentment by their children. These children, having learned at home that the world is a cold, hard, unfeeling place, are then likely to regard the world in this fashion when they leave home, and to treat people with suspicion, distrust, and hostility.

It is important to note that although Adorno and his colleagues were concerned primarily with extreme right-wing ideology, the authoritarian personality they describe can be found espousing many other (if not all) political ideologies.

Source: T. W. Adorno, E. Frenkel-Brunswik, D. J. Levinson, and R. N. Sanford, *The Authoritarian Personality* (New York: Harper & Row, 1950).

Deeply prejudiced people, psychologists have found, are prejudiced against anybody and everybody as long as it helps them feel better about themselves. If an authoritarian white man can bolster his self-image by hating, or feeling superior to, or being angry at a black, brown, or yellow man, then he will probably do so. His prejudice is thus a necessary part of his life. It is part and parcel of the way he sees himself and the world around him. If you took away his prejudices, he would have to look himself squarely in the self-image—and that can be a painful experience for even the least prejudiced among us. There is one important difference, though, between us and them. People who have a *need* to be prejudiced in order to deal with life actually perceive in a different way from other people, and thus will have very different ways of making sense of their lives.

We all have the need to live in an orderly world where we can see what we expect to see, where things happen as they are supposed to. Flying nuns and talking dogs can make amusing entertainment, but we'd find them very disturbing as reality. If we perceived such things happening, we'd try to find a rational explanation for such behavior because we *know* they can't really be happening. Perhaps we would not even "see" what was happening right in front of us; we might simply refuse to perceive it.

DEFENSE MECHANISMS

People will unconsciously defend themselves against the anxiety they feel in a disturbing situation. They do this by distorting reality and by deceiving themselves, two processes that underlie what Sigmund Freud called *defense mechanisms.* We all use defense mechanisms to protect our self-image at some time or another, and examples of their use are quite familiar to us in everyday life. We all have a need for a positive self-image, to think well of our behavior and justify it if we have to. Sometimes the only way we can do this is by unconsciously deluding ourselves and altering the facts of the situation to fit in with our positive self-image.

It is when defense mechanisms are carried to extremes and take up a large part of a person's life that psychologists consider such behavior to be abnormally disturbed. There are many defense mechanisms and psychologists differ about their exact classification, but the most commonly found include the following:

Repression

We have already come across this mechanism in action, back in Chapter 6. There was the case of the woman with the phobia about running water who had *repressed* her childhood memory of disobeying her parents' instructions not to play near a waterfall. The essence of repression is the blotting out from conscious awareness of stressful conflicts or disturbing motivations. They are submerged in the unconscious. In the extreme case of amnesia, repression is so complete that the person submerges even his identity, his sense of self.

Denial

Perhaps the simplest and most direct defense mechanism is *denial,* where someone simply refuses to accept the existence of a situation that is too painful to tolerate. Tombstones marked "Only Sleeping" can be an example of denial, and likewise the practice of parents who keep their daughter's room exactly as it was when she was a child, although she has long since grown up and left home.

Rationalization

The most familiar defense mechanism is probably *rationalization,* which we use in two different kinds of situations, involving frustration in one and guilt in the other. For instance, a student who feels frustrated at not getting into the college he wants may relieve his frustration by deciding that it was a lousy school anyway, or a snob school, or stuck in the middle of nowhere.

When people do things they know they shouldn't do, they feel guilty, and rather than admitting the real reason for their behavior they will often rationalize it by inventing plausible reasons for doing what they did. Slave owners in the United States, for instance—who kept slaves for economic gain—argued that their slaves were quite happy, needed firm discipline for their own good, and would be completely lost without their masters. A student may buy a term paper because he doesn't want to do the necessary work himself, and rationalize it by saying he needs an A to get into law school.

Projection

Sometimes people who feel very uncomfortable having certain thoughts or impulses will assign the same thoughts or impulses to someone else, *projecting* them from within themselves onto others. This is especially clear in the case of powerful impulses like sex and aggression. Adolf Hitler, who had, to put it mildly, an aggressive way of dealing with the world and a rather unusual sex life, was forever attributing all kinds of violent, sadistic, and perverted behavior to the rest of mankind. In our everyday lives, we all know of stingy people who accuse others of being tight-fisted, or habitual liars who disbelieve everyone they speak to.

Sublimation

This defense mechanism is the one most approved of in our society. When we have an impulse that cannot be expressed directly, we repress it in its raw form and let it emerge in a way that will not be upsetting to ourselves or to other people. It is often argued, for instance, that successful businessmen who work long hours in highly competitive fields are, at least partly, *sublimating* their impulses toward unacceptable aggression and competition by expressing them in ways that win them rewards and social approval instead.

Displacement

This mechanism is related to sublimation in that the original impulse is diverted from its direct expression. In this case, the impulse does not change form but gets *displaced* from its original target onto someone else. A loyal worker who finds himself laid off by his company and feels angry and hostile at the way he has been treated usually has some difficulty expressing those feelings directly. Who is the company, anyway? Who exactly is responsible for his situation? Whom can he talk to?

In this kind of predicament, it is very tempting to find a scapegoat that one can blame and thus give vent to strong feelings that won't just disappear. The scapegoat is often a minority group struggling to enter the employment market itself. When times are hard economically, displacement is at the root of a great deal of social prejudice. Terrible evidence of this was found in a study of the southern United States between 1882 and 1930. It was found that when the price of cotton fell in any given year, and with it the income of white farmers, the number of blacks they lynched increased (Hovland and Sears, 1940).

Reaction Formation

Sometimes people who are threatened by an impulse they feel might overwhelm them fight the impulse by going to the other extreme and vigorously denouncing expressions of it in other people. Men who are unsure of their masculinity and afraid of women will often jeer at other men with supposedly feminine or "sissy" traits like gentleness and kindness. Such men might like nothing better than to behave in an open and trusting fashion with a woman, but reject such feelings as a sign of weakness and vulnerability. They adopt a tough, macho disguise instead, in a process of *reaction formation* toward their real feelings.

PSYCHOTHERAPY AND LIKING YOURSELF

Psychotherapy is usually defined as the treatment of emotional and mental disturbance by psychological means. Normally, psychotherapy is a situation where a patient comes to a therapist for help in dealing with himself. The patient, for example, may wish to know why he is depressed or anxious and what he can do about these disturbing feelings.

The essence of most psychotherapy is the search for self-understanding by the patient within an atmosphere of trust, security, and support. The therapist encourages the patient to get behind his defense mechanisms; to get in touch with what he *really* feels, what his real needs and fears are, regardless of how silly, selfish, trivial, or obscene the patient may at first feel them to be. One goal of psychotherapy is therefore that the patient come to accept himself as he really is rather than the way he would like to appear, and that he come to like himself, to be content with his self-image.

There are many kinds of psychotherapy and many therapists who use more than one technique. Most, however, would acknowledge their indebtedness to the first modern psychotherapist, Sigmund Freud, and the school of psychoanalysis which he founded. Every psychotherapist operates on an assumption about how and why people behave the way they do, what makes people tick and what would make them tick better —an assumption about *personality,* in other words. Theories of personality try to explain why people are so alike in some ways and so different in others—a simply stated but tremendously difficult task.

We will examine the concept of personality further in Chapter 12. In the following sections, we will take a very brief look at some of the most important types of psychotherapy and the theories of personality associated with them.

Psychoanalysis

Freud thought of the human personality as being in three parts, the *id,* the *ego,* and the *superego.*

ID

The id is composed of powerful drives, raw impulses of sex and aggression that demand to be satisfied immediately. We are not usually aware of the id; it is unconscious.

EGO

We are aware of the ego. It is the rational, conscious, thinking part of our personality. What we have been calling our self-image would be contained within Freud's description of the ego. The ego gets its working energy from the id, but when the id impulses are too strong and threaten to take over the ego, it represses them and defends itself with the various defense mechanisms we outlined above.

SUPEREGO

The superego, like the id, is usually unconscious so that we are unaware of its workings. It is the part of our personality that deals with right and wrong, with morality, with the correct and proper way to behave, feel, and think. The superego can be just as powerful as the id in its demands on the ego that we behave the way we should or take the consequences of feeling guilty.

These three aspects of the personality are constantly interacting with each other as we move through life. Frequently they are in conflict. This conflict appears in the ego as the conscious feeling of anxiety, whose source we are unaware of because both the id and the superego, with their conflicting demands, remain unconscious. The id growls "Do it," the superego cries "No, no," and the poor old ego is caught in between, doing its best to separate them and keep the peace.

To the extent that the ego succeeds, the personality is well-adjusted, balanced, content, and happy. To the extent that the id and superego influence someone's personality, he suffers conflict, feels anxious, and therefore behaves in the kind of disturbed fashion psychologists call *neurotic,* which we encountered, for instance, in discussing defense mechanisms.

Freud believed that the first few years of a person's life were absolutely crucial in shaping his adult personality. Conflicts that inevitably arise in early childhood between id, ego, and superego are at the root of neurotic behavior in adulthood. These conflicts are repressed in the unconscious, and the job of the psychoanalyst is to help the patient become conscious of these problems and to strengthen his ego so that he may bring them squarely within the image he has of himself and face them unflinchingly.

Psychoanalysis is usually a long process, often requiring several visits a week over a period of years. A patient's unconscious does not yield its secrets to him easily. Very often when a painful area of his experience is about to be made conscious, he will resist the therapist's encouragement to keep going and will choose to leave his memories in his unconscious. If these memories are painful enough and his *resistance* is strong enough, the patient may even terminate his analysis.

To help him gain the patient's trust and overcome any resistance, the psychoanalyst has a few important tools to work with. Most important of these is the technique of *free association,* where the patient lies quietly on a couch and talks freely about whatever enters his head, no matter how irrelevant, trivial, or obscene it appears. What the patient is doing is sinking exploratory shafts into the well of his unconscious. When the free associations begin to converge on some particular area of his life, he has struck oil. The therapist now has to help the patient refine this crude oil dredged up from the unconscious and distill from it the essence of his conflict.

The therapist works in a similar manner with dreams and slips of the tongue; like the products of free association, they occur when the ego's repression, its conscious control of mental processes, is weakest, allowing unconscious thoughts and feelings to filter up and be consciously expressed. With the aid of such techniques the psychoanalyst helps the patient to reorganize, understand, and cope with his real problems.

Client-Centered Therapy

Another important but very different kind of psychotherapy is based on the work of Carl Rogers. Unlike Freud, who was a physician, Rogers was trained as a psychologist, and their different professional backgrounds are reflected in their different approaches both to an understanding of personality and to the practice of psychotherapy.

Freud's underlying view of human nature was a very pessimistic one. He believed that man is largely driven by irrational forces which only a well-ordered society can hold in check. Rogers, on the other hand, has a very optimistic view of human nature. Man, he argues, is basically rational and is motivated to fulfill himself and become the best person he can be.

Both these views of human nature may seem familiar, for we have encountered them before in this book. In our discussion of the nature-nurture controversy in Chapter 3, we noted a similar pessimistic view of human nature belonging to Thomas Hobbes and a similar optimistic one espoused by John Locke, both English seventeenth-century social philosophers. All four of these men were interested in the effects of society on the personality and its development. Hobbes and Freud on the one hand, Locke and Rogers on the other, represent the opposing answers to the basic philosophical and psychological question, "Is society harmful or beneficial to the individual personality?"

The rise of psychotherapy made psychologists and other social scientists increasingly aware of the closely entwined relationship between the way individuals function and the way their society functions. This relationship is so important that we will examine it from several different perspectives throughout the remaining chapters.

The name of Rogers' system of therapy highlights another important difference from psychoanalysis. Freud, as a medical man, regarded the therapeutic relationship as one between doctor and patient, where the patient comes to the doctor because of some sickness which the doctor identifies and tries to cure. In Rogers' system, a "client" (not a "patient") comes to a therapist (not a physician) for help with a problem.

The Rogerian therapist does not try to "cure" the client's "sickness" but rather provides a warm, accepting, sympathetic environment in which the client can examine his own thoughts and feelings in his own way. The therapist does not try to interpret what the client says or guide him along certain lines of thought; nor does he offer praise or blame. In this sense, Rogerian therapy is often called *nondirective.*

Finally, Rogers stresses the importance of the conscious self-image in his therapy; he is not very interested in the workings of the unconscious. To the extent that a client is maladjusted in his behavior, his self-image is out of touch with reality. Such a client has a rigid self-image which he tries to guard from any negative perception of himself that might threaten it. If he can relax his defenses and free his self-image, he can come to integrate within it what he *really* feels and thinks and does—and still like himself even if he is no longer perfect.

Behavior Therapy

Where Freudian therapists are mainly concerned with the workings of the unconscious and Rogerians much less so, the behavior therapist hasn't the slightest interest in it at all. Where the other psychotherapists are interested in getting behind the behavioral symptoms to the real causes of the individual's problems, the behavioral symptoms are the only things that matter to a behavior therapist.

Behavior therapy is based squarely on operant conditioning, the technique we saw B. F. Skinner employ in shaping the behavior of animals back in Chapter 6. Using the same techniques of reward and punishment to encourage or extinguish certain behaviors, behavior therapists try to foster what they and their patients consider a healthier way of dealing with their problems. A person who wants to stop smoking, for example, may be given an electric shock whenever he puts a cigarette in his mouth, until he is conditioned to avoid smoking. In the same way, behavior therapists argue, it is possible for people behaving in a neurotic fashion to learn to behave in a healthy fashion.

A great deal of controversy has been generated by the claims and techniques of behavior therapy. Its supporters argue that they have a high rate of success in getting disturbed people to change their behavior. Its opponents argue that without getting at underlying unconscious conflicts or fostering self-insight in the individual, there can be only a short-term improvement in his behavior before new symptoms of neurosis appear (see Box 10.3).

SELF-ESTEEM

All through this chapter we have noted the importance, in dealing with ourselves, of liking the person we have to deal with. Psychologists often call this feeling *self-esteem.* The higher our self-esteem, the more of a person we can become and the easier it is to deal with ourselves. Bigoted people usually have low self-esteem which has to be bolstered by feeling superior to some other group of people. People with high self-esteem, we shall see in the following chapters, tend to know who they are, to be independent, and to be happy with their self-image. They have no need to hate anyone—including themselves.

BOX 10.3

GROUP PSYCHOTHERAPY

Although individual psychotherapy remains the dominant form of treatment, in recent years there has been a tremendous upsurge of group psychotherapy. Unlike the one-to-one situation in which therapist and patient (or client) have traditionally interacted, group therapy involves the treatment of several people at the same time.

Therapy groups go under various names, and group therapists adopt a variety of approaches. The most common groups are the *encounter* groups and the *sensitivity training* or T-groups ("T" for "training"). These groups are usually nondirectively organized and led, and comprise anywhere from a few to about a dozen people. The reasons for the rise of group therapy are probably related to the relative scarcity of good therapists and the cost of individual therapy. Psychoanalysis, for example, takes several years, and psychoanalysts tend to feel that patients make better progress if they can come more often than once a week.

However, it can also be argued that the group therapy situation has some unique advantages. Patients who are anxious and unsure about going into therapy may be somewhat relieved to find other people with similar problems in a similar situation. In addition, a skilled psychologist can use the richer social interactions available in the group situation to focus on problems of interpersonal relations and ways of adapting to others. These opportunities for a direct look at such problems could not occur in individual therapy, of course, and some patients respond to this situation particularly well.

Just as in individual therapy, it is extremely difficult to judge the effectiveness of group therapy. Any attempt to do so usually bogs down in questions about the meaning of "cure" and the difference between "normal" and "abnormal." There is some evidence from a study by Lieberman, Yalom, and Miles that most people in group therapy have a positive experience, although the nature of that experience may be interpreted widely by the participants. Some people found acceptance and understanding; others gained intellectual stimulation or some useful advice.

Probably the most we can say about any therapeutic relationship at this point is that there is a very complex interaction here involving the type of therapist, the type of patient, and the type of situation. If these factors are harmonious *and the patient is ready to change,* then psychotherapy will be most effective by any criteria.

Source: M. A. Lieberman, I. D. Yalom, and M. D. Miles in L. Blank, G. G. Gottsegen, and M. G. Gottsegen eds., "The Group Experience: A Comparison of Ten Encounter Technologies," *Encounter Confrontation in Self and Interpersonal Awareness* (New York: Macmillan, 1971).

SUGGESTED READINGS

Axline, V. *Dibs: In Search of Self.* Boston: Houghton Mifflin, 1965. An account of how client-centered play therapy helped a five-year-old boy who had been diagnosed as mentally retarded but who turned out to be very bright.

Freud, S. *Psychopathology of Everyday Life.* New York: New American Library, 1952. A discussion of the way the unconscious pops up in daily living. Many interesting examples.

Green, H. *I Never Promised You a Rose Garden.* New York: New American Library, 1964. A novel about the life of a schizophrenic girl in a mental institution.

Kesey, K. *One Flew Over the Cuckoo's Nest.* New York: Viking Press, 1962. A novel about life in a mental institution, centered around a "sane" hero who gets himself admitted and tries to change things.

Lindner, R. M. *The Fifty Minute Hour.* New York: Bantam Books, 1954. Descriptions of five case studies in psychoanalysis.

Rogers, C. *On Becoming a Person.* Boston: Houghton Mifflin, 1961. Presents Rogers' client-centered therapy in action, discussing his view of personality that people can only be happy if they understand and accept themselves and take responsibility for their own lives.

Rubin, T. *The Angry Book.* New York: MacMillan, 1970. Rubin argues that repressed anger is at the root of a lot of emotional problems. Discusses how to identify anger and what to do about it.

PART FOUR

THE PERSON AND SOCIETY

In the final part of this book, we will switch our focus of attention to the psychological aspects of social living. I have talked throughout this book of our environment; the most important fact about this environment is that there are other people in it. In a sense, all psychology is social psychology, a point of view that will become clearer as we see how persons make a society and how a society makes a person.

CHAPTER 11

Society and the individual

THE SOCIAL APPROACH TO PSYCHOLOGY

Textbooks in the field of social psychology have titles like *Individual in Society, The Social Animal,* and *Psychology and Social Behavior.* These titles impart the essential nature of a social approach to psychology, where we are concerned not so much with the behavior of people as with the behavior of people *together.* Since most of our behavior involves other people, it is absolutely crucial for us to examine the relations between people and the social world they have to live in and try to make sense of.

In adopting this social approach we will be concerned with two different issues. First, there are psychological effects, such as conformity to social pressure, that only emerge in situations where people interact with each other in groups. Second, we have already come across many aspects of individual behavior which can also be looked at from the point of view of society as a whole. The process of learning, for example, is obviously of far-reaching importance in a society that expects everyone to be able to read, write, and count. In this chapter we will examine this latter aspect of the social approach, in particular as it relates to the growth and development of children.

SOCIALIZATION

The process by which an individual child becomes a person, and that person a member of his or her society, is called *socialization.* This term is sometimes used as though it described something that was done to people, without their consent or participation. We talk of people "being socialized" into society but never of people "socializing themselves" into society. In fact, however, socialization is very much a two-way process. People influence their social world and are influenced by their social world from birth on.

Psychologists have observed, for example, that some newborn infants are more active than others. This simple difference means that people will react to them differently. The infant will in turn react to their reactions, and the socialization process will have begun. In a very real sense, children can socialize parents just as parents socialize children. Each can influence and even manipulate the other's behavior (see Box 11.1).

Socialization is particularly important of course during the early, formative years of life. In this area of psychology, the concerns of the social approach and of the individual developmental approach intersect. Both are particularly interested in how the child learns what is expected of him and what he does about it. Studies of this *social learning* process have produced some striking results that help us understand the importance of socialization.

BANDURA AND SOCIAL LEARNING: MODELING BEHAVIOR

As we saw in Chapter 9, children learn to speak in the same way as their parents by imitating them with the parents' encouragement. The parents thus serve as a *model* for the children. This kind of modeling behavior is so universal and so familiar to us that we don't usually notice it—and thus it has enormous influence on our behavior.

Albert Bandura has tried to examine the process of modeling, under controlled conditions in the laboratory (Bandura, Ross, and Ross, 1961). He was especially interested in the way that children model the aggressive behavior of adults. The subjects in Bandura's experiments were nursery school children who saw an adult beat up a Bobo doll (an inflatable plastic doll that bounces back up after it is knocked down) with hands, feet, and mallet. The adult finally kicked the doll around the room, shouting at it aggressively as she did so.

When they were allowed to play with the same doll, the children imitated the adult model they had seen, and attacked it violently. When given a choice of aggressive toys (like guns and mallets) or unaggressive toys (like cars, animals, and crayons), the children preferred to play aggressively and beat up the Bobo doll. In addition, they invented new ways of mistreating the doll and of playing aggressively. Thus, they did not simply imitate the actions of the adult and copy her exact behavior but rather *modeled* her behavior, generalizing from it to a wider range of similar behaviors.

Bandura also discovered that when children saw an aggressive adult being rewarded for his actions, they were more likely to copy his

BOX 11.1

BRINGING UP PARENTS

In a very scholarly and stimulating little book called *Socialization* (now, alas, out of print), Kurt Danziger has reviewed a great deal of research on child rearing and pulled together some interesting conclusions.

Danziger points out that in real life parents do not always act as models for children to imitate; sometimes parents imitate their children, as when they coo and gurgle at their infant's cooing and gurgling, or ask their teenagers what fashions are "in." These aspects of family life are simply the more obvious examples of the two-way interaction between parents and children where each side can influence the other.

This influence takes the form of making demands and acceding to demands of compromise and give-and-take. Parents and children form a social system; they need each other. As Danziger puts it, "Children are ingenious at discovering ways of controlling their parents and parents are heavily dependent on their children for all kinds of rewards difficult to obtain outside this relationship."

Right from birth, parents (and especially mothers) react to the behavior of their child, treating him according to his level of activity or irritability. Parents adapt their behavior to their child's needs—for food, comfort, warmth, and so on—and to the extent that they meet the child's needs successfully, they exert influence on *his* behavior. Thus, a *reciprocal* relationship is established between parent and child.

Danziger suggests that both sides make positive and negative demands on each other. Parents, he argues, demand control of the child's behavior. They urge children to do certain things and to refrain from doing other things. At the same time, the child's demands also take both positive and negative forms, as when he demands that his parents pay attention to him or when he objects to arrangements his parents have made for him.

Danziger points out that if this reciprocity of influence is not kept in mind, studies that attempt to observe and explain actual parent-child relationships may be seriously distorted. For example, behavior on the part of the parent that might be recorded by an observer as "annoyance" is often attributed to the parent's preexisting hostile feelings. In fact, says Danziger, the parent's behavior might well have been deliberately provoked by the child.

Recognizing this kind of manipulation is only possible if we stop thinking of children as passive recipients of a process called socialization and regard them as active participants in bringing up their parents.

Source: Kurt Danziger, *Socialization* (Baltimore: Penguin Books, 1973).

behavior, but when the adult was punished they were less likely to copy his behavior. As we saw in Chapter 8, young children judge the morality, the "rightness" of an action, in terms of its outcome. Behavior that is rewarded is therefore good; behavior that is punished, bad.

LEARNING ANTISOCIAL BEHAVIOR

Ever since television became a widespread phenomenon, there has been a continuing debate about its effects on the behavior of children (see Box 11.2).

People are particularly worried about the effects of televised violence, and Bandura's studies have added to this controversy. On the one hand, the argument is made that as long as the villains in TV dramas are clearly punished, then children will not be encouraged to imitate them.

On the other hand, it is pointed out that the good guys are often as violent as the villains, and that what children may be learning from this situation is that violence is successful if you're good, and that violence is the natural way of dealing with conflict between people. What children learn about the world is not always what they're supposed to learn. As with everything else they see, children make sense of what they see on television in their own way.

Almost all psychologists who are interested in this problem believe that seeing violence on television does cause children to be more violent in their real-life behavior. A study done by Liebert and Baron illustrates the kind of evidence that supports this belief. Two groups of children were shown a TV program; one group saw a sports program and the other group saw an episode of "The Untouchables," a crime series packed with violent action. Each group was then allowed to play with some other children who hadn't seen either of the programs. The group that had seen "The Untouchables" was much more aggressive and ready to be violent toward other kids than the group that saw the sports program (Liebert and Baron, 1972).

The kind of research on modeling that we have just been discussing has contributed a great deal to our understanding of how children learn to be antisocial. One effect has been to make psychologists take another look at what children learn from their families. If complete

BOX 11.2

THE POWER OF TELEVISION

From time to time in the history of mankind, an invention is introduced whose effects are felt in every area of social life, changing the way people live. The wheel was one such invention; so was the printing press; and television may well be another. Television is such a recent invention that we are just beginning to assess its impact on our lives.

The most important fact about television in the United States is that virtually everyone watches it. Over ninety-five percent of homes have at least one TV set, and many have more than one. This means that even in homes where there are no books, magazines, or newspapers, there is television. It also means that even when people don't have telephones or indoor plumbing, they may still have television.

Not only do most people have television, but they watch television more than they do anything else except work and sleep. In the average American home, the TV set is on for almost six hours a day, *every day.* To put it another way, the average viewer spends nine complete years of his life watching television. It has been estimated that before a child enters kindergarten, he will have spent more time in front of the set than he will spend in the classroom during his college career. In adolescence, he will spend more time watching TV than he spends in school.

After digesting these statistics, the obvious next question is "What are people watching for all these hours?" In dealing with this question, we must bear in mind both the goal and the means of the commercial TV companies. The goal is to make money, and the means is by entertaining. The TV industry makes its money from selling advertising spots to sponsors. Sponsors want their ad to be seen by as many people as possible; they haven't the slightest interest in the substance of the program their spot is on.

The TV companies define "entertainment" in terms of movement, action. Very often this gets translated as violence. If there are a half dozen detective series on television and they all run for years, week after week, the writers soon run out of ways to make their programs exciting and different based on the story alone, especially as they must make sure to hold the viewer's attention *through* the commercial breaks (the whole point of the program). The simplest and surest way to meet this need is by introducing exciting, *violent* action at the right time.

This is especially true of children's programs, for children, of course, have a shorter attention span than adults. The results are inevitable. Most children's programs contain violence, and cartoons (which are the most popular of all children's programs) are composed nearly entirely of violence. Between the ages of five and fourteen, the average child watches something like 12,000 people being killed.

strangers can get kids to model their aggressive behavior, it seems more than possible that their own parents can have the same effect. In fact, it has been found that if a person has power over others, they are more likely to imitate his behavior, and to a young child parents are all-powerful (Danziger, 1971).

There is indeed some evidence that the fathers of aggressive delinquent boys are themselves highly aggressive and subject their children to harsh physical punishment (Danziger, 1971).

LEARNING PROSOCIAL BEHAVIOR

Modeling, like all other psychological processes, is quite neutral in its social effects. Just as children can learn antisocial behavior by modeling, so can they learn prosocial behavior. For example, in a laboratory setting children were allowed to win some money in a game. They were then induced to give part of their winnings to charity by the behavior of an adult model whom they respected. The sacrifice was real—the children would not willingly have parted with any of their winnings—and the effect of the model in eliciting this prosocial behavior was all the more impressive for it (Grusec, 1971).

It appears likely that television is also capable of influencing children in a prosocial as well as an antisocial direction. A study has been done on the effects of the program "Mister Rogers' Neighborhood," which is mainly intended for preschool children in poor urban areas (Friedrich and Stein, 1973). The program approvingly illustrates such prosocial activities as consideration for others, sharing, cooperating, and controlling aggression. Apparently, the program's models did influence the behavior of the children studied in such prosocial directions.

While modeling is an extremely powerful factor in social learning, a great deal of a child's behavior can be shaped (in both pro and antisocial directions, of course) simply by the rewards and punishments of classical and operant conditioning. Children learn very quickly in this way that swear words are powerful. Whenever they want to tease or shock an adult, they have an effective range of four-letter weapons at their disposal. In a similar fashion, they can quickly learn the attention-getting rewards of aggression.

However, if given the right conditions children are just as capable of learning prosocial behavior. In a study where some children were rewarded for constructive, cooperative play and others for aggressive, competitive play, the investigator was interested in seeing what would happen if both groups were severely frustrated. The frustration consisted of stopping a highly enjoyable movie in mid-reel and reclaiming the candy given out to the children earlier. The children were then allowed to play, and reacted in the expected manner. The kids who had been trained to play constructively and unaggressively did so, while those who had been rewarded for being aggressive displayed a lot more aggression (Davitz, 1952).

INSTITUTIONS

All of us live our lives among groups of people. Some of these groups are more important to us than others. A few groups are important to everybody and are officially recognized as such by our society. What happens in these groups is crucial to the working and to the future of our society, so it watches over them carefully, passes laws and creates regulations dealing with them, and thus turns them into *institutions.* The institutions that have the most powerful influence in a child's socialization are the *family,* the *school,* and the *nation-state.*

Figure 11.1 illustrates the individual's progress toward being recognized as a fully adult member of his society.

Family

Most children in our society, until they go to school, live their lives mainly within their family. Freud was not the first to argue that the child's family experiences are crucial in determining his adult personality, but he was certainly the most influential. The great majority of psychologists would still agree with him on this point, especially with regard to the influence of parents.

That is why in Figure 11.1 I have represented parental influence as two parallel lines that accompany the individual from birth on. In the first few years of life the behavior of his parents is of constant daily concern to a child. They are all-powerful. They always know the answers. They know what to do in every situation.

As the child grows up and increases his contacts outside the home, the child can begin to put his own parents, his family, within a wider social framework. He acquires a perspective on his family as he comes into contact with other families and other models of behavior. As he widens his social horizons, his parents become less and less of an immediate, daily, physical presence, and their influence is diluted by other social influences. But in a psychological sense the child's parents will be with him in some form for the rest of his life, for he will have internalized what he learned from them.

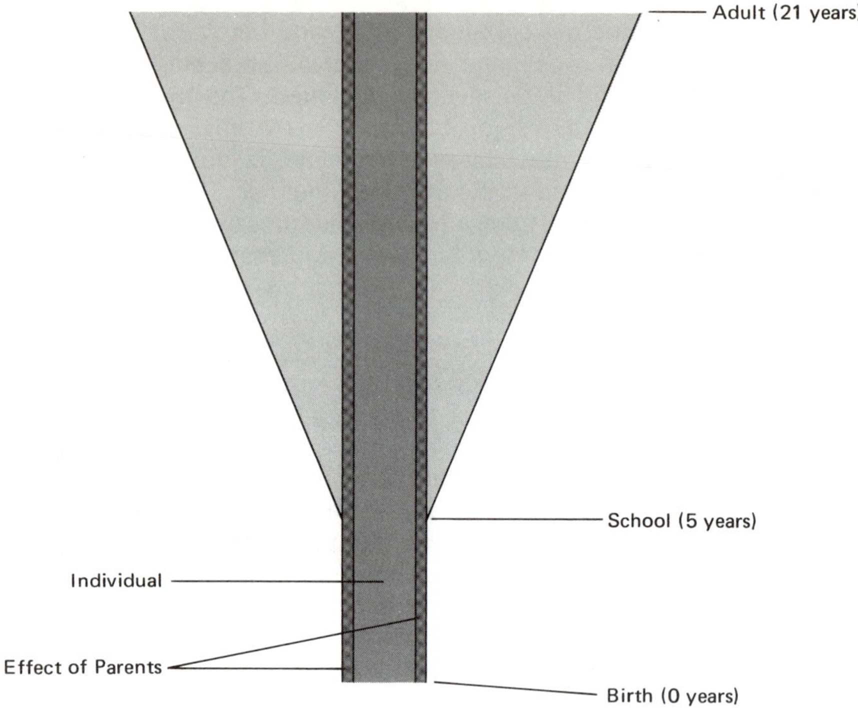

Figure 11.1 Statt Cone representing socialization process.

School

The next important institution the child meets is the educational system. Our society requires certain levels of academic skills of its members—at least the ability to read, write, and count—and we tend to regard this as being the function of school. This is obviously an essential part of the socialization process and nobody can be a fully accepted member of our society unless he can read, for instance. But to a psychologist, schools have a much more important task—they prepare the child for his adult role in society.

In his family setting the child was probably used to having someone around to whom he could turn for information or explanation about the world as it filtered through to him; for example, in the form of comic books or television. But in school he actually becomes part of the world and he must deal with it alone. Play gradually gives way to work, and even play must be done in a certain way at a certain time with other people. And this is the child's first nonacademic lesson in socialization: how to behave in an extremely complex mass society where everyone's life is ruled by the clock.

Schools reflect the values of the society around them and instruct their students in those values. As we are dealing here with the psychological process of learning, that process will operate regardless of the social desirability of the outcome. What some children may learn is that they are failures who are not expected to achieve anything in life. Since the women's liberation movement focused their attention on the problem, psychologists have found evidence that girls at all levels of the educational system have been encouraged, as part of the female role, to hide their intellectual abilities and not appear brighter than the boys (see Box 11.3).

As the child goes through the school, the other children who accompany him from grade to grade (his peer group) will assume an ever-increasing importance to him, and eventually their opinions will influence him more than those of his parents.

Nation-State

At a certain point in his life, society recognizes that the individual has become a fully adult human being—socially. Psychologically, of course, individuals of adult age may be at various stages of maturity in their development as persons. The official age for becoming an adult varies with time and place as well as with the particular social behavior you choose to look at, but certainly by the age of twenty-one people in our society are regarded as adult. They can now fulfill all aspects of citizenship, and they come into direct contact with the third key socializing institution, the *nation-state.*

The most important single fact about the way people of this planet are divided up socially is that virtually everyone is the citizen of some national government. The few people who are not really have no social existence; they cannot travel (having no passport) nor do they have the right to live and work in any country. National governments are the only legitimate source of power in a country (controlling the army) with the ability to raise taxes and regulate laws.

The individual in his role of citizen comes into contact with these social influences as a taxpayer, voter, soldier, and signer of all kinds of legal documents. These are all signs that the socialization process has achieved its purpose and produced an adult social being who can behave in the ways expected of him. But different nations produce different kinds of adult social beings. People are taxed, vote, and fight under different systems of values. These values in turn are reflected in very different educational systems and family patterns.

There is some evidence that even nations with such similar institutions as the United States and Canada can produce people who regard the world, and their own place in it, in very different ways (Statt, 1972). To a psychologist, such differences are neither good nor bad;

BOX 11.3

WHY SEX ROLES ARE SEXIST

Until fairly recently the performance of sex role behavior went virtually unexamined. Boys were expected to behave like boys and girls like girls. Boys were "naturally" noisier, more aggressive, and more rational, while girls were "naturally" more gentle, more emotional, and more dependent. Boys grew up wanting to be doctors; girls aspired to be nurses.

These differences in masculine and feminine sex roles are based on differences in male and female gender. That is, because boys and girls are biologically different they are also expected to be socially and psychologically different. These expectations begin with parents, of course, and children very quickly learn what these expectations are and how they can be fulfilled. Suzy is encouraged to play with her dolls and toy washing machine, her brother Sam with his toy guns and cars. Any attempts by the children to trade toys are swiftly and firmly discouraged.

But what difference does it make which toys kids play with? As long as they're at home it doesn't make much difference. But when they start school and go out into the wider social world, this early sex role training is of enormous importance. The child's world of play is analogous to the adult's world of work. The way children learn to play is the way they learn to behave in society like men or women.

The social importance of this learning to be different lies in the value judgments of our society where "different" invariably means "unequal." This inequality is epitomized by the boy/doctor and girl/nurse role differences. Girls very quickly learn that their social role is to be inferior—secretary, not boss, and teacher, not principal.

So pervasive is this stereotype of correct feminine behavior that girls often grow up hiding their ability and intelligence because these are not "womanly" attributes to have. In fact, Matina Horner reports in a study of female college students that bright women seem to have a "motive to avoid success." This finding is all the more striking in a culture which places great value on achievement and in which males show a well-established need to achieve success.

Horner asked her subjects to write a story around the theme: "After first-term finals, Anne finds herself at the top of her medical school class." Nearly two-thirds of the women in the study reacted negatively to this hypothetical example of a woman being successful. Some stories even denied the facts as given, claiming that Anne hadn't really finished first; a man had actually finished first, one woman said, but that was fine and Anne didn't mind it.

Anne was generally seen as unfeminine, unattractive, and, of course, unmarriageable. When Horner tried the same situation on males, substituting the name "John" for "Anne," less than ten percent of the subjects showed any anxiety about success. Women, Horner concludes, are victimized in our society both coming and going. They have to worry about failure, and they have to worry about success.

Source: Matina Horner, "Fail: Bright Women," *Psychology Today* 3 (6): 36–38, 1969.

they just are. But whatever the effects that socializing institutions have on people, whatever kind of people they are meant to produce, they form the boundaries within which the psychological development of the person takes place, and they select from the vast range of psychological possibilities those aspects of behavior that they consider most valuable.

The institutions of family, school, and nation are all linked together, of course, and normally share the same social values and reinforce the same kinds of behavior. Typically, the basic ways of relating to the world which are laid down in the family are expanded upon and related in school to actual behavior, behavior which the individual then engages in as an adult. The young child in our culture, for instance, learns certain attitudes in his home about the rightness of obeying authorities. The schools offer examples (both in school life and in history and civics lessons) of what this means in terms of appropriate behavior. As an adult, our individual will be very likely to pay his taxes. In societies that value this kind of authority less highly, fewer people may pay their taxes.

SUGGESTED READINGS

Golding, W. *Lord of the Flies.* New York: Putnam, 1959. A novel about a group of English schoolboys stranded on a deserted island who resort to primitive behavior with the lack of social restraints.

Mead, M., and Wolfenstein, M., eds. *Childhood in Contemporary Cultures.* University of Chicago Press, 1955. An anthropologist and a psychoanalyst examine the lives of children in various times and places.

Orwell, G. *1984.* New York: Harcourt Brace Jovanovich, 1949. A novel that describes the socialization influences of a totalitarian country on its citizens.

Read, P. *Alive.* Philadelphia: Lippincott, 1974. The real-life story of survivors from a plane crash in the Andes mountains and how they are pushed to the extreme of their socialization in a fight for survival.

CHAPTER 12

Making social sense

THE MEANING OF PERSONALITY

The term *personality* is commonly used both in psychology and in everyday speech, and like most terms that have this dual usage it does not mean quite the same thing in each context. Psychologists are interested in what makes someone *unique,* the *characteristic* ways in which he behaves, the overall *pattern* of how he relates to other people and how they react to him.

In everyday speech we talk about someone as being "tough and aggressive" or having "an attractive personality," showing that we try to discern characteristic patterns in his behavior. These patterns are categories of behavior, as defined by our society, that we have learned to recognize from our previous experience with people. Where the difference lies is that unlike the psychologist we do not normally try to assess the uniqueness of an individual at the same time as we place him in categories that emphasize his "sameness."

It is interesting to note that one of the attributes of a great novelist or playwright is the ability to create characters of some psychological subtlety and complexity. But we don't have the time in living our lives to be as subtle as novelists or playwrights. In fact, our society encourages us not to be subtle in relating to others.

We know little or nothing about many of the people we come across in the course of our lives, and very often we have nothing to go on but appearance—someone's color, clothing, size, gestures, and so on. When you get on a bus, for instance, how much uniqueness does the driver have for you as opposed to his sameness to all the other bus drivers you've seen? If you stopped to appreciate the uniqueness of this individual, the people standing behind you in the rain might not appreciate *your* uniqueness.

Both the psychologist and the man in the street use the term *personality* to make sense of an individual's behavior. It is only an individual's behavior, after all, that we have to go on. We can never know for sure why somebody acts in a certain way; all we can do is observe their behavior and infer what inner processes motivated them to do it. We will look at how the psychologist makes sense of personality in Chapter 14. Here we are concerned with the way our society influences *our* judgment of individual behavior, both our own and that of other people.

NORMS AND NORMALITY

As children grow up and go through the process of socialization they learn that certain kinds of social behavior are approved of in their society while others are not. At each level of development, certain standards of behavior are expected of the individual in the way he relates to others. These standards of expected and approved behavior are called *norms.*

By the use of these norms a society ensures that most people do what is expected of them most of the time. By learning the norms of a society people can predict the behavior of others with a high degree of accuracy. In America we expect people to drive on the right-hand side of the road and to speak English. If they drove on the left and spoke Chinese we would be very disturbed—unless we happened to be in Hong Kong where the norms are different.

These kinds of norms are obviously very practical. Everyone accepts them as right and proper standards of behavior without question—without even being aware of them. But there are other norms which are subject to social change and therefore to a great deal of debate and controversy. Until very recently it was the unquestioned norm in our society for men to go out to work while women stayed home with the kids. While this pattern of behavior is no longer unquestioned and is certainly changing, it remains the norm in one sense—most families still have a father who goes out to work and a mother who stays home with the kids. Thus another way of finding out the social norms is to find out what most people actually do in a given situation.

In the Middle Ages, for instance, there was a widespread belief that demons and witches were the cause of mental and physical illness, poor harvests, and general bad luck. People saw the devil quite frequently, along with any number of ghosts, elves, hobgoblins, and assorted evil spirits. In these times before the existence of modern science and medicine when the disease known as the Black Death swept through Europe and killed off one-third of a defenseless population, it must have been difficult *not* to believe in evil spirits. At any rate, we can see why this belief was the norm and why such behavior was considered quite *normal.*

We no longer have the same social norms and therefore we no longer consider it normal for people to see evil spirits. In fact, if somebody claims to have done so we would consider him decidedly abnormal. And here we come to the question of defining what is meant by normal. There are two main ways in which this problem is approached; one is psychological, the other social. We will consider the psychological definition of normality in Chapter 14; here we are concerned with the social definition.

The social view of what is normal is sometimes referred to as statistical normality, meaning simply that if most people (a statistical majority) do it, it's normal—with the corollary that if most people don't do it, it's abnormal. By this definition the people in the Middle Ages who believed that witchcraft caused disease were normal, and the people who believed that germs caused disease were abnormal.

Norms therefore represent social normality in a given place at a given time. If the socialization process works, then social norms are passed on from one generation to the next. However, because they operate to keep things the way they are in a society, norms of behavior can still persist after everyone has forgotten the reason for their existence. This is true of any social group or organization, for they all have norms of behavior.

The transmission of social norms over time from one group to another has been studied in the laboratory (Jacobs and Campbell, 1961). Subjects were asked to judge how far a light had moved. By themselves, the subjects estimated the movement at an average of 3.8 inches. When a confederate of the experimenter was introduced, he persuaded the subjects to agree that the distance was much longer—15.5 inches. This judgment became the new group norm, and even after the confederate had left the experimental situation the new norm persisted, with one group of subjects persuading the next that the light had moved 15.5 inches. This effect lasted through several complete changes of subjects before people returned to the original group norm.

DEVIANCE, DISORDER, AND DISSENT

Social norms, even when they are completely accepted and unquestioned, are not meant to be absolutely rigid and unbreakable. If a fire truck has to drive on the wrong side of the road to get to a fire, no one is likely to be outraged. In fact, this *deviation* from the norm is just as accepted as the norm itself. Accompanying every norm, therefore, there is a range of acceptable behavior that deviates from it.

Deciding when deviant behavior is too deviant to be acceptable cannot be an all-or-nothing question. It is a matter of the circumstances surrounding the behavior and of the motivation of the people involved. We accept the norm that it is wrong to kill, just as we accept the deviation that killing in self-defense is right. But what exactly is self-defense? Supposing you think someone might want to kill you, and you kill him before he makes a move; is this acceptable deviant behavior?

Perhaps the issue is clearer at the level of international relations. Every nation accepts the norm that acts of aggression against another nation are wrong. In this century alone, national governments have been involved in two world wars and dozens of local ones, killing people by the tens of millions. To you and me that seems like a lot of aggressive acts, but no leader has ever appeared before his people and argued that "we have to commit aggressive acts to protect our investments . . . expand our markets . . . give our generals something to do . . . increase our power and territory . . . put a damper on unrest at home." These are often the real reasons, but the argument they actually make is the only acceptable deviation from the norm against aggression —self-defense. Even Hitler claimed he was forced to go to war in self-defense.

It is important to note that behavior considered to be too deviant is so defined by the interests of the *majority,* the same process as the original definition of the norm itself. Therefore, what is an unacceptable deviation in one time and place can, if the interests of the majority are different, be quite acceptable in another. Practically all the behavior currently considered deviant in our society, from men wearing earrings to incest and child abuse, has been the norm in some place at some time. Of course, when *most* people informally agree to deviate from a stated norm, a new norm has actually been formed. This seems to be what happened during Prohibition in the United States when liquor, although officially unobtainable, was actually consumed in vast quantities (see Box 12.1).

Usually deviation from a widely held group norm is perceived by the group as a threat. There is a well-known practice in industry where workers will informally set the speed at which they will work and the amount of work they will do in a given period of time. Workers who violate the group norm, by working much harder or much more slowly, for instance, will usually be punished by the group for their deviation. This punishment may be either psychological (name-calling, ridiculing, and ostracizing) or, if the group feels sufficiently threatened, physical.

As a rule, people will comply with a group norm they don't like because of the implicit threats regarding deviant behavior. However, if the norm in question deals with a matter of principle or belief that is important enough to a group member, he may be willing to risk punishment in order to express his *dissent* from the group.

Such is the case with people who espouse unpopular beliefs, like pacifism in time of war, or monarchism in a time of political revolution. Many religions began as a form of dissent by a few people from the

BOX 12.1

DEVIANT SUBCULTURES

People who deviate in a disapproved fashion from a social norm may do so only once, or just occasionally, or perhaps habitually. But unless the rest of society singles out certain kinds of deviant behavior as being especially important and dangerous, people who deviate from a certain norm in a similar fashion will be found living all through the society. Deviants will only be pushed to live in a separate social world by the actions of nondeviants.

Such is the case in our society with drug addicts and homosexuals, for instance. In 1915, authorities in the United States began trying to suppress the drug trade. There were drug addicts before that date, but it was only after their supplies were threatened that they began to move away from regular societal activity and form a separate, complex subculture of their own to smuggle drugs into the country and distribute them to users.

As a member of this subculture was now automatically a criminal, there was an even more powerful mechanism holding the subculture together. In most Eastern countries, where drug addiction is considered a medical rather than a criminal problem, no comparable subculture has emerged.

The same is true of homosexuality. In ancient Greece and many other cultures where homosexuality was as acceptable as heterosexuality, there was no separate subculture composed of homosexuals. It is only because homosexuality (whether or not it is considered psychologically sick) is regarded as deviant from the norm of heterosexuality that there are social phenomena like gay bars, clubs, and newspapers.

In an attempt to observe some of the psychological dynamics that may be at work here, Freedman and Doob attempted to create social deviants in the laboratory. Subjects were given personality questionnaires and then fed back a false set of scores on various scales, together with the supposed scores of 1000 similar people. "Deviants" were created by telling some of the subjects their scores were at the end of the scales. "Nondeviants" were led to believe that their scores were at the center (i.e., the normal or average part) of the scales.

This procedure was repeated three times, with the "deviants" becoming increasingly anxious about their situation. Furthermore, they tended to act in a manner reminiscent of real-life subcultural groups. When they were told other people's scores and asked to choose a group, they chose other "deviants." When asked to engage in a tedious letter-writing task, twice as many "deviants" were willing to do it as "nondeviants," a finding interpreted as an attempt by the "deviants" to make themselves more socially acceptable.

Source: J. L. Freedman and A. N. Doob, *Deviancy: The Psychology of Being Different* (New York: Academic Press, 1968).

existing religions of their society. People who dissent strongly enough from a social norm may be willing to die for their beliefs—and many have.

Both deviance and dissent from accepted norms can lead to social *disorder.* Disintegrating neighborhoods with old abandoned buildings and dwindling, destitute, frightened populations often contain at the same time high proportions of drug addicts, alcoholics, and other people who exhibit very deviant behavior. People who were active in the American civil rights movements of the 1950s and 1960s dissented strongly from prevailing norms of segregation and discrimination against blacks. The ensuing reactions by people who supported these norms resulted in a great deal of social upheaval and disorder.

To a psychologist, social disorder in and of itself is neither good nor bad. It implies that group norms are being challenged and may be in the process of changing. However, the existence of social disorder often leads to a great deal of psychological disorder where people feel afraid, anxious, and insecure, unable to make sense of what is happening in the society around them.

Historians looking back on past social disorders can see them in a different light, one that shows the effects of changing norms. Two hundred years ago, the disorder in Britain's American colonies led to the birth of a new nation. In Germany, after the First World War, disorder led to Hitler and the Nazis. Had Jefferson and company been unsuccessful, they would have been hanged as traitors. Had Hitler been successful . . . ?

BENEDICT, MEAD, AND CULTURAL RELATIVITY

Just as social norms have varied enormously from one time to another, so also is there a tremendous variation between one society and another. Anthropologists have shown us the great variety of answers that different societies provide to the universal questions of life. One such set of questions concerns the creation of the world, the creation of the society, and the society's place in the world.

The answers a society provides to *these* questions can determine whether it will use magic, science, religion, myth, politics, or economics to explain all the other facts of life. In some societies the cause of rain is understood in magical terms, in others, scientific. Some societies attribute a person's status in society to religious forces, others to economic forces. But no society leaves such vital aspects of life unexplained. The questions "Why is the world the way it is, why is our society the way it is?" have to be answered. If they are not, the members of a society will not be able either to make sense of the way things are or to pass this information on to their children.

Different answers to the universal questions produce different kinds of societies which encourage different kinds of responses from their members. As the anthropologist Ruth Benedict has pointed out, societies organize themselves around their view of what human qualities and ways of relating are most important. She found a society where aggression was stressed and where people were very suspicious of each other's intentions, another society where competition and the amassing of goods were considered important, and a society where moderation and lack of competition were encouraged above all (Benedict, 1934). Observers of American society have frequently noted the dominance of competitiveness and individualism and the stress on achievement.

A person whose psychological predisposition is out of tune with his society may be considered socially abnormal by his own society, but we should refrain, Benedict argued, from judging other people in other societies by our own standards. There are no absolute standards by which all societies can be compared. They are all *relative,* and so one society's answers are as good as another's. In studying an individual's behavior, it cannot be understood unless it is seen in the context of his society's behavioral norms.

Other anthropologists have shown us that behavior *we* regard as inborn and natural may in fact be learned through the process of socialization. We tend to regard the behavior of men and women as being very different "by nature." Margaret Mead has studied a society called the Tchambuli in which the dominant sex went out to work, fishing and trading, while the weaker sex stayed home, dancing and painting and prettying themselves up (Mead, 1935). Contrary to our expectations, though, the dominant sex here was female and the weaker sex male (see Box 12.2).

CHANGES OVER TIME

So far in this chapter we have been considering ways in which a society can influence the behavior of its individual members. But there are also ways in which both we and the society we live in can be shaped independently of each other. One of these ways involves simply the passage of time. Psychologists are interested in *psychodynamics*—how and why people change—so they must therefore be

BOX 12.2

ONE PERSON'S MEAT IS ANOTHER PERSON'S TABOO

Two of the most important aspects of every culture are the attitudes taken toward food and sex. These areas of human behavior are usually the subject of a great number of clearly understood "dos" and "don'ts." And very often what is done in one culture is offensive to people from another culture. Many people will not eat pork, beef, or meat of any kind, while some people will eat anything, including other people.

The Buka people of the South Pacific were noted by anthropologists to be much freer about sexual behavior than Western societies. However, they did have some strong food taboos against people of the opposite sex eating together—thus reversing our own taboos. But there are also great cultural differences between people who consider themselves to have a lot in common with each other. The French are forever shaking their heads sadly at the incomprehensible refusal of the English-speaking world to appreciate such delicacies as ants, snails, brains, and rabbit.

There do seem to be some universal attitudes toward sexual behavior. Rape and incest, for example, are prohibited and punished in every culture. Exactly what constitutes rape or incest, however, can vary widely. The brother-sister marriages of ancient Egypt would be unthinkable to us, while sexual relations with a girl of fifteen would not be considered rape in many non-American societies.

Ford and Beach surveyed the sexual behavior of over 200 societies and found that American customs were atypical in many ways. While stable partnerships are found everywhere, the American concept of marriage as being the only officially recognized sexual relationship was relatively rare, being found in about sixteen percent of the cultures studied.

Similarly, our traditional disapproval of women approaching men was rarely found. Where there was no social pressure against it, women initiated sexual behavior as often as men did. Attitudes about sexual behavior involving animals ran the whole range from acceptable to disgusting. Likewise, there are about as many societies which approve of homosexuality as disapprove of it, although heterosexual behavior is the universal favorite.

One sexual practice that seems to be officially condemned almost everywhere (and often ridiculed as well) is masturbation. Unofficially, most people in most cultures probably do masturbate.

Perhaps the reason for the official disapproval is that masturbation, while it is harmless physically and psychologically, is not usually a social behavior. It may even be interpreted as antisocial.

Source: C. S. Ford and F. A. Beach, *Patterns of Sexual Behavior* (New York: Harper & Row, 1951).

aware of the effects of time, for change refers to the differences that are observed between one time and another.

Change over time is important in three ways: in terms of the individual's own *life cycle;* the prevailing norms and events, or *zeitgeist,* of any given period in his life; and his age group or *cohort.* Figure 12.1 shows how these three aspects of time are related to each other.

Life Cycle

One obvious but very important aspect of the life cycle is that the longer we've lived, the less of our life cycle lies in the future. A glance at Figure 12.1 will show how this relates to society. People of seventy-five probably do not expect to see the end of this century, whereas people of fifty may well do so, and people of twenty-five will certainly expect to do so. Therefore, the younger a person is, the longer his image of the future. If the end of the world is posted for the year 2000 A.D., the people least likely to worry about it are those who will be dead when it happens.

Psychologists have actually tested this kind of assumption, and discovered that older people do indeed favor shorter-range solutions to social problems than do younger people. (Gergen and Back, 1965). Hardly a news bulletin, you will yawn, but how old do you suppose the people are who make decisions about our future? And what will be the effects of a short-run solution (on, let's say, poverty, pollution, population, or prejudice) in the long run?

At different points in the life cycle people are expected to behave in different ways. An adolescent behaving in a manner more appropriate to a child is likely to be told, "Act your age." A child in a solemn mood may look like "a little old man"; a middle-aged person having a fling is entering a "second childhood." There are definite age norms of behavior and they are just as powerful in shaping our lives as any other norms.

Zeitgeist

The German word *zeitgeist* means literally "spirit of the times." It is used to denote the prevailing social and political mood of an era, the conventional wisdom, the fads and fashions in everything from hair

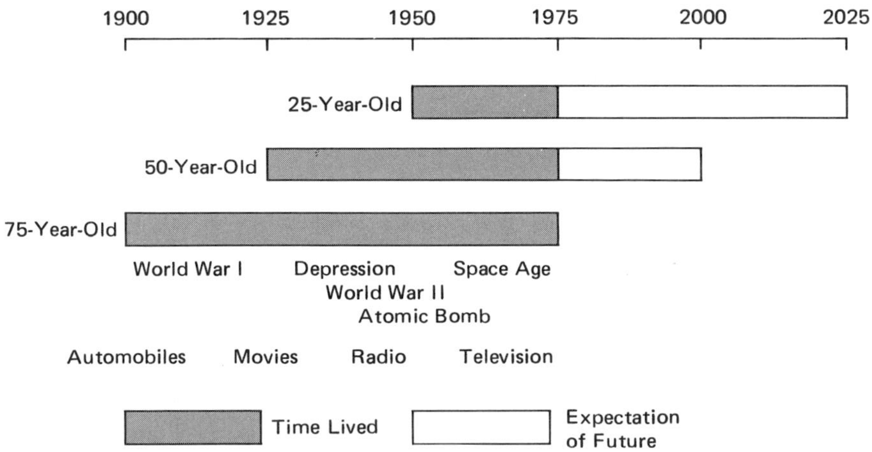

Figure 12.1 Changes over time.

length to psychology. Sometimes a zeitgeist is characterized by widespread social upheaval (the First World War, the French Revolution), and at other times by events less easy to categorize (the Roaring Twenties, the Silent Fifties, the Space Age).

Whatever the zeitgeist might be, it affects the emotional and mental life of the people living through it, and one particularly important form this takes is in the prevailing norms about rearing children. There used to be a governmental agency called the United States Children's Bureau which from time to time would publish a bulletin called *Infant Care.* This bulletin relayed the considered opinions of child rearing experts to any parents who were interested.

In 1914 and 1921 the bulletins advised parents to treat such behavior as masturbation and thumb sucking very severely, even instructing that the offending limbs be tied down and immobilized. By 1929 the advice in this area was less dramatic, recommending simply that the infant's attention be diverted. At the same time, though, parents were advised to be very rigid about weaning and toilet training, subordinating everything to a time schedule that ideally should be followed to the exact minute. From the end of the 1930s on the advice becomes increasingly more tolerant in all areas, with the emphasis on individual differences rather than rigid scheduling.

Cohort

The life cycle and zeitgeist effects can be linked by focusing on an individual's cohort, the group of people who were born at the same time as he was. If we look at Figure 12.1 we can see for each of our three cohorts where they are in the life cycle and what kind of zeitgeist they have shared. The point of their being a cohort is that they experienced the same zeitgeist at the same point in their lives.

This is the basis for our talking about the differences between generations—like the older generation and the younger generation. Indeed, if parents of a certain age live through a very different zeigeist from their children there often is also a very substantial psychological difference, leading to a difficulty in communication about how to make sense of life that is sometimes referred to as a generation gap. Research on socialization patterns in Russia, for example, has suggested that the generations which grew up before and after the Bolshevik Revolution of 1917 had very different kinds of social relationships and ways of coping with society which effectively ended a great deal of traditional Russian life (Inkeles, 1955) (see Box 12.3).

Most psychologists believe that cohort influences are most important during childhood and adolescence when the self-image is still being formed and when the individual is most susceptible to the peer pressures of his age group.

PLURALISTIC IGNORANCE

Throughout this chapter we have been looking at ways in which people make sense of their society together. But people in every society have differences in what they perceive to be happening—to say nothing about whether what's happening is good or bad. In addition, there is always a sizable difference, of course, between what is supposed to happen in a society and what actually does happen socially, politically, ethically, and every other way.

In our society public behavior is very predictable. We know how people behave in stores, offices, buses, theatres, schools, streets, and factories. It is easy to check our own behavior in these situations to see if we're doing the "right" thing, to make sure we're socially normal. However, we know remarkably little about each other's private lives. We really don't know if our private behavior is as "normal" as our public behavior. Where people in a society are all in this position, they are said to be in a state of *pluralistic ignorance.*

At least one study of how pluralistic ignorance functions has been conducted—with some amusing results (Schanck, 1932). The research was done in a small rural community with strict Christian norms about abstaining from drinking and gambling and about observing the Sabbath. The people were very hospitable, and every Sunday after church the investigator was invited back to a different home for the rest of the day. Each visit followed the same routine; after lunch the Good Book was put back on the shelf, the blinds were drawn, and the guest was invited to drink and gamble with the only family in town that broke the rules.

BOX 12.3

THE GENERATION GAP

In most societies children will closely model their parents. When adolescence is reached and the individual is at the transition stage between childhood and adulthood, there may well be a breakdown in the modeling relationship. This is often the case when a social upheaval takes place as the result of war, migration, or technological change—and sometimes all three.

When this happens there is a discontinuity in the socialization process. People may be left behind by new ways of doing things, unable to cope and unable to help their children cope in the changed society. The adolescents who will form the new generation have to look elsewhere for help and support in making sense of a social world unknown to previous generations. In such circumstances the help and support may be sought from each other, with young people becoming very conscious of their generation and differentiating it sharply from their parents' generation.

There is nothing new about this phenomenon, although every new generation thinks there is and every generation of parents bemoans the impossibleness of the younger generation. In the 1960s there appeared to be a particularly striking generation gap between college-age people and their parents. Kenneth Keniston outlined the processes involved by interviewing a number of radical college students.

Keniston had previously suggested that one result of the widespread and rapidly increasing social change that our society was going through was the difficulty of identifying with anyone or anything. If values and ideas are constantly changing, how could young people identify with adults whose values and ideas looked as if they had already been overtaken by history?

In interviewing his subjects, Keniston found that they tended to identify strongly with people of the same age and distrust not just anyone over thirty, but organizations and ideologies of all kinds. They did not regard the older generation as incurably evil and corrupt and ready to be overthrown by the forces of light, but rather as irrelevant to the needs of the time.

Source: Kenneth Keniston, *The Uncommitted: Alienated Youth in American Society* (New York: Harcourt Brace Jovanovich, 1960), and Kenneth Keniston, *Young Radicals: Notes on Committed Youth* (New York: Harcourt Brace Jovanovich, 1968).

SUGGESTED READINGS

Benedict, R. *Patterns of Culture*. New York: New American Library (Mentor Books), 1949. Discusses the relationship between individual and society and argues that an individual's behavior must be looked at in the light of his society's values.

Ellison, R. *Invisible Man*. New York: New American Library (Signet), 1952. A novel that portrays the meaning of being black in a society that considers black to be deviant.

Kanter, R. *Communities and Commitment*, Cambridge, Mass.: Harvard University Press, 1972. A study of American communes, highlighting the conflict between individual control and social control of behavior.

Mead, M. *Sex and Temperament in Three Primitive Societies*. New York: New American Library (Mentor Books), 1950. Shows how male and female roles are learned in different societies and how these roles relate to individual needs.

Polsky, N. *Hustlers, Beats, and Others*. Chicago: Aldine, 1966. A collection of essays on various kinds of deviants and the worlds they live in.

CHAPTER 13

Organizing social cues

In the last chapter we surveyed the effects on our lives of the large-scale influences that change in time or place can have. We noted there how our psychology, the way we think, feel, and behave, is shaped in general terms by these factors. In this chapter we will take a closer look within these boundaries and focus on the interactions between an individual and his social world in our own time and place.

EFFECTS OF SOCIAL INFLUENCE

The behavior of an individual can be affected, under certain conditions, by the mere presence of other people. Even when the other people are not trying to influence the individual's behavior he may act differently than when he is alone. Psychologists have known since 1897, for example, that an individual will work harder on simple tasks (like winding a fishing reel) when other people are sitting watching him, without saying or doing anything (Triplett, 1897).

The individual's behavior has been stimulated by having other people pay attention to him. By acting as an audience for his performance they provided him with social cues to which he responded with increased production. This process is called *social facilitation* and it has been observed in an actual work setting, a factory where telephone equipment was assembled. The investigators who did this study were not looking for the effects of social facilitation, though; they were interested in seeing whether changes in the working conditions themselves would increase productivity.

Various changes in lighting, rest breaks, hours of work, and system of payment were tried on a group of five workers. After every change the result was the same—productivity increased. Even when one of the changes involved a return to the original conditions, pro-

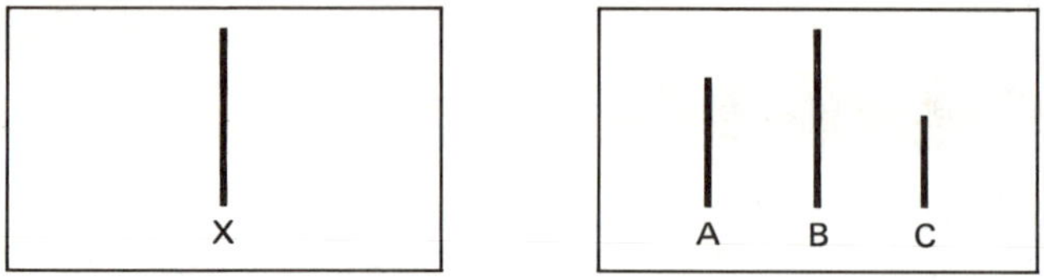

Figure 13.1 Asch conformity situation.

ductivity still increased. Finally it dawned on the investigators that none of the working conditions made any difference one way or the other. What mattered to the workers was that someone was interested in observing their performance. The psychologists had increased productivity by the mere fact of doing their study, an effect that is known by the name of the town where the factory was located as the *Hawthorne effect* (Roethlisberger and Dickson, 1939).

Conformity

Perhaps the most important social interaction is that of *conformity* to social pressure. We have already seen the tremendous importance of social norms in influencing our lives and how people usually conform to the behavior expected of them; here we will examine the psychological mechanism that makes this social engine work. Several studies will help illuminate the many different ways in which conformity operates.

In the early 1950s, Solomon Asch did a series of studies on the effects of group pressure on the individual which startled other psychologists, and even Asch himself. The typical Asch experiment had seven people seated around a table judging lengths of lines (Asch, 1956). Only one of the seven subjects in Asch's experiment was a real (i.e., naive) subject. The other six were paid confederates of the experimenter, and it was their job to produce the group pressure directed at the naive subject. The study was billed as an exercise in visual perception, and the subjects were supposed to compare the length of a line on one card with three lines on another card, as in Figure 13.1.

The experimenter then asked the subjects whether line X was equal in length to lines A, B, or C. Asch deliberately made the task very easy so that subjects when they were alone would always give the right answer. What Asch wanted to find out was this: what would happen if his six confederates all gave the same wrong answer? Would the naive subject say what he really saw, or would he be influenced by the unanimous judgment of the group to conform and give the same wrong answer as everyone else?

Asch had arranged things so that the naive subject was always seated in the number six position where he would hear five other judgments before his own turn came. In *over a third* of the cases the naive subject conformed to the group pressure and gave an answer he knew to be wrong.

There are two ways we can interpret this finding. We can say that most people refused to yield to group pressure even though they were going against the norm. But we can also say that over a third of the subjects were willing to deny the evidence of their own eyes in order to comply with the norm, and it is this unexpected result that psychologists found so startling.

Asch's experiments have been repeated many times by other psychologists and the findings have usually been the same. A great deal of work has also gone into studying the various factors involved, and these are commonly divided into individual factors and group factors.

A study of the people who yielded to group pressure shows that they are much lower in self-esteem and have a poorer image of themselves than the people who did not yield. The most important group factor is whether or not the majority making the wrong judgment is unanimous. If even one other person agrees with the naive subject, his likelihood of yielding to group pressure is greatly reduced (see Box 13.1).

A different type of conformity was the object of research by Stanley Milgram (1963). In Milgram's work, the conformity studied was not compliance with a norm set by a group of people in the same room as the subject, but compliance to a general norm of society—obedience to authority. But Milgram's studies were similar to those of Asch in at least one respect: they caused a great stir among psychologists. In fact, his dramatic findings have also caused a great stir among nonpsychologists.

Like Asch, Milgram was interested in observing the behavior of one naive subject at a time, in a controlled setting. The subjects thought they were taking part in a learning experiment where they were to play the role of a teacher, while another person (Milgram's confederate) took the part of a learner. The learner was supposed to memorize lists of nonsense syllables which the teacher was supposed to help him learn by giving him an electric shock whenever he made an error. The more errors the learner made, the stronger the voltage he was given—up to 450 volts, at which point the switch was marked "Danger! Severe Shock XXX."

In fact, no electric shocks were actually given, although the subject thought they were. The situation was rigged. Communication between teacher and learner was by means of an intercom, for the supposed learner was supposedly strapped into an impressive-looking electronic apparatus in the next room, out of sight of the teacher. The

BOX 13.1

BELIEFS AND GROUP PRESSURE

While Solomon Asch was performing his important series of studies on conformity, other psychologists interested in the same phenomena adopted a somewhat different approach. Richard Crutchfield, for instance, developed a technique that dispensed with the need for confederates and gave him a great deal of control over the conformity situation.

In Crutchfield's experiments, five people were each making their individual judgments of the stimuli. The subjects were seated side by side, each person seated in his own cubicle facing a switchboard and out of sight of the others. Verbal communication was not allowed, and the only way a subject could communicate with the others or with the experimenter was by flicking a switch in front of him that lit up signal lights on everyone else's switchboard.

Each subject was asked to indicate in this way whether he agreed or disagreed with various statements that were presented to the group. The switchboard in front of him registered the answers of the other group members. Unlike the Asch situation, however, each of the people in the group was a naive subject whose responses to group pressure were being studied. In fact, there was no communication between the subjects in the group. Crutchfield systematically controlled the situation by providing each subject with false information on his switchboard about the judgments of the other four people.

At certain points, each subject found himself faced with what looked like a unanimous group choice supporting the wrong answer to a particular statement. Where the statements dealt with the same level of difficulty as in the Asch study—that is, easy perceptual comparisons or arithmetical problems—Crutchfield obtained about the same level of conformity as Asch, about one-third of the subjects.

But when Crutchfield made the arithmetical problem difficult, up to 80 percent of the subjects were persuaded to conform to the false group consensus and agree with an answer that was clearly wrong. In this situation, Crutchfield also induced bright college students to agree with a great number of odd statements: for example, that most Americans are over 65 years old, that the average person only has a life expectancy of 25 years, and that this same average American eats six meals a day—perhaps accounting for the fact that he only sleeps four hours a night.

Most striking of all, perhaps, was the reaction to the statement

"Free speech being a privilege rather than a right, it is proper for a society to suspend free speech whenever it feels itself threatened." In a control group free of group pressure, only 19 percent of the subjects agreed with this statement; in Crutchfield's situation of group pressure, 58 percent agreed.

Source: R. S. Crutchfield, "Conformity and Character," *American Psychologist* 10: 191–198, 1955.

responses the subject thought he was getting from the learner were actually a tape recording with prearranged right and wrong answers. As the errors increased and the punishment along with it, the subject heard howls of pain, demands to be let out, and finally silence from the room next door. The real purpose of the experiment was to see how far the subject would go in giving someone electric shocks when prompted to do so by an authority, the experimenter.

When people are asked to guess how many subjects continued on up to the 450-volt mark, the usual estimate is about one percent. In fact, some 65 percent, *almost two-thirds* of the subjects, did so. Milgram is careful to point out that the subjects in his study were not sadists who enjoyed inflicting pain on other people. Far from it; they were extremely uncomfortable about the whole situation, and often expressed a desire to terminate the experiment. Yet only a third of the subjects were willing to defy the experimenter's authority and refuse to continue.

As with the subjects in the Asch experiment, the people who did not succumb to the conformity pressure tended to be higher in self-esteem than the people who did. The most important situational factor was the amount of personal responsibility the subject had to accept for his or her actions. In one part of the study, the subject had to force the learner's hand down on a shockplate in order to deliver the maximum 450 volts. Under these conditions, the amount of conformity was more than halved; less than one-third of the subjects were willing to go this far.

Another kind of conformity to a general social norm has been suggested by Elliot Aronson in his book *The Social Animal* (1972). The kind of behavior that Aronson is interested in also involves conformity to a general social norm, but in this case the norm is that people do not interact with others—what has come to be known as *bystander apathy.* It is often argued that when someone is attacked or has an accident in a public place, the norm is for other people not to get involved, to walk away from the scene. Some research studies have also supported the notion of bystanders conforming to a norm of apathy.

At the same time, there are instances where people do get involved. But why do people help out in some situations and not in others? A study done in the New York subway system gives us some clues (Piliavin, Rodin, and Piliavin, 1969). This experiment was designed to see if people would come to the aid of a man who had collapsed on the floor of a subway car. The man was an accomplice of the experimenters, of course; in some cases he appeared to be ill and in other cases drunk.

The results of this experiment surprised a lot of people. Where the man appeared to be ill, people came to his aid 95 percent of the time. When the man reeked of liquor, he was still helped 50 percent of the time. Aronson suggests that the situation in this experiment provided two conditions that changed the social norm from apathy to intervention. First, everyone in the subway car felt part of the same situation, sharing a common predicament. Second, they couldn't walk away. They were part of the scene and had to deal with the fact that someone had collapsed in front of them.

Our final example of conformity involves the ingenious use of an optical illusion. If you sit in a room that is completely dark except for a tiny pinpoint of light, the light, although it is completely stationary, will appear to move about. This illusion of movement is called the *autokinetic effect*. Muzafer Sherif (1936) discovered that when he put three people in the room at the same time, their individual estimates of how far the light had moved began to converge until a consensus was reached, thereby establishing a group norm.

When each subject then judged how far the light had moved when he was alone in the room, he did not return to his original judgment but opted instead for the group judgment. The subject thus conformed to the group norm, although we should note that he had a hand in setting that norm. This study is about as clear an example of conformity pressure as one can imagine. An outside observer would see nothing happening, no apparent pressure from either the experimenter or the other subjects, merely a group of people sitting in the dark deciding how far a stationary light had moved. What these people were doing was deciding how to make sense of something that had absolutely no meaning by itself.

There is another interpretation we can make of Sherif's findings. It appears that people organized the perceptual cues (tiny light against dark, formless background) in two different ways. By themselves they judged that the light was only moving a little; in a group they judged it as moving further. By themselves they could only rely on their own senses (which were of course being deceived), but in the group situation they had some extra, social cues in the form of other people's judgments.

Conformity to group norms may therefore be thought of as a process where people organize social cues to help them understand how one is expected to respond, and what the consequences would be if one responded differently. In an ambiguous social situation, with no laws or physical coercion to direct our behavior, social cues are all-important.

Individual Solutions and Group Solutions

The theme we perceived in Sherif's work, that individuals and groups come up with different solutions to the same problem, deserves a little more amplification. From the research on decision making and problem solving, for instance, it appears that ideas and solutions provided by individuals tend to be more diverse and creative than those provided by groups. At the same time, though, once the ideas have been generated a group decision seems to be more effective in selecting the best one for the problem at hand.

A great deal of research has also been done on risk-taking behavior. Contrary to what we might expect, it seems that groups are inclined to adopt a much more risky solution to a problem than individuals are. Why this happens is a matter of some debate. A typical problem in this kind of experiment asks the subject to think of himself as a man with a secure but modest income who gets the chance to go into business for himself, in a venture that promises great financial gain but involves some risk. The question is, how much risk is he willing to take? Usually a group of subjects is willing to take more risks than the same set of people making individual decisions. This change in behavior from an individual to a group condition is called the *risky shift* (Wallach et al., 1962).

What Do People Get from Groups?

We have already encountered one of the most important functions that groups have for individuals: they help us decide what is really happening and how we can make sense out of it. In Chapter 8 we discussed an experiment by Stanley Schachter and Jerome Singer (1962) in which the subjects were unsure of their feelings until they saw another person (the experimenter's accomplice) acting happy or acting angry, and then decided that what they felt was happiness or anger. The accomplice provided the cues and the subjects structured a *social reality* out of it.

Leon Festinger (1954) has suggested that we use groups for purposes of *social comparison,* to see where we stand in terms of ability and status. We seem to need such information in trying to understand ourselves. Moreover, the comparisons we make about our abilities have to be realistic and relevant to our own situation. A Little League baseball player does not compare himself to Hank Aaron but to the other kids on the team.

An earlier contribution by Stanley Schachter (1959) illustrates another function that groups provide individuals. Schachter told his subjects that as part of an experiment they were to receive some painful electric shocks. Then they were given the choice of waiting by themselves or with others for ten minutes until the experiment began. Another group was told the electric shock would be so mild as to be enjoyable, and was given the same choice of waiting by themselves or with others.

About a third of the group which believed the experiment would be enjoyable wanted to wait with others, but about two-thirds of the group which was expecting an unpleasant experience opted for company. The presence of other people (especially if they're in the same situation) seems to be comforting in times of stress. Schachter referred to this effect as *the need for affiliation* (see Box 13.2).

JUDGING OTHERS: OPINION AND ATTRIBUTION

In Chapter 7 we stressed how important the process of perception is in our predicting and understanding the world around us. This is also true of the social world where the process of *person perception* is crucial in our attempts to make sense of other people's behavior.

In Chapter 7 we looked at a study by Fritz Heider (1944) where people attributed human motivations to the movements of two triangles and a circle. Heider was intrigued by the implications of this behavior, and in 1958 he wrote a book called *The Psychology of Interpersonal Relations* in which he set out some very influential ideas on the way we make sense of our social perceptions.

Heider suggested that we have a great need to predict the events that are likely to happen in the world around us, to understand what causes things to happen. In our social world, where we deal with other people, the ability to predict what others might do is of crucial importance, for we often work on the assumption that events are caused by people.

Interpersonal relations are built on the ability we have to predict each other's behavior. Living with other people is not always easy, but imagine what it would be like if you never knew what to expect of them. In order to predict the behavior of others as accurately as possible, Heider argued, we try to figure out what their personalities are like and what their dominant characteristics are. We seem to operate with an implicit theory about someone's personality; from observing his behavior we *attribute* various qualities to him. Once we have attributed a certain personality to someone, we can figure out how he is likely to behave in situations we haven't seen him in.

Solomon Asch (1946) believed that we form our impression of people on the basis of certain key personality traits or characteristics. Once we have made a judgment about these few traits, Asch suggested,

BOX 13.2

BIRTH ORDER AND THE NEED FOR AFFILIATION

Schachter's study on the psychology of affiliation contains evidence that different people need different amounts of affiliation with others. In particular, the order of a subject's birth into the family seemed to be clearly related to the need for affiliation. When Schachter's subjects were placed in the unpleasant condition of waiting to be given an electric shock, those who were first-born or only children were most likely to seek the company of others.

There was a decline in the need that people showed for affiliation with later birth order, the latest-born children displaying the least need for affiliation. The way these findings are usually interpreted is that first-born children are socialized to be more dependent on others than later-born children. Parents are probably more concerned about their first children, more aware of their needs, paying more attention to them, and planning their upbringing more intently.

Parents usually have less time to devote to their younger children than they had with the first. They themselves are also that much more experienced. They may be less intensely concerned about having a later-born child, feeling that they were too anxious and overprotective with the first one. For whatever reason, it seems to be the case in our society that parents are around less often to comfort their later-born children through the inevitable fears and unpleasant situations encountered in growing up.

Therefore, first-born children may learn to find comfort in affiliating with others much more than do later-born children who are forced to find some other way of coping. Furthermore, the first-born child may often experience a sudden withdrawal or at least a reduction of parental attention with the arrival of a new baby. This is likely to sensitize him to the whole issue of his dependence on others for approval and affection and support, making him all the more likely to seek the comforting presence of others when he is feeling anxious.

Another psychologist, A. P. MacDonald, has shown more recently that (at least for males) first-borns are socialized differently from later-borns. Firstborns are simply more socialized to the adult society, meaning that they are more likely to conform to the wishes and expectations of adults in order to satisfy their affiliation needs. As a matter of fact, first-borns in our society (and others, too, for that matter) are much more successful in terms of occupation, status, and prestige than later-borns—but less popular with other people.

Source: Stanley Schachter, *The Psychology of Affiliation* (Stanford University Press, 1959), and A. P. MacDonald, Jr., "Anxiety Affiliation and Social Isolation," *Developmental Psychology* 3 (2), 242–254: 1970.

they form the framework within which we perceive all of a person's behavior. To test his idea, Asch gave two groups of subjects a list of personality characteristics and asked them to give their impression of the person described.

The two groups received the same list of traits, with one important difference:

Group 1: intelligent, skillful, industrious, *warm,* determined, practical, cautious
Group 2: intelligent, skillful, industrious, *cold,* determined, practical, cautious

The single difference between "warm" and "cold" led to very different impressions being formed. An impression about the "warm" person was "a scientist . . . driven by the desire to accomplish something that would be of benefit." The "cold" person was described as "rather snobbish . . . calculating and unsympathetic."

Halo Effect

The process of generalizing about someone's personality from very limited information has come to be known as the *halo effect.* As the name implies, this process is usually employed in making a *favorable* judgment about someone, although negative halo effects can operate in the opposite direction. The first impression we have of someone we meet is likely to be made on the basis of very limited information and will therefore be susceptible to the halo effect.

In our society, physical attractiveness is considered a particularly important characteristic. When we meet someone for the first time, this is likely to be the basis for our first impression of that individual. Research has shown that a halo effect will probably occur and we may attribute all kinds of desirable qualities to that person simply because of the way he or she looks.

So pervasive is this effect that it has been found in all kinds of social situations, starting as early as nursery school. When Karen Dion (1972) asked some female college students to judge the misbehavior of a group of young children, the more attractive children were judged tolerantly and the less attractive were judged harshly. Moreover, children themselves tend to make similar judgments on the basis of appearance.

Measuring Status in Inches

A process similar to the halo effect can influence our judgment of physical size. Several college classes were introduced to a stranger by one investigator who then asked them to judge the man's height. When the stranger (the experimenter's accomplice, of course) was introduced as a student, the average estimate of his height was about five feet, ten inches. When the same man dressed the same way was presented as a full professor, the average estimate of his height was just over six feet (Wilson, 1968).

Being tall (up to a point) is considered a desirable characteristic for men in our society. The more important we consider someone to be socially, the more ready we are to ascribe physical "importance" to him as well.

LERNER: MAKING SENSE OF CHANCE

In perception we make order out of the sensory chaos that surrounds us, just as in social perception we make order out of the social chaos that surrounds us. If the social order breaks down we are very disturbed; if someone behaves "out of character" toward us we are taken aback. Disorder is psychologically upsetting. We have already seen that highly prejudiced people or individuals under great stress can perceive or misperceive anything if the psychological disorder is sufficiently threatening to them. But Melvin Lerner (1965) has shown how deeply rooted this need is in all of us all the time.

Lerner had a group of subjects observe two people working at some task. The two people worked equally hard at the task but they were not equally rewarded. In fact, the reward was decided on the flip of a coin, with one person receiving the whole reward and the other person nothing. When the observers were questioned about this they argued that the person who received nothing had not in fact worked as hard as the other—even though it was quite clear that he had. But the need to see order in the giving of rewards (so that nobody gets "cheated" and nobody gets "something for nothing") was so deeply ingrained in these observers that they were willing to deny the evidence of their senses in order to make the social cues add up the way they wanted.

SOCIAL CUES: INTENDED EFFECTS

We have already come across several situations where people's expectations determined what they would perceive and how they would behave as a result. It is therefore possible in some situations to manipulate a person's behavior by providing him with the social cues he expects. When people are in the hospital, for example, they usually expect to be given some kind of medicine. But there are times when no medicine can or should be given. On such occasions a doctor may meet the patient's expectations by giving him "medicine" such as sugar water or a salt tablet, which has no physiological effect but may well have a powerful psychological effect.

There have been many cases where a patient's health improved after this kind of treatment, apparently because two of his deep-rooted expectations had been fulfilled. The patient "knew" that in the hospital he would receive medicine and he "knew" that this medicine would make him better. This is called the *placebo effect* and it works best with people who have faith and trust in the medical care they receive.

SOCIAL CUES: UNINTENDED EFFECTS

There are times, of course, when the manipulation of familiar social cues does not have the intended effect. The American novelist Upton Sinclair found this out rather strikingly at the beginning of the twentieth century. Sinclair was a socialist who wanted to better the lot of American workers, and to further his goals he wrote a book called *The Jungle* (1973) about the dreadful working conditions in the Chicago stockyards.

Sinclair expected that his account of workers and rats falling into the machinery and being ground into hamburger meat would produce a public outcry for safer, more humane working conditions. But Sinclair's audience did not share his expectations. There was an outcry, all right, but it had nothing to do with the plight of the workers. The outcry was for better food hygiene laws.

SELF-IMAGE AND SOCIAL STATUS

Psychologists have long known that the social groups in which people live can shape their perceptions, both social and physical. People at the top and the bottom of the social status ladder tend to make fewer distinctions than people in the middle (Davis et al., 1941). Those at the bottom can't afford to care while those at the top can afford not to care. But observers have found that to people in the middle of the ladder it may be of some importance whether they or other people are classified as lower middle class, middle class, or upper middle class.

Self-image is particularly important in the way we perceive others. People who are unusually tall or short are often very conscious of another person's height, for instance. Psychologists have also found evidence that black people, in this predominantly white society, judge the skin color of other blacks in relation to their own (Martin, 1964). In this study, people ascribed higher status to lighter coloring.

MEMBERSHIP GROUPS AND REFERENCE GROUPS

In every human society, a baby is born into the same social groups as his parents. He is automatically a member of their religious or social class or language grouping, for example. Someone's group memberships are therefore of great importance in shaping his psychology. But when an individual is old enough to compare his groups with other groups in his social environment, his group memberships may no longer be automatically acceptable to him.

In the past, when the self-images of black people were more negative, many light-skinned blacks rejected their blackness and tried to "become" white. Their membership group was black but the group they compared themselves to, and to whose norms they referred for guidance in their behavior, was white. Their *reference group* was different from their *membership group.* To the extent that blacks or any other group of people feel positive about their membership group and value its particular qualities, their reference group is the same as their membership group. In that case people will not refer to other groups when they wish to compare their individual abilities or achievements with others; they will compare themselves with other people in the same membership group.

Differences between membership groups and reference groups are most noticeable in people who are trying to climb the social ladder. Poor people who aim to become middle class, middle class people striving to be recognized as upper class, will often adopt the values and norms of their reference group. The group we choose to compare ourselves with will determine how contented we feel with our own lot. If we are poor but our standard of living is as good as the other poor people we compare ourselves with, we will not feel deprived. If we compare our prosperity with that of the wealthy, we certainly will feel deprived. To a psychologist *deprivation* is entirely relative; if a person *feels* deprived, he is deprived.

SELF-FULFILLING PROPHECY

Throughout this chapter we have been dealing with examples of the way we organize social cues to make a coherent picture of the world around us. We have seen how people will distort the evidence of their senses to make what they actually perceive fit what they expect to perceive. Now we will follow this process a step further and take a look at how people make their expectations happen.

Gustav Jahoda (1954) has made a very interesting discovery about the Ashanti of West Africa. They believe that people born on different days of the week have different personalities. To accompany this belief they tend to name their children according to the day of the week on which they were born; thus Kwadwo was born on a Monday and

Kwakwu on a Wednesday. Kwadwos are supposed to be quiet and even-tempered, Kwakwus aggressive and quarrelsome.

Apparently the Ashanti had their expectations fulfilled, for when Jahoda checked the police records he found that the Kwadwos born on Monday had a very low rate of criminal offenses, while the Kwakwus born on Wednesday had a very high rate. This study suggests not only that people tend to behave the way they are expected to but that if the expected behavior becomes part of their self-image, this is the kind of behavior they will also tend to choose for themselves. Both the individuals concerned, and their society in general, were involved in the process called *self-fulfilling prophecy.* Making our images of ourselves and of other people come true is a process that affects all areas of our behavior. We will come across it again before the end of this book.

SUGGESTED READINGS

Janis, I. *Victims of Groupthink: A Psychological Study of Foreign-Policy Decisions and Fiascos.* Boston: Houghton Mifflin, 1973. Includes the Cuban missile crisis and the Vietnam war.

Milgram, S. *Obedience to Authority.* New York: Harper & Row, 1974. Milgram summarizes a decade of research into the conditions that encourage or discourage people to obey an authority.

Orwell, G. *Animal Farm.* New York: New American Library, 1954. A satire on the social psychological effects of political revolution.

Schachter, S. *The Psychology of Affiliation: Experimental Studies of the Sources of Gregariousness.* Stanford, Calif.: Stanford University Press, 1959.

CHAPTER 14

Placing the individual in society

TESTS AND MEASUREMENTS

Throughout this book we have observed how the constant struggle to make sense of the environment leads us to seek definiteness and avoid ambiguity, to value predictability as the rule, with novel stimuli as the exception. In the last chapter we examined the ways in which the process of making comparisons can help us make sense of our social world. By comparing ourselves to others, we know where we stand; by using this compass we can orient ourselves in what would otherwise be an endless, featureless, turbulent sea of people.

To satisfy this psychological need, our society has developed an increasingly elaborate system for categorizing everybody, whether it be by age, income, education, occupation, color, religion, creed, ethnic origin, or sexual preference. We seem to feel more secure in a stable social order where everybody can be pigeonholed in the "right" box. In this chapter we will discuss those aspects of social order that have been of greatest concern to psychologists—*tests and measurement* of mental abilities and emotional disturbance, and the social significance of their use.

BINET, IQ TESTS, AND THE POLITICS OF EDUCATION

The most common of all psychological tests are the ones that are supposed to measure intelligence. There must be very few people in the industrialized world who did not take at least one intelligence test in school. Intelligence testing began in France at the beginning of this century. The education authorities of Paris were concerned with the problem of identifying children who would be likely to fail in school, and they turned to a psychologist named Alfred Binet for help.

Binet was interested in measuring cognitive mental processes in adults and children. He wanted to compare how people thought, imagined, understood, and remembered, and by combining their performance in these areas, he hoped to come up with a single test that would rank everyone according to intelligence. The purpose of Binet's work for the Paris school system was to provide such an intelligence test that could be given to all the children. The results of the test would enable the authorities to predict the children of low intelligence who would be average in school and the highly intelligent children who would do well.

Binet's intelligence test was composed of many subtests of mental abilities that increased in difficulty. When a child could go no further, the subtests he had successfully passed were added up to provide his *mental age.* The mental age was then compared with the child's actual or chronological age. If the two ages were similar, the child was considered of normal intelligence, meaning that he'd done as well on the test as the average child of his age—a social definition of normality, in other words. To the extent that the child's mental age was younger than his chronological age, he was abnormally dull; the other way around, he was abnormally bright.

Binet's subtests were chosen because they were found to separate dull children from bright children. This meant that he had to know before he started which children were bright and which were dull. He obtained these judgments from teachers, who based them on previous performance in school, an important point to which we will return shortly.

Other psychologists have simplified the comparison process by dividing the mental age by the chronological age, giving a *mental quotient:*

$$\frac{\text{mental age}}{\text{chronological age}} = \frac{\text{5 years 0 months}}{\text{6 years 8 months}} = \frac{\text{60 months}}{\text{80 months}} = \frac{60}{80}$$

When the mental quotient is multiplied by 100, the result is a single figure:

$$\frac{60}{80} \times 100 = 75$$

This figure is called the *intelligence quotient,* or *IQ.*

In the example above, the child has an IQ of 75. If the child's IQ were five or ten points lower, he would probably be taken out of the regular school system (both now and in Binet's time) and placed in a special environment for retarded children. If his IQ were about 100, the child would be considered normal; if substantially higher (over 125, for example), he would be considered bright.

Binet's original intelligence test has been revised several times and adapted, at Stanford University, for use in English-speaking countries where the *Stanford-Binet* is now the most widely used of all psychological tests. In fact, Binet's influence rapidly spread throughout the world. There are now many intelligence tests, for individuals and groups, adults and children. Countries with systems of mass education seem to have a great need for mental tests in general and intelligence tests in particular. If mass education is regarded as an investment in a nation's future it becomes important to obtain the best return for that investment, which usually boils down to the goal of giving as many people as possible as many years of schooling as they can take (see Box 14.1).

Self-Fulfilling Prophecy Again

The social importance of intelligence tests is that whatever else they can or cannot do, they seem to predict fairly accurately how well children will do in school. I say "seem to," because relating cause and effect here is more complex than it looks. The implicit assumption is that children with high IQs (who will probably go further) are worth more of a teacher's time and skill than other children. But there is some evidence that this assumption is misguided and simplistic.

Intelligence tests are usually given for the first time when a child is very young and his self-image is being formed. If the child is upset by the test experience, or didn't sleep well the night before, he might perform far below his capacity. But if the IQ score he is given is accepted by his teachers and parents as an accurate measure of his intelligence, he has little alternative but to accept their judgment and incorporate it into his self-image. Based on his IQ, his teachers and parents will form certain expectations of his school performance, and so will he. A process of self-fulfilling prophecy may then come into effect, leading the child to do as well or as badly as everyone expects.

There is some experimental evidence from the classroom to support this argument. At the beginning of a school year, a group of teachers were told that twenty of the children in their classes had high IQs and were "late bloomers" intellectually who were expected to fulfill their promise in the year ahead (Rosenthal and Jacobson, 1968). Sure enough, by the end of the year these twenty children had done very well, fulfilling their teachers' expectations—and that is just the point, for the children were all of *average* IQ. The teachers had been deliberately misled to see whether their expectations of the children's performance would actually lead to the performance they expected.

Back in chapter three we discussed intelligence in the light of the

BOX 14.1

CONFESSIONS OF AN IQ TESTER

There have been times when I earned my living by administering the Stanford-Binet IQ test to children in elementary schools. It was a salutary experience and gave me an insight into the meaning of an IQ score that is unobtainable in academia.

One of the most important things I learned is that whatever a child scores on the test, he or she is capable of scoring higher. The vagaries of most testing situations are enough by themselves to render a low score meaningless. The importance of rapport between tester and child was solemnly impressed upon me, but nobody quite explained to me how to establish rapport when the child is a scared, sullen, inarticulate little seven-year-old daughter of a drunken mother, and the test is being conducted on an orange box in a freezing broom closet surrounded on all sides by classrooms breaking up into various stages of chaos.

Slum schools being what they are, I've had to conduct tests in staff rooms with teachers wandering in and out, classrooms with kids wandering in and out, and open halls with everybody and his dog wandering in and out. I was once invited to do an IQ test in the wings while a play was being rehearsed onstage.

You are supposed to start the Stanford-Binet by assessing the child's vocabulary, asking him brightly, "What is an orange? . . . envelope? . . . straw?" As the answer is often an opaque and unrelenting stare, you change gears and give the kid some materials to get his hands on (like wooden blocks or a string of beads) in an attempt to break the ice.

This ploy often works, up to a point, and you can check off the items dealing with counting ability, attention span, and so on. But the Stanford-Binet is largely verbal, and sooner or later you have to edge into "What is the difference between a bird and a dog?" Silence. "A bird flies, a fish . . . ?" Silence. If you scored each silence as a wrong response, you would finish the test in five minutes and the child would have an IQ in the imbecile range. So you bend the rules and jolly the poor child along until something scorable emerges.

There are also kids who are anything but dumb but decide to play games on you, ironically taking out years of frustrated hatred of authority by deliberately upsetting your most earnest efforts to help them. This was especially true of some black kids, who showed more intelligence in avoiding the right answer than most kids did in finding it—not realizing, of course, the significance that a low IQ score could have for their future. Once the magic number is entered in a child's folder, how it got there (and the accompanying remarks of the tester) can be conveniently forgotten.

Jensen nature-nurture controversy and noted that intelligence tests, being made up by white middle class psychologists, are biased against children who are not white or not middle class. This bias alone probably accounts for much of the lower IQ scores found among nonwhites and poor people. The effects of self-fulfilling prophecy would do the rest.

We should also note that an IQ score is meaningless in itself. It is not like height, for instance, which tells you something definite about someone. We compare our height to that of other people because of our need to know how we compare with others. But we don't need to compare our height with other people *in order to know how tall we are.* For that we simply use a tape measure. There is no tape measure of intelligence. An IQ score simply tells you how you compare with other people who have taken the same test. *It does not tell you how intelligent you are.* But then, an intelligence test is not meant to tell the testee anything; it is meant to discriminate, to differentiate *between* people for the purpose of assigning them to various educational, occupational, and social categories.

Finally, it is worth noting that after almost a century of scientific investigation psychologists still cannot agree on what intelligence is.

PERSONALITY TESTS

The other branch of psychological tests and measurement is concerned with assessing various aspects of personality. As with Binet and the creation of intelligence tests, techniques for assessing personality were developed in response to a social demand. This demand, as in the case of intelligence tests, took two forms.

There was first of all a widespread concern that disturbed individuals, whose behavior might disrupt the life of a community, be identified for treatment. Second, the occurrence of two world wars meant a total commitment of national resources for the countries involved and ensured that the ingenuity of their scientists would be stimulated and encouraged. For psychologists, this provided a number of unique opportunities and challenges, one of them being the need to assess the human resources represented by the millions of men and women in uniform.

After the Second World War there was a tremendous increase in the amount of personality testing done, and there are now over 500 different tests available. There are two kinds of tests in use, the *paper-and-pencil,* or questionnaire, method, and the *projective* technique. The creators of these tests were interested in distinguishing people who were abnormal in some way from normal people. Like Binet, they first had to find an abnormal group and compare them with a normal group on each item. Items which brought out differences in the way the groups responded were kept and the rest discarded. Unlike Binet, their judgment of who was normal to begin with rested on a psychological definition, which we will come to shortly.

Paper-and-Pencil Tests

The most popular example of this technique is the Minnesota Multiphasic Personality Inventory, usually known as the MMPI. The MMPI now exists in 19 languages and is used all over the world. It consists of 550 items to which the subject has to answer "true," "false," or "cannot say." The items deal with a vast range of thought, feelings, and behavior as the following few examples show:

I am bothered by acid stomach several times a week.
I like to read newspaper articles on crime.
I never worry about my looks.
I often feel as if things were not real.
If I were an artist, I would like to draw flowers.

The MMPI can help a trained clinical psychologist form a general impression of someone's personality, the area of any disturbances he might have, and how severe these disturbances are.

Projective Tests

As the name implies, projective tests make use of the process of projection, the same process we encountered in Chapter 10 where we discussed defense mechanisms. In that context we noted how people who feel uncomfortable at having certain thoughts or impulses will assign these thoughts or impulses to someone else, projecting them from within themselves onto others. In a projective test, the subject or patient is presented with an ambiguous situation and asked, in effect, how he would make sense of it. In doing so, we assume that he projects his own feelings, values, and desires onto the situation.

1. RORSCHACH INK BLOT TEST

Named after its inventor, Herman Rorschach, this test may well be the most famous of all psychological tests. Ten pictures of actual ink blots are used, five of them in color. The subject is asked what he sees in the ink blot, what it reminds him of. There are no right or wrong answers, of course, and the theory is that each person will see people or things that are important to him. Clinicians experienced in the use of the Rorschach claim that the subject's responses to the shape and color and detail of the ink blot can reveal a great deal of his unconscious life as it is projected onto the picture.

2. THEMATIC APPERCEPTION TEST (TAT)

The TAT is another widely used projective test, where the situation the subject is shown is a little less ambiguous than an ink blot. The test consists of 20 pictures, each containing one or two people. The emotions portrayed and the relationships of the people in these pictures are made deliberately ambiguous, and the subject is asked what is happening in each picture, what led up to it, and what the outcome will be. The psychologist then looks through all 20 stories to see what *themes* can be *perceived* (hence the name of the test) that may give him some clues about his patient's problems.

Usually, if someone were being diagnosed in a clinical setting, none of the personality tests we have mentioned would be given by itself. A whole battery of different tests might be given, depending largely on which tests the psychologist had found most useful in his own experience. The aim is to obtain as much information as possible about the subject in the time available.

DIAGNOSIS: WHAT IS ABNORMAL?

In Chapter 12 we broached the question of defining normality and saw that there were two ways of arriving at such a definition, the social and the psychological. The social definition of what is normal depends on social norms and changes with time and place; the psychological definition does not. Regardless of when and where he lives, if a person is so mentally or emotionally impaired that he cannot cope with his feelings and with the daily business of living, cannot work, cannot communicate with those around him, or does harm to himself or others, then he is considered to be *psychologically abnormal.*

But psychologically abnormal behavior is not always clear-cut enough to be easily identified. Normal behavior shades into abnormal behavior without any dividing line between them. There are times when even a trained psychologist using all the tests at his disposal may not be able to say for sure whether someone is abnormal, or if so, how abnormal he is. Furthermore, the judgment of the psychologist is affected by *his* time and place, just like that of anyone else. He makes his diagnosis of psychological normality and abnormality within a context of social normality and abnormality.

We don't know if there is a universal psychological standard of normality that is unaffected by time and place because the *interpretation* of any behavior is always affected by time and place. When we discuss psychological abnormality in this chapter, therefore, we should bear in mind that we're actually limiting our focus to our own society. The definitions and categories of abnormal behavior I will describe *may* be applicable to behavior in other times and places, but that judgment should be left to the psychologists in those other times and places.

DIAGNOSING DISORDER: NEUROSIS

Not only is it difficult to tell when normal behavior has become abnormal, but the symptoms of abnormal behavior are also found in people who would be regarded as perfectly normal. The roots of disturbed behavior are to be found in feelings of anxiety and depression, but everyone feels anxious or depressed at some time. The only distinction we can make is one of degree. People who would be described as abnormal are much more anxious and depressed than most, so much so that it shows up systematically in the way they behave. Such behavior is called *neurotic.*

A great deal of neurotic behavior results from the extreme use of the normal defense mechanisms against emotional conflict that we reviewed in Chapter 10. *Anxiety* is present in all neurotic behavior. The psychologist defines it as irrational fear, a vague chronic sense of uneasiness for which there is no apparent reason. Neuroses can be classified in different ways. We will consider four of the most important types: *anxiety, obsessive-compulsive, hysterical,* and *dissociative* neuroses.

Anxiety Neurosis

In many neuroses anxiety, while always present, may be masked by other symptoms. Cases where anxiety is openly displayed are called simply *anxiety neuroses.* People suffering from such neuroses are constantly and consciously tense and apprehensive. At times they are overwhelmed with a sense of panic that can leave them sick, dizzy, and faint.

Sometimes the feeling of anxiety is associated with a particular situation. There are people who are afraid, for example, of being confined in a narrow space like an elevator. This kind of anxiety is called a *phobia*—in this case, *claustrophobia.*

Obsessive-Compulsive Neurosis

If someone has a disturbing thought that keeps coming into his mind, he has an *obsession.* If he has an irresistible urge to repeat the same behavior over and over again (like washing his hands or checking the mailbox), he is being *compulsive.* Obsessions are often dramatic fantasies dealing with powerful and unacceptable emotions of sex and aggression. Compulsions are often attempts to deal with these unacceptable emotions in an acceptable way, such as the people who feel guilty about masturbating and spend half the day washing their hands (like Lady Macbeth) in an attempt to cleanse themselves of their sin.

Hysterical Neurosis

The word *hysteria* has a particular meaning in psychology. It is used to describe the neurosis where internal emotional conflicts become *converted* into external physical symptoms of illness. Medically these symptoms have no physical basis, and when the conflict is resolved they simply disappear. War and combat conditions are known to produce cases of hysterical neurosis where people are afraid of their dangerous situation but cannot consciously admit this fear to themselves.

Their unconscious takes over and dramatically provides them with unimpeachable medical evidence of a disability that will have them removed from the dangerous situation. Such is the case of a Marine who suddenly finds his arms or legs paralyzed, or a pilot who goes blind. These cases of hysterical paralysis and hysterical blindness are medically unreal in the sense that they did not result from any physical injury. But psychologically they are completely real to the patient, who has no control over his condition. The physical symptoms are indeed strikingly real. If a paralyzed limb is jabbed with a needle the patient feels nothing. Hysterical ailments remain until the underlying conflicts are brought out and dealt with, at which time they disappear as dramatically as they appeared.

Hysterical illness is rarely found outside of combat in our present-day society. Much more common are the physical symptoms resulting from *conscious* anxiety and conflict. It has long been known that people living in urban industrial environments are subject to a great deal of stress and tension of which they are quite aware. If these conditions are chronic they can affect the physical functioning of the body, for example, by speeding up the heart rate, blood pressure, and the workings of the digestive system.

Several common illnesses are known to be caused in this fashion, such as asthma, dermatitis, and stomach ulcers. These are known as *psychosomatic* illnesses, from the Greek words *psyche* (mind) and *soma* (body). A psychosomatic basis has been claimed for many other ailments, including heart disease and cancer. It is at least arguable that if mind and body, feelings, thoughts, and actions, are tied up in the same human package, every illness has some psychosomatic component.

Dissociative Neurosis

Feelings, thoughts, and actions normally go together. They are harmoniously *associated* with each other in an individual personality. But when serious conflicts are repressed into the unconscious, people may try to separate their conflicts from the rest of their personality, to *dissociate* them. We have already come across one example of extreme dissociation. When we discussed memory in Chapter 6 we noted the occurrence of *amnesia* in people who had a need to forget some painful memories. Such extreme repression is an attempt by the individual to cut himself off, to dissociate himself from an emotional conflict too severe for him to deal with consciously.

An even more dramatic example of dissociative neurosis is the case of *multiple personality.* In this condition repression leads to the dissociation of what appear to be two or more complete personalities within the same individual. This is what people usually mean by "split personality," the idea captured by Robert Louis Stevenson in his fictional account of Dr. Jekyll and Mr. Hyde where one man could be both evil and good at different times. Multiple personality is a very rare condition and should *not* be confused with schizophrenia, which we will consider in the next section on psychosis.

DIAGNOSING DISORDER: PSYCHOSIS

Psychologists used to believe that neuroses and psychoses were completely different kinds of disorder that stemmed from different roots. It is now thought likely that psychoses are simply more severe reactions to the same kinds of personality problems—just as neuroses are more severe reactions to the normal personality problems that most people encounter. People with psychotic disorders are often so severely disturbed that they cannot cope with their everyday lives and have to be hospitalized. Psychosis is a relatively common condition; in fact, about half the hospital beds in the United States are filled by psychotic patients.

Psychosis is characterized by a *loss of contact with reality,* accompanied by *thought disorders* and an *inability to communicate* with other people. A distinction is often made between *organic* psychoses that result from physical brain damage, and *functional* psychoses that have been considered psychological because no physical cause could be found. There is now considerable debate in psychology as to whether the functional psychoses might not have a genetic or biochemical basis to them. If mind can affect body as in the case of psychosomatic illness, it does not appear unreasonable that it could also work the other way around. Functional psychoses are usually divided into three categories, *schizophrenia, manic-depression,* and *paranoia.*

Schizophrenia

The term *schizophrenia* is derived from the Greek words *schizo* (split) and *phrenia* (mind), and right here we have the source of a popular misconception. We have already seen that multiple personality is the condition that is popularly thought of as "split personality" or "split mind." The split in that case is between two different personalities within the same individual. The split in schizophrenia is between the processes of thinking and feeling within the same individual.

Schizophrenia is usually characterized by a breakdown in the normal harmony between a person's thoughts, feelings, and actions, so that each of these three components of personality seems bizarre and unrelated to each of the others. A schizophrenic may smile when discussing a tragic event, for instance, or he may show no emotion at all.

Schizophrenia is also marked by disorders of thought and speech, making communication with other people very difficult, and a schizophrenic may even withdraw completely and refuse to communicate at all. The patient often has difficulty distinguishing between reality and his own fantasy world. He may have delusions that other people are persecuting him or trying to control him. He may hallucinate and hear voices that aren't there.

Many different types of schizophrenia have been suggested, but there is a raging controversy among psychologists about the reliability of these classifications and even about the usefulness of diagnosing someone as schizophrenic at all. At the present time schizophrenia is the most commonly diagnosed psychosis, accounting for perhaps half of all the people in psychiatric institutions. These patients are the least responsive to treatment and have a very low rate of recovery.

Manic-depression

This psychosis is marked by sharp changes of mood, ranging from a *manic* state where the patient is intensely excited, through a normal mood, to a *depressive* state where the patient mopes about feeling hopeless and sad. Some patients swing from one extreme to the other, but most vary between a normal condition and one of the extremes, usually depression. Manic-depressive psychosis often disappears without any treatment, though in some patients it can recur several times.

Paranoia

Paranoia is a rare psychosis, but because of the *delusions* that characterize it, it has captured the popular imagination. These delusions often take the form of *persecution,* where the patient believes that people are out to get him for some reason or other. There are also *delusions of grandeur,* beloved of cartoonists, where a patient believes he is Napoleon or some other great historical figure.

ANTISOCIAL PERSONALITY

There is one kind of abnormal personality that cannot be classified as either neurotic or psychotic because the individual does not feel the anxiety, tension, and conflict associated with these disorders. In fact, he doesn't seem to feel any anxiety, tension, or conflict at all, even though his behavior may be seriously disturbed. People in this category persistently engage in socially deviant behavior like alcoholism, drug abuse, and criminality of all kinds. The extreme *antisocial personality* is the individual who commits murder almost casually with no feeling of guilt or remorse.

This kind of behavior is often referred to as *psychopathic* or *sociopathic* and is applied to people who seem to have no conscience whatsoever. On the surface such people can often appear to be honest, charming, and convincing, but they have no compunction about doing anything that will further their own ends. Nor are they capable of feeling any warmth or love for another person. Psychologists know little about the cause of such a personality disorder, although it appears possible that its origins lie in early childhood where the child may have been treated as an object, without love, and so never learned how to form normal kinds of relationships with other people.

SZASZ AND THE POLITICS OF MENTAL HEALTH

Some of the basic statistics on serious psychological abnormality reveal the extent of its effects on society. More people are hospitalized for mental illness than all other diseases put together. Some 750,000 people are currently in mental institutions in the United States, and it has been estimated that one out of every ten babies born today will be hospitalized with mental illness at some time in his life.

The prevalence of mental illness has led some professionals to reexamine the whole process of defining, diagnosing, and treating behavior disorders. Traditionally the *medical model* has been used where mental illness, abnormal behavior, and personality disorders were viewed as forms of a disease like any other. If other diseases can be cured by medical treatment in a hospital, why should this one be any different?

In his book *The Myth of Mental Illness* (1961) Thomas Szasz argued that what is called mental illness is not a medical disease at all. Physical illness is dealt with in terms of biological criteria like germs, bacteria, fever, and so on; mental illness is not. By labeling large numbers of unhappy and anxious people in a certain way, Szasz suggested, we can put them into medical categories and place them in an institution. But what if people are unhappy and anxious simply because they're poor and unemployed and don't know where their next meal is coming from?

Even if labels like schizophrenic or paranoid were accurate, reliable, and fully understood by everyone, the act of labeling and classifying itself (as we have seen in other social contexts) sets up certain expectations of the way people will behave, and with it the tendency to make these expectations come true. If we treat people as schizophrenics we will find lots of evidence of schizophrenic behavior in their activities (see Box 14.2).

BOX 14.2

HOW CAN YOU RECOGNIZE A CRAZY PERSON?

A professor of psychology and law named D. L. Rosenhan decided to put this question to the test. In particular, Rosenhan wondered what would happen to normal people who managed to get themselves admitted to a mental institution. Would they have any trouble convincing the psychiatrists that they were sane and should be released?

Rosenhan arranged to have eight normal people (including himself) admitted to a variety of institutions on the east and west coasts of the United States. No one in these institutions had any idea what these pseudopatients were up to. The subjects were both men and women and represented a variety of occupations. They all had themselves admitted to their institution by walking into the admissions office and reporting having hallucinations where they heard voices saying to them over and over again words like "hollow" and "empty."

Apart from these supposed hallucinations, everything else the subjects reported about themselves was entirely true. On the basis of this information all eight of our intrepid explorers were admitted to a mental institution, and seven of them were classified schizophrenic.

Once they had been admitted, the pseudopatients behaved in an entirely natural manner (or as far as they were able to under the circumstances) and never again reported hearing voices or having any other kind of symptom of abnormality. The subjects had decided beforehand that they could only be released by convincing the hospital psychiatric staff of their sanity. But this was not as easy as they had imagined. Their average length of stay was 19 days, and one person was in for 52 days.

Even when they were released it was not because their normality was glaringly obvious to the psychiatrists. They were released because their schizophrenia was diagnosed as being in remission, meaning that while they had been mentally sick, they were now well enough to try living in the outside world again. Apparently nobody on the staffs of the institutions ever thought of questioning the original diagnoses.

Interestingly enough, the real patients were often aware of what was happening. About one-third of them spotted the imposters in their midst, making comments like, "You're not crazy. You're a journalist, or a professor." But then, the pseudopatients had much more contact with the real patients than they had with the psychiatrists. In fact, they spent an average of 6.8 minutes per day being cured by the professional staff.

While there are people who would be described as mentally sick by anyone's definition, an increasing number of psychologists would argue that the typical inmate of a mental institution suffers mainly from being *labelled* mentally sick. Rosenhan's study is compelling evidence for their point of view.

Source: D. L. Rosenhan, "On Being Sane in Insane Places," *Science* 179: 250–257, 1973.

Once again we have encountered the enormous importance of self-fulfilling prophecy in our attempt to make sense of the individual's place in society—and how that place becomes his.

SUGGESTED READINGS

Gross, M. *The Brain Watchers.* New York: Random House, 1962. A comprehensive attack on tests and testing.

Kaplan, B., ed. *The Inner World of Mental Illness: A Series of First-Person Accounts of What It Was Like.* New York: Harper & Row, 1964. Describes a wide variety of disorders.

Lyman, H. *Test Scores and What They Mean.* Englewood Cliffs, N.J.: Prentice-Hall, 1963. A discussion of the ways in which psychological tests are used and their results interpreted.

Neill, A. *Summerhill.* New York: Hart, 1960. A radically permissive approach to education in a famous residential school.

Schreiber, F. *Sybil.* New York: Warner, 1974. A case history of a woman with (to put it mildly) a split personality. At last count she had sixteen.

Szasz, T. *The Myth of Mental Illness.* New York: Harper & Row, 1961. A rejection of the concept of mental illness by a psychiatrist who believes that people labeled as sick should be regarded instead as having inadequate strategies for coping with life.

CHAPTER 15

Attitudes and how they change

ATTITUDES AND OPINIONS

Most people would use the words *attitudes* and *opinions* interchangeably, along with *values* and *beliefs.* Psychologists have found it useful, however, to make a distinction between these terms. *Opinions* (and beliefs) are mainly *cognitive* and would be offered in answer to the question "What do you *think* about X?" *Attitudes* (and values) are mainly *affective,* with a high emotional content, and would be given in answer to the question "What do you *feel* about X?" The difference is between saying "New York City is big" and "New York City is bad." An attitude, while it includes a cognitive, evaluative component, is also emotionally charged, making it more powerful than a relatively emotionless opinion.

ATTITUDES AND BEHAVIOR

As well as cognition and affect, the third component that psychologists look for in trying to understand an action is *behavior.* It has often been observed by social researchers that what people feel and think about something, as stated on a questionnaire, does not always correspond to the way they actually behave; their *intentions* must also be taken into account.

Knowing someone's *opinions* on an issue, like a presidential election, for instance, will tell you something about the way he will actually behave. Knowing his *feelings* about the candidates as well will tell you more; and if you can find out whether he intends to *act* on his opinions and feelings by actually voting, you may have a very accurate prediction of which candidate will receive his vote on election day.

Modern polling organizations are aware of these factors, and partly by phrasing their questions precisely so as to get at them they can make very accurate predictions about election results. External factors can also be important. The shorter the time gap between finding out someone's intentions and the actual event taking place, the more accurate will your prediction be. Polls increase in accuracy as the election draws near, and those taken on the eve of an election will be the closest to the final results.

There are other external factors which are somewhat more subtle. Asking someone if he would cheat on an examination may produce the answer no. When that person actually takes the exam and cheats, does that mean he deliberately lied to the questioner? Probably not. When the subject stated his intention of not cheating, he was not faced with the actual exam situation. He may quite honestly have considered himself beyond the temptation of cheating even in a stressful situation, but when he was actually in that situation, he learned that he was not (Wicker, 1969).

Actually, we have already come across an even more striking illustration of the discrepancies between attitude and behavior. When we discussed Stanley Milgram's research on obedience to authority in Chapter 13, we noted that a wide range of people found it hard to believe that anyone (including presumably themselves) could administer a 450-volt shock to another human being. They predicted that less than 1 percent of subjects would do so, while the actual figure was about 65 percent.

We can be quite confident that many of the people making these predictions would themselves have administered the shocks if they were put in the same position. In fact, some of Milgram's subjects were shaken up by what they had discovered about themselves. The more similarity there is between the situation where a person is asked about his intentions and the situation where he must actually do something, the more accurate will be the prediction from one to the other. In the Milgram experiment the subject had to deal publicly with the stress of causing pain to another human being, a situation whose pressures he could not have anticipated. In the privacy of a voting booth a person is not usually subject to other pressures and simply has to pull a lever or mark an X beside someone's name.

Finally, in order for attitudes to be expressed in behavior, people have to know what the appropriate behavior is. Everyone shares the attitude that war and hunger are evils which should be eradicated. But how can we translate these attitudes into actions? This problem has been studied experimentally by Leventhal, Singer, and Jones (1965). A group of university students was told about the dangers of getting tetanus. Half of them were given very specific instructions on how to get inoculated against the disease and the other half were given no instructions. Just over 3 percent of the people who didn't receive any instructions actually got themselves inoculated as compared with almost 28 percent of the people who knew what action to take.

ATTITUDE CHANGE

Attitudes are entirely learned, and they are learned the way most other human behavior is learned. We imitate our parents and are rewarded for it, we respond to the influence of our peers and other social groups, we discover what attitudes are appropriate to our social situation, and what attitudes we find compatible with our self-image.

Once again we must deal with both the cognitive and the affective parts of an attitude. The important point here is not what attitude is being expressed but how deep the emotional roots behind it are. Most people, for example, regard the shape of the earth as a cognitive matter, a matter of factual information to be decided by scientific research. Their belief that the earth is more or less round has no emotional content whatsoever.

But there are (or have been) people who believed, despite all the scientific evidence, that the earth was flat. These people could not be convinced by rational argument to change their belief or opinion because it was actually a deeply rooted, emotionally held attitude which they *needed* to believe. And if psychologists have discovered anything about attitudes, they've discovered that when it comes to reason versus emotion it's no contest. Beliefs about issues that people regard as matters of fact are easy to change; attitudes that are social expressions of powerful individual emotions are very difficult to change.

It's easy to laugh at the flat earthers, but how about people who believe (despite scientific evidence to the contrary) that men are physically and intellectually superior to women? These attitudes—commonly held by both men and women—are probably learned from parents in early childhood. They are part of the emotionally charged package that comes with learning the difference between male and female. And even where people are convinced *intellectually* that these attitudes are factually untrue, it may be very difficult for them to change their *feelings*—and therefore their behavior.

Self-Justification

We've already discussed the experiment done by Schachter and Singer (1962) where they injected subjects with adrenalin. In that study some of the subjects were told that adrenalin led to symptoms of excitement like sweating and heart palpitations. When the symptoms appeared they knew why and attributed their feelings to the effects of the drug.

Where the subjects were not told what to expect, they were in effect confronted with some powerful feelings that came out of nowhere. But they couldn't just be there all by themselves, they had to be fitted into some framework that made sense; their existence had to be justified. When the experimenters provided the subjects with a model who was happy or angry they justified their feelings in terms of anger or happiness.

The subjects in this experiment were experiencing several aspects of the need to make sense, one of which is the need to justify our own beliefs, attitudes, feelings, and values so that we can convince ourselves and everyone else that our behavior really did make sense. We need to feel rational and consistent, to know that our thoughts, feelings, and actions are in harmony. A lack of such harmony, you will recall from the last chapter, is a prime characteristic of psychological abnormality.

Popular catch phrases like "The devil made me do that," "It's in my blood," or "It must be the weather" are very revealing in this context. Behavior that is left unexplained is very disturbing; it upsets our sense of order and predictability. We find it more comfortable to provide a superficial or silly justification than to have no justification at all.

Festinger and Cognitive Dissonance

In 1957 Leon Festinger proposed a simple but far-reaching theory to account for the process of self-justification. Noting the powerful drive toward consistency or *consonance,* Festinger suggested that if an individual holds two psychologically inconsistent cognitions (beliefs, attitudes, values, ideas) at the same time, he will be in a state of *cognitive dissonance.*

Because cognitive dissonance is a state of psychological tension it is inherently unpleasant, Festinger argued, and we are strongly motivated to reduce it. We should note here that the dissonance theory does not deal with *logical* inconsistency but *psychological* inconsistency. In other words, people are not so much concerned with actually *being* consistent as with *feeling* consistent.

Suppose you've come to New York City to work, and in thinking things over one day you decide that New York City is a horrible place to live. Presumably you regard yourself as a sensible person. If so, you're now in a state of cognitive dissonance. Your cognition "I am a sensible person" is inconsistent with your cognition "I'm living in a horrible place when I don't have to." Now logically there's only one thing you can do—leave—but psychologically you have a choice.

To reduce dissonance you could follow the logical route and argue "I am sensible; sensible people don't choose to live in horrible places, so I'll move." Your cognitions would then be consonant, but of course your attitudes toward New York would not have changed. Or you could work on the other cognition (that New York City is horrible) which would give you two choices. It is the different consequences of making these choices that interests psychologists most.

You could say "Yes, it is horrible, but I stay here because I have a great job," thereby reducing dissonance with an *external* justification for your behavior. But your attitude toward New York would remain the same. Suppose, however, that you couldn't find any such justification in your situation yet you continued to live in New York. Perhaps you would become defensive and argue "Well actually, if you think about it, the city is not too bad; in fact, it's rather attractive, and it has exciting people and places that exist nowhere else."

Once more your dissonance would be reduced and your cognitions would be consonant; you would be a sensible person who chose to live in an attractive place. But notice what else has happened—you've changed your attitudes about New York. In fact, you have *convinced yourself* that New York is an attractive place. That kind of *internal* justification underlies the most powerful kind of attitude change.

Festinger tested his theory experimentally (Festinger and Carlsmith, 1959). He had a group of students engage in some very boring, repetitive tasks for a long period of time. When they had finished the tasks the subjects were placed in a situation of cognitive dissonance. They were asked to tell other students waiting to participate in the study that the tasks they had just finished were very interesting and enjoyable. Some of the subjects were paid twenty dollars for telling this lie and some were paid only one dollar.

The subjects were then asked to report how they themselves felt about the tasks. The group which had been paid twenty dollars found it boring and dull, just as it was. But the group that was paid one dollar claimed the task was interesting and enjoyable. The first group had reduced dissonance by an external justification—it was worth twenty bucks to tell someone that a boring task was enjoyable. But they didn't believe it themselves, of course, and so their attitude toward the task didn't change.

The other group had no such external justification for their behavior so they had to look internally to make sense of what they had done. Their cognition "I am a truthful person" was dissonant with their cognition "I told someone a boring task was enjoyable." One of these cognitions had to change, and as their self-image was deeply felt and strongly implanted it was easier to change the other attitude. So these people persuaded themselves that the task really had been enjoyable, just as they had told the other students it was.

There are a couple of points of special interest to us here. One point is that these findings run contrary to common sense, which would presumably argue that if you want somebody to adopt a certain attitude, the more you pay him, the more likely he is to do so. In this study, the *less* people were paid, the more readily did they change their attitudes.

The second point concerns the relationship between attitudes and behavior again. We've already seen that a person holding certain attitudes does not necessarily act on them; there are many other factors involved. Similarly, a change in behavior will not necessarily follow from a change in attitude. However, the cognitive dissonance studies have shown that if the appropriate *behavior comes first,* then a change in *attitude can follow.* This is a process we will come across more than once in this chapter. It has important social implications which we will examine at the end of the chapter (see Box 15.1).

Newcomb and Bennington College

In the late 1930s, Theodore Newcomb studied the way attitudes change over time in a community setting. The study was done at Bennington College in Vermont, which was then a small liberal arts school for women. Newcomb noted the social and political attitudes of the people who entered the college in 1935 and recorded them every year thereafter until they graduated in 1939 (Newcomb, 1943).

The students came from wealthy, conservative backgrounds, but the Bennington College community was very liberal. Newcomb found that the conservative attitudes toward the political and social issues of the day that the students brought with them became steadily more liberal as they went through college. Living in a close-knit community where the norm was to have liberal attitudes, most of the women became liberal themselves.

What's more, these attitudes were not just temporary ways to conform or be popular. When Newcomb did a follow-up study 20 years after his subjects had graduated, he found that most of them had retained their liberal attitudes and had married men who felt the same way (Newcomb, 1957).

STEREOTYPES AND SOCIAL PREJUDICE

We have looked at some striking instances of attitude change and the conditions under which the change took place. But many widely held attitudes seem incapable of change. They appear to be frozen into *stereotypes.* Stereotypes are grossly oversimplified attitudes toward other social groups, where all the members of a group are regarded as having the same characteristics. No attempt is made to treat the members of these groups as individuals. However, stereotypes may be quite neutral and even helpful to us, like our working images of bus drivers or mailmen as people who perform a certain social function. Stereo-

BOX 15.1

PROPHECY: HOW TO BE RIGHT WHEN YOU'RE WRONG

It is not often that psychologists who develop a theory by working in the laboratory have a chance to test it on a real-life situation. Such was the case with Leon Festinger and his colleagues Stanley Schachter and Henry Riecken. These investigators very ingeniously arranged a test of Festinger's cognitive dissonance theory with a study of religious beliefs in an unusual situation.

They read about a religious sect whose prophet, a Mrs. Marion Keech, had made the interesting prophecy that the world would be destroyed by a flood at dawn on December 21. The lady claimed to have received word of the impending catastrophe from outer space—the planet Clarion, to be exact. Mrs. Keech did not publicize her information. Her Clarion contact had warned her that she must only divulge the coming doom to people who came to her for guidance. Only such people would be imbued with the right spirit.

The true believers who gathered around Mrs. Keech identified with her message, disposed of their possessions, and waited with her for the world to end as she had prophesied. When the flood started, according to Mrs. Keech, they would be picked up by a spaceship and whisked to safety. They had publicly committed themselves to an irrevocable course of action. What would happen when the appointed hour came and the world did not come to an end? Obviously, they would have a lot of cognitive dissonance to resolve.

Festinger and company meanwhile had infiltrated the group and were accepted as true believers. They now had ringside seats to the end of the world, or whatever might take its place. The advertised time came and, of course, went. As it became clear to even the most fervent believer that nothing was about to happen, the group became confused and bewildered, at a loss to make sense of the situation. After much soul-searching, Mrs. Keech received another message from outer space: The planet Earth had been saved because of the faith shown by the believers.

The group was enraptured with this explanation—and their faith was strengthened. Now they went out into the world and actively sought converts to Mrs. Keech's mission. And this outcome was precisely what the investigators had predicted. When faced with the two dissonant cognitions, "I am a normal, sane person" and "I have given up all my possessions and am sitting around like a lunatic waiting for the world to end," something had to give. The individual could either say "I'm not really sane" or (as Festinger, Riecken, and Schachter hypothesized) he could say "What I've done is not crazy, and here's the reason why. . . ."

By reinterpreting the prophecy they had turned failure into success, and by recruiting new members to their group they provided increasing evidence to support the validity of the original prophecy and the wisdom of their own decision to join the group.

Source: Leon Festinger, Henry Riecken, and Stanley Schachter, *When Prophecy Fails* (Minneapolis: University of Minnesota Press, 1956).

types can also be either positive or negative—"Scotsmen are honest" is just as much a stereotype as "Englishmen are aloof."

When stereotypes are negative, they become the basis for social prejudices, usually against minorities. There are many roots to prejudice, of course: social, economic, political, religious, and cultural, as well as psychological. When times are bad economically, when there is a great deal of unrest and discontent, prejudiced attitudes as well as prejudiced behavior surface more easily. But some people are more likely to be prejudiced than others, and some social situations are likely to produce more prejudice than others. These are psychological issues, and they are often discussed in terms of the *personality* and *situational* factors in prejudice (see Box 15.2).

In Chapter 10 we discussed the need to be prejudiced and saw how an authoritarian home environment can lead to an authoritarian personality with a predisposition to be prejudiced against other people. In hard times, it doesn't take much frustration for such an individual to distort reality and displace his anger onto a convenient social scapegoat.

In recent chapters, we have noted the powerful pressures on people to conform to social norms. If these norms are prejudiced, there will be a great deal of prejudiced behavior. It has often been noted, for example, that there were always more instances of prejudiced behavior by whites toward blacks in the southern United States than in the North. A study of authoritarian personalities by Thomas Pettigrew (1959) found there was about the same amount of personality prejudice in both northern and southern whites, so the difference in prejudiced behavior is presumably to be found in the different social context.

Pettigrew argues that most of the prejudice in the South can be accounted for simply by people conforming to prejudiced social norms. For historical reasons these norms are different from other parts of the country, and the power of conformity has helped to keep them going.

BOX 15.2

OLD STEREOTYPES NEVER DIE—THEY ONLY CHANGE

In 1933 Daniel Katz and Kenneth Braly published a pioneering study in the formation of racial stereotypes. Their subjects were Princeton college students, and their study has been repeated with two succeeding generations at Princeton—by C. M. Gilbert in 1951, and by Karlins, Coffman, and Walters in 1969. The subjects in each case were white Anglo-Saxon Protestant males.

In the original study, Katz and Braly found their subjects quite ready to make stereotypical judgments about the characteristics of other groups, and there was a great deal of agreement about what these characteristics were. Jews were labeled "shrewd" and "mercenary," Italians were "artistic" and "impulsive," and Negroes (this was 1933, remember) were "lazy" and "superstitious."

When Gilbert repeated the study 18 years later in 1951, he found some notable changes. To begin with, his subjects were extremely reluctant even to take part in the study, many of them regarding it as silly and childish to be required to make generalizations about other groups of people. Consequently, stereotypes expressed in this study seemed to be subject to what Gilbert called a *fading effect.* They were a lot weaker than those of the 1933 sample, especially with regard to the negative traits associated with bigoted stereotypes.

Eighteen years after Gilbert's work, the study was repeated for the third time in 1969 and the picture changed again, becoming, inevitably, more complex. This time the investigators discovered that the old stereotypes had not so much faded away as changed. The bigotry that had faded from the 1951 stereotypes did not increase in strength in 1969. But what did return was the tendency of many people to make stereotyped judgments of other groups.

What had changed between 1933 and 1969 was the nature of these commonly held stereotypes. Presumably in line with social and political changes affecting college students over the years, the content of their minority group stereotypes had changed. No longer were blacks "superstitious" and "lazy"; they were now "musical" and "pleasure-loving."

Moreover, the *object* of certain stereotyped attitudes had changed. The judgments "ambitious" and "materialistic" were no longer attributed to Jews, as they had been in 1933. In the social climate of the late 1960s these judgments formed part of a different stereotype—that of the white Anglo-Saxon Protestant male, who dropped from his previous most-favored status to fifth place out of ten groups.

Source: D. Katz and K. W. Braly, "Racial Stereotypes of 100 College Students," *Journal of Abnormal and Social Psychology* 28: 280–290, 1933, C. M. Gilbert, "Stereotype Persistance and Change Among College Students," *Journal of Abnormal and Social Psychology* 46: 245–254, 1951, and M. Karlins, T. L. Coffman, and G. Walters, "On the Fading of Social Stereotypes: Studies in Three Generations of College Students," *Journal of Personality and Social Psychology* 13: 1–16, 1969.

PREJUDICE AND SOCIAL CONTACT

For a time it was thought that increased contact between different groups of people would lead to increased liking and a decrease in prejudice. It was at one time fashionable to sponsor such contact and to believe that increased travel and tourism would gradually break down stereoptypes and prejudiced behavior.

It hasn't happened, of course, and there was never any real evidence for believing that it could. Prejudice can exist with any amount of contact or with no contact at all. When Shakespeare wrote "The Merchant of Venice" his portrayal of Shylock the Jew as a cruel and sniveling miser was a stereotype that his Elizabethan audiences could recognize—but not from personal experience, for the Jews had been expelled from England hundreds of years earlier.

Southern blacks and whites have always had the closest contact with each other and it certainly did not lead to any breakdown in prejudice. But these contacts were usually in situations where the blacks were in a subservient role, as slave, servant, porter, or washerwoman. Psychologists have since discovered that if barriers of prejudice are ever to be overcome the first essential is that both groups meet in a situation of *equal-status contact.*

An example of such contact was provided by the experience of having black soldiers fight alongside whites in World War II. Whites who had shared the battlefield situation with black soldiers seemed to lose some of their prejudiced attitudes. A study done when the war ended found that 62 percent of the white troops who had not had this experience objected to the idea of integrated units. But only seven percent of those who had fought beside blacks expressed any objections (Star, Williams, and Stouffer, 1965). Here again is an example of a change in behavior leading to a change in attitudes.

COMMUNICATION AND PERSUASION

We live in a society where people are constantly trying to change our attitudes. Whether we are being asked to vote for a political candidate or buy a new brand of toothpaste, communications are directed at us whose object is to have us do something we might not otherwise do. The mass media of communication—and especially television—are therefore of tremendous interest to psychologists working in the field of attitude change.

We've already seen (in Chapter 11) that television has a powerful persuasive effect on the attitudes of young children, especially in the area of aggression. Presumably this kind of influence is not as strong with adults who are less impressionable, but adults are just as subject to more subtle influences on their attitudes and behavior.

One important influence that television has is in the way it presents popular stereotypes of our society. Until quite recently this was very obvious in the parts played by women and blacks on fictional TV programs. Only now are professional roles and hero roles being created for anyone other than the all-American white male. Relationships too are generally presented in stereotypic form. It is still rare to find husbands and wives or parents and children who have the problems of real people.

These televised stereotypes represent to almost 100 percent of the population who own TV sets an image not only of the way life is, but implicitly of the way life is supposed to be. Inevitably these images will not always fit with the reality of people's lives, resulting in psychological and social tension.

By conforming to the norm of social stereotypes, the television industry mirrors, legitimizes, and perpetuates existing stereotypes. By adhering to something it calls "community standards," the industry presents life the way people might like it to be—and creates a new set of stereotypes—where nobody swears and where Archie Bunker, the stereotypic bigot, never uses the ethnic insults that every other bigot in America uses.

These unintended influences on our attitudes are not immediately obvious, but what about situations where there is a clear attempt to persuade us to buy something? Surely we can recognize a commercial sales pitch no matter how cleverly it's packaged? Can we possibly be affected by advertising if we're suspicious of it? The answer seems to be that we can. There is no question that heavily advertised products sell better than others, even at five times the price for exactly the same thing.

Robert Zajonc (1968) has suggested that an effect he calls "mere exposure" may go a long way toward explaining this finding. Zajonc found that the more familiar people became with various objects, words, or pictures, the more they liked them. The sheer familiarity of heavily advertised products may influence us to pick them out of a crowd. When we're confronted with a dozen brands of toothpaste or detergent, all virtually identical, we tend to pick the one whose name we know best, especially as the decision itself is not exactly of earth-shaking proportions. However, if we have an important decision to make, and it affects some deeply emotional attitudes, factors other than familiarity come into play.

We would be mistaken in assuming that televised communications always have a direct and immediate effect on the viewer. When young children watch TV, many of the things they see are quite unfamiliar to them, so they ask their parents for help in interpreting the communication. Parents can therefore perform an important intermediary function between the communication and the child.

Similarly, Katz and Lazarsfeld (1955) have suggested that a *two-step flow of communication* exists for adults where the mass media influence the opinions and attitudes of certain members of a community who in turn influence the opinions and attitudes of others. These key figures are often individuals of high status in the community, but not always. Teenagers can be opinion leaders in such areas as fashion and popular entertainment.

Credibility of a Source

The study of attitude change is often dealt with in three segments: the *source* of a message, the nature of the *message,* and the *audience.* We have seen something of communication messages and their effects on the audience; now we will look at the source of these messages.

It has been well established that the more *credible* a source, the more chance his message has of influencing an audience. Credibility in this case includes an attitude of respect and trust on the part of an audience, coupled with the belief that the communicator knows what he's talking about. When Tom Hayden and other figures of the radical Left warned about the power of the military-industrial complex in the United States, they did not influence many people. When President Eisenhower said the same thing in his farewell address to the nation he was seen as highly credible, and the impact was therefore far more powerful.

In this example, President Eisenhower was more effective than Tom Hayden for two additional reasons. First, he was not perceived as arguing in his *own interest.* In fact, as an ex-military man he could be perceived as arguing against his self-interest. Second, he was a popular and *well-liked* figure to a great many people, and there is some evidence that people we like can influence us to change our attitudes in their direction (Aronson, Turner, and Carlsmith, 1963).

We can think of this effect in terms of cognitive dissonance. If we like X but don't like his attitude toward something, we are in a state of dissonance which can be resolved either by not liking X or by liking

X's attitude. It is often easier and more pleasant to keep liking somebody and to change our attitudes to be more in line with his.

SHERIF AND SHERIF: SUPERORDINATE GOALS

We have touched on several aspects of a very complex process in this chapter, and we have looked at a handful of studies from the enormous body of research on attitude and attitude change. There is one very important study in this field which may help to illustrate some of the processes we have mentioned and suggest a possible solution to the problems of group living caused by antagonistic attitudes.

Muzafer Sherif and his colleagues (1953) conducted a study of a boys' summer camp (for 11- and 12-year-olds) at Robbers Cave, Oklahoma. The boys were divided into two rival groups, the Rattlers and the Eagles, and encouraged to compete with each other at sports. The experimenters arranged things so that ingroup solidarity and intergroup hostility were increased to the point where name-calling, fighting, and other signs of aggression broke out.

The experimenters' task then was to break down the hostile attitudes that had been established and restore harmony all around. Their first attempt involved contact between the Rattlers and the Eagles in pleasant situations, like watching a movie. But this had little effect. Then they presented the two groups with goals that had to be achieved for the camp to function, but which required the participation of all the campers at the same time. These are called *superordinate goals*.

The goals, like emergency repairs to the water supply or pulling a truck uphill, were beyond the capacity of either group by itself, and in working together to achieve them the Rattlers and the Eagles began to lose their stereotypes of each other and their hostile attitudes. Gradually the boys developed new friendships across group lines and cooperated with each other spontaneously.

Combat as a Superordinate Goal

Earlier in this chapter we discussed the effects of sharing combat situations on the attitudes of white soldiers toward blacks. For these two groups combat was also a superordinate goal. They had fought together, been dependent on each other, and had achieved a common objective. Unfortunately, the existence of superordinate goals seems to be rare outside of combat or emergency conditions.

Perhaps that is why these conditions are often evoked, in an attempt to attain harmonious attitudes, with such slogans as "the spirit of '76," "war on want," or "war on poverty." But these are attempts to change people's *attitudes* so that they will then be motivated to change their *behavior.* As we have seen throughout this chapter, it seems to happen more easily the other way around.

One aspect of living in a society that claims to be democratic is that social change will only come about when enough people are persuaded that their social attitudes should change. First change the attitude, then hope the behavior will follow, in other words. As we've already seen, this is much less efficient than changing behavior first, then letting attitudes catch up.

But if we advocated the more efficient course psychologically, we would have to deal with the social implications. Totalitarian governments, for instance, can simply give orders and create social situations that will change the *behavior* of their citizens, whether their *attitudes* have changed or not; a much more effective course of action, but what does it cost? The findings of psychology, like those of any other science, are neutral in themselves. But their social implications and applications are not, and they are much too important to be left to the psychologists alone.

SUGGESTED READINGS

Allport, G. *The Nature of Prejudice.* New York: Doubleday (Anchor Books), 1958. A comprehensive but highly readable account of prejudice in all its aspects.

Bem, D. *Beliefs, Attitudes, and Human Affairs.* Monterey, Calif.: Brooks/Cole, 1969. A short account of the formation of attitudes and their social significance.

Brown, J. *Techniques of Persuasion: From Propaganda to Brainwashing.* Baltimore: Penguin Books, 1963. Discusses the manipulation of our attitudes in such areas as advertising and politics.

McGinniss, J. *The Selling of the President 1968.* New York: Pocket Books, 1970. A practitioner's account of how politicians are packaged and sold through the mass media.

EPILOGUE

If you've been with me so far, you should be thoroughly convinced by now of how crucial to our psychology is the need to make sense. And when I say "our" I mean everybody—including psychologists. People who study people for a living have the same needs, values, limitations, and frailties as anyone else, and this is reflected in the way they study and try to understand human behavior.

CHAPTER 16

The psychologist's need to make sense

THE PSYCHOLOGIST AS SCIENTIST

Throughout this book we have seen examples of the crucial role that order plays in our need to make sense. Disorder is disturbing and disorienting; order represents security and predictability. But nobody has a greater need for order than a scientist. The very essence of scientific research is finding order where there was none before. The first essential in studying a problem scientifically is to go about it in a systematic, orderly fashion.

A scientist goes about his work *as though* everything that happens has a cause that he can discover by looking long enough and hard enough in the right places. This assumption of *causality* distinguishes science from religion. Religion deals with faith, with beliefs that cannot be proved or disproved scientifically.

A scientist trying to understand the creation of the universe can look for the physical causes while believing that God started the whole thing off and not experience any dissonance because the existence of God is a matter of faith, and the existence of physical causes is a matter of science. When a psychologist approaches his subject in this manner, he is a scientist. Whatever he discovers about the causes of human behavior is a scientific finding.

If a scientist bases his work on the principle of causality, he believes that all happenings (including human behavior) are *determined.* If something is determined (or predetermined), its fate is inevitable and decided in advance. The scientist's job is to find out how and why it happened when it did, like meteorologists trying to understand the origin and progress of a hurricane, or Newton trying to figure out why the apple fell down.

When applied to human behavior the principle of determinism implies that people have no free will, no control over their actions. Whether or not we really have free will is a philosophical question that cannot be proved or disproved scientifically. Again it is a matter of belief. But when the psychologist is studying human behavior as a scientist he acts *as if* his subjects have no free will, regardless of what he actually believes. We will return to this point near the end of the chapter, for the way it is followed in practice marks a basic distinction between theories of psychology.

THE EXPERIMENTAL METHOD

When people imagine scientists at work, they probably think of experiments being done in a laboratory. This is certainly true of most sciences, but not all. Anatomy and astronomy are two perfectly respectable sciences that have no experimentation. It is worthwhile to note that the *science* of psychology started far earlier than the first psychological experiments on sensation and perception in the 1870s. In fact, many psychologists regard the Greek philosopher Aristotle, who lived over 2000 years ago, as the first member of the profession.

However, the application of the experimental method to psychological problems marked an important stage in the development of psychology as a science. What the experimental method does for a scientist is to allow him to test his ideas or *hypotheses* about a problem and see if they are correct. Only by doing an experiment can he be sure that something *caused* something else to happen. This claim cannot be made by any other kind of study.

The key factors in experimentation are *control* and *randomness.* A hypothesis is carefully defined and the situation arranged so that the hypothesis is either accepted or rejected. For example, in doing Asch's conformity experiment the psychologist could hypothesize that pressures to conform to others would affect a subject's perceptual judgment. The experimenter would control the subject's social environment by arranging his confederates in certain positions around a table and by instructing them to give wrong responses in a prearranged fashion.

Control would be exerted in two other ways. First, all the experimental arrangements would be standardized so that each trial of the experiment could be compared with every other trial. Second, in order to know that the experimental situation really was having a unique effect on the subjects, it would have to be compared with a *control situation* where there was no experimental manipulation. In the Asch experiment this would mean testing subjects' ability to judge lengths of lines when entirely alone.

However, the same subjects could not be in both the experimental and the control conditions. They would be two different sets of people. But suppose the people in the experimental condition had more conforming personalities than the others; would this not bias the results? Yes, it would, unless the experimenter took care of the most important part of any experiment and *randomly assigned* the subjects to either the control group or the experimental group.

By doing so, every one of the subjects has an equal chance (one out of two), when he or she walks into the lab, of being in the experimental situation. The effect of this randomization is to neutralize whatever individual characteristics the subjects bring with them. If they've been randomly chosen, then for the purposes of the experiment it doesn't matter how conforming or nonconforming they may be.

CORRELATION AND CAUSATION

By using the experimental method psychologists can confidently specify cause and effect in the behavior they are studying. In repeating (or replicating) the Asch experiment a psychologist can say that conformity pressures—and nothing else—caused certain subjects to deny the evidence of their eyes and yield to the false judgment of the group.

In psychology it is not always possible, of course, to study a problem experimentally, and therefore it is not always possible to specify causation. Suppose the psychologist is interested in the effects of school attendance on children's grades. He has a hunch that high attendance leads to high grades. So he checks the figures and finds that, sure enough, the kids who get high grades have a high attendance record. His hunch has now been proven, right? Wrong. Absolutely wrong. He has not found that high attendance *causes* high grades, he has found that high attendance *correlates* with high grades, and that is a very different proposition.

When two things correlate they change together at the same time. There is, for example, a high correlation between a boy's mental age and the length of his pants. What can we conclude from this correlation that makes any sense? Nothing at all, because it tells us nothing about causation. The cause lies elsewhere—in chronological age. As boys get older their intellectual abilities grow, and so do their legs.

But doesn't our educational example sound much more plausible? It seems quite logical that if some children go to school more often than others, their work will benefit and their grades will be higher. In actual fact it may well be true—but it hasn't been proved by our psychologist. In fact, it might be equally plausible to argue the opposite conclusion, that giving children high grades makes them like school more, so they go more often.

THE PSYCHOLOGIST AS SOCIAL THINKER

A great deal of our understanding of human psychology has come from psychologists who either did not regard themselves as scientists or who went far beyond their scientific role. The prime example, of course, is Sigmund Freud, who based a tremendous amount of original thought on his observations of a handful of late nineteenth-century middle class Viennese patients.

Some of Freud's ideas are not to be taken too literally, and he made sweeping generalizations about human behavior based on very little evidence. Yet our understanding of the human condition probably owes more to Freud than to any other psychologist. He noticed things about human behavior, like slips of the tongue and the occurrence of hysterical paralysis, that many other people had noticed before him. But the nature of his genius was to fit these processes into a pattern that made sense and that led him to outline the workings of the unconscious and the power of irrational motivation in the human personality. This discovery has changed the way societies deal with mental illness, child raising, criminal behavior, sexual behavior, and formal education, to name some of the more obvious areas of Freudian influence.

Jean Piaget is another case in point. While it had always been known that children make mistakes as they acquire intellectual concepts about the world, no one had been able to make any sense out of them. Piaget found an order to these childish "mistakes." By simply asking children about various concepts he made sense for us out of the way children make sense.

To an adult the idea of conservation, for instance, is perfectly obvious. When the shape of an object changes, its contents are conserved; they stay the same. Adults did not understand how children could make a mistake with such a simple fact. Piaget had the insight to ask children the right questions. When he poured the contents of a small fat jar into a tall thin jar, he discovered that for young children he was also changing the contents. By careful observation of a small number of children, coupled with the psychological imagination to follow wherever his insight led him, Piaget has greatly increased our understanding of human development and of the relationships between children and their social and physical universe.

Psychologists whose achievements are of this magnitude have passed beyond the world of psychological science to enrich the history of ideas. Because their subject matter is of such immediate concern to everybody, the impact of the psychologist as a social thinker is probably more direct and powerful than that of any other scientist.

THE PSYCHOLOGIST AS HUMAN BEING

At various points throughout this book we have seen the phenomenon of self-fulfilling prophecy in action. Psychologists and other social scientists have discovered many instances where our expectations help to determine what we find. But psychologists, as human beings, are just as likely to be affected by self-fulfilling prophecy as anyone else. The particular importance of this observation is, once again, that psychologists study human behavior and they must therefore be especially careful in the interpretation of their findings. This is particularly true in areas of society where psychologists are frequently asked for advice and guidance.

In Chapter 14 I mentioned a study on the effects of teacher expectations on a child's school performance. When the teachers were told that normal children had high IQs and were expected to do well, the children actually did well. Robert Rosenthal, who conducted that study, had previously noticed a similar process affecting investigators doing psychological research (Rosenthal and Lawson, 1964).

In this study a class of psychology students was given the project of training rats to perform a simple response. Half the class was told their rats were "bright" and the other half was told they had "dull" rats. In fact, as you've already guessed, all the rats had a normal IQ. The results of the study showed that the performance of the "bright" rats was much better than that of the "dull" rats.

The interpretation made of these findings is very much like that of the classroom study. Expectations of "brightness" evoked enthusiasm, interest, and affection on the part of both teachers and experimenters. Their subjects apparently responded to this treatment by performing up to their best capacity. This illustration of *experimenter bias* should make us aware that even the most rigorous of experimental studies is still conducted by fallible human beings.

A striking example of the social importance of such fallibility has come to light as a result of recently raised feminist consciousness (Aronson, 1972, pp. 177–178). A study done in the 1950s suggested that women are more easily persuaded than men (Janis and Field, 1959). For a number of years this interpretation went unchallenged; it seemed to fit the commonly accepted definition of female personality.

Then female psychologists took a closer look at the study and found that the examples used (like civil defense) were not the most exciting of subjects to most women. As people are generally more persuadable when they don't have a strong emotional investment in an attitude, it is no surprise that the female subjects in this study were more easily persuaded by the arguments than the males.

Presumably, since male psychologists have been made aware of the issue, such a study would be done very differently today. But who can say what universal, implicit assumptions now affecting psychological research will appear to be blatantly wrong in ten years' time? The psychologist as human being belongs in a specific context of time and place, and only a genius (in any field of endeavor) can rise above these limitations. In the 1930s American psychologists were finding all sorts of evidence for the psychological superiority of the democratic way of life. At the same time, psychologists in Germany were discovering that the healthiest type of personality was the authoritarian model espoused by Hitler and the Nazis.

THE PSYCHOLOGIST AS THERAPIST

When most people hear the word *psychologist* they probably imagine a therapist talking to a patient. And with good reason. The largest single group of psychologists in the United States are the clinical psychologists; they account for about a third of all psychologists.

In Chapter 10, I defined psychotherapy as "the treatment of emotional and mental disturbance by psychological means." As such, psychotherapy dates at least as far back as the ancient Greeks. Until well into the twentieth century psychotherapy was the exclusive preserve of the medical practitioner or psychiatrist. With the flourishing of scientific psychology and research on human behavior in the universities, psychotherapy became a branch of the psychology profession (see Box 16.1).

At the end of Chapter 14 we looked at the social meaning of mental illness and saw how disturbed behavior was in part related to the process of labeling someone's behavior, then expecting him to behave according to the label. In his work with schizophrenics R. D. Laing has gone a step further and argued that there is no such illness; people are labeled schizophrenic when their ideas about the world are out of step with the majority (Laing, 1967).

The problem, he holds, is one of communication and understanding. In effect he is suggesting that schizophrenics may make sense of the environment in a different way from the rest of us, but that their way of making sense is as good as ours and sometimes better. With help from sympathetic and understanding therapists, Laing believes that people can emerge from a condition diagnosed as schizophrenic not merely cured but enriched by their experience.

Not many therapists would go all the way with Laing, but he has helped to focus attention once more on the age-old problem of defining abnormality, at a time when social values are being widely reexamined and when the psychologist as therapist is being asked to undertake an increasingly important role in dealing with the causes and effects of deviant behavior.

THE PSYCHOLOGIST AS THEORIST

Psychologists have always been concerned with theories of human behavior, with constructing a system that would explain why people behave the way they do under any given conditions. Many such theories and systems have been proposed, and in this book we have met with

BOX 16.1

PSYCHONFUSION

Psychologists are often asked the question, "What's the difference between a psychologist and a psychiatrist?" and in self-defense they will often reply "About $30,000 a year." The question, however, is not an unreasonable one and it requires a serious answer. But the confusion doesn't stop there. There remain at least two other distinctions to be made, the difference between psychologist and psychotherapist, psychologist and psychoanalyst.

All of these terms refer to the study and treatment of people who are emotionally and mentally disturbed. The professional field involved is known variously as abnormal psychology, clinical psychology, psychopathology, psychiatry, or simply mental health. If we examine the background of the people who work in this field, their similarities and differences should become clearer.

1. Psychologist

A psychologist working in the mental health field will usually have a Ph.D. in clinical psychology. He will have taken courses and done research in the graduate psychology department of a university, followed by an internship at a mental institution where he would treat patients under the supervision of an experienced staff member.

2. Psychiatrist

A psychiatrist has been trained as a physician, going through medical school and receiving the M.D. degree. He has chosen psychiatry as his medical specialty and will also treat patients in a mental institution under the supervision of a senior professional. The psychiatrist will therefore perform virtually the same function as the clinical psychologist, with the exception that, being a physician, he can prescribe drugs and other medical treatment which the psychologist can't. In addition, he often has a higher status in the institution, and he always makes more money.

3. Psychotherapist

Both the clinical psychologist and the psychiatrist may wish to go into private practice, in which case they will usually seek further training in *psychotherapy*—the treatment of emotional and mental disturbance by psychological means. But to become a psychotherapist you don't have to have either a Ph.D. or an M.D. Social workers who have a master's degree in social work (M.S.W.) and some experience working in a clinical setting are also eligible to be trained as therapists. As we noted in the text, there are many different kinds of psychotherapy, but probably the most widely used techniques are psychoanalytic.

4. Psychoanalyst

A psychoanalyst is a psychotherapist who has received specific training in the theories and methods of psychoanalysis. Such training requires a thorough grounding in the work of Sigmund Freud, of course, but will also include exposure to the work of later psychoanalysts like Anna Freud, Melanie Klein, and Karen Horney. The psychoanalyst in training will also undergo a personal analysis.

examples of the three most famous ones—behaviorism, Gestalt, and psychoanalysis. Few psychologists adhere to any one theory, though most would probably agree there is some merit to each of them.

Theories of psychology tend toward two opposite poles commonly known as hard-nosed and soft-nosed. A hard-nosed theorist does not merely act as if all human behavior were determined, he believes it really is. Man has no free will, according to this theorist, and as all human behavior is predetermined by environmental influences and our reactions to them, psychologists should concentrate entirely on specifying these influences and these reactions. A prime representative of the hard-nosed theorist is a behaviorist like B. F. Skinner. Hard-nosed psychologists are mostly found in such areas as learning, perception, and physiological psychology.

Soft-nosed theorists accept the determinist principle as a working rule of thumb for doing science, but they don't believe that human behavior actually is predetermined. They believe there is more to human psychology than can be observed in behavior; that even if you could observe and specify all the stimuli and responses between people and their environments there would be something vital missing. To the soft-nosed theorist a person's past history of subjective experience also affects his or her actions and, by definition, no one can observe another person's subjective experience. This nasal disagreement among psychologists will not be resolved because one side cannot prove that anything other than behavior exists, and the other side cannot prove that nothing other than behavior exists.

Most psychologists are probably more comfortable with the soft-nosed theories, and there are certainly plenty of them around. Practically all theories of personality, thinking, and development are soft-nosed. One of the most prominent theoretical trends in recent times has been the growing interest in *humanistic* psychology. Humanistic psychologists concentrate their attention on those aspects of human behavior which are uniquely (or particularly) human, like love and creativity.

Carl Rogers, whose nondirective therapy we encountered in Chapter 10, is a member of this school. His interest in the enhancement of the self is typical of humanistic psychologists. One of the most important proponents of humanistic psychology was Abraham Maslow, who argued that people have a drive for *self-actualization.* Maslow suggested there is a hierarchy of motivations, and that after the basic physiological drives are satisfied people have more specifically human needs, the highest of which is self-actualization, where one strives to become all that one is capable of becoming (Maslow, 1970).

Parallel to the growing interest in humanistic psychology is the increased focus on the self (especially among young people) and its possibilities for growth via drugs, mysticism, or religion. The focus on change and on the process of *becoming* seems to have united an increasing number of psychologists and nonpsychologists alike in finding new ways to deal with the oldest of human problems—how to make sense of ourselves and our environment.

SUGGESTED READINGS

Anderson, B. *The Psychology Experiment.* Belmont, Calif.: Brooks/Cole, 1971. A short introduction to the scientific method that goes through all the steps from designing an experiment to writing it up.

Bruno, F. *The Story of Psychology.* New York: Holt, Rhinehart and Winston, 1972. A very brief history of the people who have influenced the development of psychology.

Dustin, D. *How Psychologists Do Research: The Example of Anxiety.* Englewood Cliffs, N.J.: Prentice-Hall, 1969. Goes through the steps involved in the process of research.

Jung, J. *The Experimenter's Dilemma.* New York: Harper & Row, 1971. The first part of this book deals with the behavior and the viewpoints of experimenters and of subjects and the relationship between them. The second part consists of readings that deal with crucial issues in psychological experimentation.

Lyons, J. *A Primer of Experimental Psychology.* New York: Harper & Row, 1965. A nontechnical introduction to the methods of experimental inquiry that are used in psychology. The book focuses on a number of long-standing controversies.

Maslow, A. *Toward a Psychology of Being.* New York: Van Nostrand Reinhold, 1968. A discussion of the way psychology can help an individual achieve self-actualization, fulfillment of his potential.

McCain, G., and Segal, E. *The Game of Science.* Belmont, Calif.: Brooks/Cole, 1969. A short discussion of the world of science and scientists.

Severin, F., ed. *Humanistic Viewpoints in Psychology.* New York: McGraw-Hill, 1965. Selections from the work of a wide variety of people sympathetic to the humanistic viewpoint.

References

Adorno, Theodor; Frenkel-Brunswik, Else; Levinson, Daniel; and Sanford, R. Nevitt. *The Authoritarian Personality.* New York: Harper & Row, 1950.

Allport, Gordon, and Postman, Leo. "The Basic Psychology of Rumor." Reprinted in Newcomb, T., and Hartley, E., eds., *Readings in Social Psychology.* New York: Holt, Rinehart and Winston, 1947.

Aronson, Elliot. *The Social Animal.* San Francisco: Freeman, 1972.

Aronson, Elliot; Turner, Judith; and Carlsmith, J. Merrill. "Communication Credibility and Communication Discrepancy as Determinants of Opinion Change." *Journal of Abnormal and Social Psychology* 67: 31–36, 1963.

Asch, Solomon. "Forming Impressions of Personality." *Journal of Abnormal and Social Psychology* 41: 258–290, 1946.

Asch, Solomon. "Studies of Independence and Conformity: A Minority of One Against a Unanimous Majority." *Psychological Monographs* 70 (9): 416, 1956.

Bagby, English. *The Psychology of Personality.* New York: Holt, Rinehart and Winston, 1928.

Bandura, Albert; Ross, Dorothea; and Ross, Sheila. "Imitation of Film-Mediated Aggressive Models." *Journal of Abnormal and Social Psychology* 66: 3–11, 1961.

Barker, Roger; Dembo, Tamara; and Lewin, Kurt. *Frustration and Regression: An Experiment with Young Children.* University of Iowa Studies in Child Welfare, no. 386, 1941.

Benedict, Ruth. *Patterns of Culture.* New York: New American Library Mentor Books, 1934.

Berkowitz, Leonard, and Le Page, Anthony. "Weapons as Aggression-Eliciting Stimuli." *Journal of Personality and Social Psychology* 7: 202–207, 1967.

Blakemore, Colin, and Cooper, Gordon. "Development of the Brain Depends on the Visual Environment." *Nature* 228: 477–478, 1970.

Burtt, Harold. "An Experimental Study of Early Childhood Memory." *Journal of Genetic Psychology* 58: 435–439, 1941.

Clark, Kenneth B., and Clark, Mamie. "Racial Identification and Preference in Negro Children." Reprinted in Newcomb T., and Hartley, E., eds.,

Readings in Social Psychology. New York: Holt, Rinehart and Winston, 1947.

Danziger, Kurt. *Socialization.* Baltimore: Penguin Books, 1971.

Davis, Allison; Gardner, Burleigh; and Gardner, Mary. *Deep South: A Social Anthropological Study of Caste and Class.* University of Chicago Press, 1941.

Davitz, Joel. "The Effects of Previous Training on Postfrustration Behavior." *Journal of Abnormal and Social Psychology* 47:309–315, 1952.

Dion, Karen. "Physical Attractiveness and Evaluations of Children's Transgressions." *Journal of Personality and Social Psychology* 24: 207–213, 1972.

Festinger, Leon. "A Theory of Social Comparison Processes." *Human Relations* 7: 117–140, 1954.

Festinger, Leon, and Carlsmith, J. Merrill. "Cognitive Consequences of Forced Compliance." *Journal of Abnormal and Social Psychology* 58: 203–210, 1959.

Freedman, Jonathan. *Crowding and Behavior.* New York: Viking Press, 1975.

Friedrich, Lynette, and Stein, Aletha. *Aggressive and Prosocial Television Programs and the Natural Behavior of Preschool Children.* Monographs of the Society for Research in Child Development, 38, 4 serial no. 151, 1973.

Gardner, Allen, and Gardner, Beatrice. "Two-way Communication with an Infant Chimpanzee." In Schorer, A., and Stollnitz, F., eds., *Behavior of Nonhuman Primates,* vol. 4. New York: Academic Press, 1971.

Gergen, Kenneth, and Back, Kurt. "Aging, Time Perspective, and Preferred Solutions to International Conflicts. *Journal of Conflict Resolution* 9: 177–187, 1965.

Gibson, Eleanor and Walk, Richard. "The Visual Cliff," *Scientific American,* April 1960, 64–71.

Grusec, Joan. "Power and the Internalization of Self-Denial." *Child Development* 42: 93–105, 1971.

Harlow, Harry. "The Formation of Learning Sets." *Psychological Review* 56: 51–65, 1949.

Harlow, Harry. "The Maternal Affectional System." In Foss, B. M., ed., *Determinants of Infant Behavior,* vol. 2. New York: Wiley, 1963.

Hebb, Donald O. *Textbook of Psychology.* 3rd Ed. Philadelphia: Saunders, 1972.

Heider, Fritz. "Social Perception and Phenomenal Causality." *Psychological Review* 51: 358–374, 1944.

Heider, Fritz. *The Psychology of Interpersonal Relations.* New York: Wiley, 1958.

Heron, Woodburn. "The Pathology of Boredom." *Scientific American,* January 1957, pp. 52–56.

Hilgard, Ernest, Atkinson, Richard, and Atkinson, Rita. *Introduction to Psychology,* 6th ed. New York: Harcourt Brace Jovanovich, 1975.

Hovland, Carl, and Sears, Robert. "Minor Studies of Aggression: Correlation of Lynchings with Economic Indices." *Journal of Psychology* 9: 301–310, 1940.

Hraba, J. and Grant G. "Black is Beautiful: A Re-examination of Racial Preference and Identification. *Journal of Personality and Social Psychology* 16: 398–402, 1970.

Inkeles, Alex. "Social Change and Social Character: The Role of Parental Mediation." *Journal of Social Issues* 11: 12–23, 1955.

Jacobs, Robert, and Campbell, Donald. "The Perpetuation of an Arbitrary Tradition Through Several Generations of a Laboratory Microculture." *Journal of Abnormal and Social Psychology* 62: 649–658, 1961.

Jahoda, Gustav. "A Note on Ashanti Names and Their Relation To Personality." *British Journal of Psychology* 45: 192–195, 1954.

James, William. *Principles of Psychology.* New York: Smith, 1890.

Janis, Irving, and Field, Peter. "Sex Difference and Personality Factors Related to Persuasibility." in Hovland, C., and Janis, I., eds., *Personality and Persuasibility.* New Haven: Yale University Press, 1959.

Jensen, Arthur. "How Much Can We Boost IQ and Scholastic Achievement?" *Harvard Educational Review,* 31: 1–123, 1969.

Kagan, Jerome. "Cross-cultural Perspectives on Early Development." Paper presented to the annual meeting of the American Association for the Advancement of Science. Washington, D.C., 1972.

Katz, Elihu, and Lazarsfeld, Paul. *Personal Influence: The Part Played by People in the Flow of Mass Communication.* New York: Free Press, 1955.

Kohlberg, Lawrence. "Development of Moral Character and Moral Ideology." In Hoffman, M., and Hoffman, L., eds., *Review of Child Development Research,* vol. 1. New York: Russell Sage Foundation, 1964.

Kohler, Wolfgang. *The Mentality of Apes.* New York: Harcourt Brace Jovanovich, 1925.

Laing, Ronald. *The Politics of Experience.* New York: Pantheon Books, 1967.

Lerner, Melvin. "Evaluation of Performance as a Function of Performer's Reward and Attractiveness." *Journal of Personality and Social Psychology* 1: 355–360, 1965.

Leventhal, Howard; Singer, Robert; and Jones, Susan. "The Effects of Fear and Specificity of Recommendation Upon Attitudes and Behavior." *Journal of Personality and Social Psychology* 2: 20–29, 1965.

Liebert, Robert, and Baron, Robert. "Some Immediate Effects of Televised Violence on Children's Behavior." *Developmental Psychology* 6: 469–475, 1972.

Linton, Ralph. *The Cultural Background of Personality.* Englewood Cliffs, N.J.: Prentice-Hall, 1945.

Lorenz, Konrad. *Evolution and Modification of Behavior.* University of Chicago Press, 1965.

Martin, James. "Racial Ethnocentrism and Judgment of Beauty." *Journal of Social Psychology* 63: 59–63, 1964.

Maslow, Abraham. *Motivation and Personality.* 2nd ed. New York: Harper & Row, 1970.

Mead, Margaret. *Sex and Temperament in Three Primitive Societies.* New York: Morrow, 1935.

Michotte, Albert. *The Perception of Causality.* New York: Basic Books, 1954.

Milgram, Stanley. "Behavioral Study of Obedience." *Journal of Abnormal and Social Psychology* 67: 371–378, 1963.

Miller, George. "Psychology as a Means of Promoting Human Welfare." *American Psychologist* 24 (12): 1063–1075, 1969.

Newcomb, Theodore. *Personality and Social Change: Attitude Formation in a Student Community.* New York: Dryden Press, 1943.

Newcomb, Theodore. *Persistence and Change: Bennington College and Its Students After 25 Years.* New York: Wiley, 1967.

Pavlov, Ivan. *Conditioned Reflexes: An Investigation of the Physiological Activity of the Cerebral Cortex.* New York: Oxford University Press, 1927.

Pavlov, Ivan. *Lectures on Conditioned Reflexes.* 3rd ed. New York: International Publishers, 1928.

Pettigrew, Thomas. "Regional Differences in Anti-Negro Prejudice." *Journal of Abnormal and Social Psychology* 59: 28–36, 1959.

Pfungst, Otto. *Clever Hans.* New York: Holt, Rinehart and Winston, 1911.

Piaget, Jean. *The Child's Conception of Number.* Boston: Routledge & Kegan Paul, 1952.

Piliavin, Irving; Rodin, Judith; and Piliavin, Judith. "Good Samaritanism: An Underground Phenomenon?" *Journal of Personality and Social Psychology* 13: 289–299, 1969.

Roethlisberger, Fritz, and Dickson, William. *Management and the Worker.* Cambridge: Harvard University Press, 1939.

Rosenthal, Robert, and Jacobson, Lenore. *Pygmalion in the Classroom: Teacher Expectation and Pupils' Intellectual Development.* New York: Holt, Rinehart and Winston, 1968.

Rosenthal, Robert, and Lawson, Robert. "A Longitudinal Study of the Effects of Experimenter Bias on the Operant Learning of Laboratory Rats." *Journal of Psychiatric Research* 2: 61–72, 1964.

Schachter, Stanley. *The Psychology of Affiliation.* Stanford, Calif.: Stanford University Press, 1959.

Schachter, Stanley, and Singer, Jerome. "Cognitive, Social, and Physiological Determinants of Emotional State." *Psychological Review* 69: 379–399, 1962.

Schanck, Richard. "A Study of a Community and Its Groups and Institutions Conceived of as Behaviours of Individuals." *Psychological Monographs* 43 (2): 195, 1932.

Sherif, Muzafer. *The Psychology of Social Norms.* New York: Harper & Row, 1936.

Sherif, Muzafer. *Groups in Harmony and Tension: An Integration of Studies on Intergroup Relations.* New York: Harper & Row, 1953.

Sinclair, Upton. *The Jungle.* New York: New American Library (Signet), 1973.

Sinnott, Edmund; Dunn, Leslie; and Dobzhansky, Theodosius. *Principles of Genetics.* 5th ed. New York: McGraw-Hill, 1958.

Skinner, B. F. *The Behavior of Organisms: An Experimental Analysis.* Englewood Cliffs, N.J.: Prentice-Hall, 1938.

Sperry, R. "Hemisphere Deconnection and Unity in Conscious Awareness." *American Psychologist* 23: 723–733, 1968.

Star, Shirley; Williams, Robin; and Stouffer, Samuel. "Negro Infantry Platoons in White Companies." In Proshansky, H., and Seidenberg, B., eds., *Basic Studies in Social Psychology.* New York: Holt, Rinehart and Win ston, 1965.

Statt, David. "National Identity in United States and Canadian Children." In Massialas, B., ed., *Political Youth, Traditional Schools.* Englewood Cliffs, N.J.: Prentice-Hall, 1972.

Szasz, Thomas. *The Myth of Mental Illness.* New York: Harper & Row, 1961.

Tinbergen, Nikolaas. *The Study of Instinct.* New York: Oxford University Press (Clarendon Press), 1951.

Triplett, Norman. "The Dynamogenic Factors in Pacemaking and Competition." *American Journal of Psychology* 9: 507–533, 1897.

Wallach, Michael; Kogan, Nathan; and Bem, Daryll. "Group Influence on Individual Risk Taking." *Journal of Abnormal and Social Psychology* 65: 75–86, 1962.

Walster, Elaine, and Berscheid, Ellen. "Adrenaline Makes the Heart Grow Fonder." *Psychology Today* 5 (1): 46, June 1971.

Watson, John B., and Rayner, R. "Conditioned Emotional Reactions." *Journal of Experimental Psychology* 3: 1–14, 1920.

Wicker, Allan. "Attitudes Versus Actions: The Relationship of Verbal and Overt Behavioral Responses to Attitude Objects." *The Journal of Social Issues* 25: 41–78, 1969.

Wilson, Paul. "Perceptual Distortion of Height as a Function of Ascribed Academic Status." *Journal of Social Psychology* 74: 97–102, 1968.

Zajonc, Robert. "Attitudinal Effects of Mere Exposure." *Journal of Personality and Social Psychology* 9 (2): 1–27, 1968.

Index of Names

Subject Index

77 78 79 80 9 8 7 6 5 4 3 2 1